41.68

D1567135

ATLAS
of the
UNITED STATES

EDITORIAL

Editorial consultant
Michael Dempsey B.A.

Editors
Jilly Glassborow B.Sc.,
Gillian Freeman B.A.

Assistant editor
Annabel Else B.A.

Contributors
Norman Barrett B.Sc.
Neil Grant M.A., F.R.G.S.
Guy Arnold M.A.

Researchers
Kathy Westcott
Pat Curran

Visual conceptualizer
Phil Jacobs

Cartographer
Pat Barber

Artistic coordinator
Jillian Burgess

Artists
Janos Marffy
Malcolm Porter

Production director
Peter Sackett

Production manager
John Baker

Production controller
Jim Clemson

ATLAS
of the
UNITED STATES

MACMILLAN PUBLISHING COMPANY
A Division of Macmillan, Inc.
NEW YORK

Macmillan Publishing Company
A Division of Macmillan, Inc.
866 Third Avenue, New York, N. Y. 10022

Collier Macmillan Canada, Inc.

Library of Congress Catalog Card Number: 85-675603

Printed in the United States of America

printing number
1   2   3   4   5   6   7   8   9   10

Library of Congress Cataloging-in-Publication Data

Nomad Publishers Limited.
  Atlas of the United States.

    1. United States—Economic conditions—Maps.
2. Geography, Economic—Maps.   I. Title.
G1201.G1N6 1985   912'.73   85-675603
ISBN 0-02-922830-1

INTRODUCTION

In Greek mythology, Atlas was one of the Titans, a group of the older gods of ancient Greeks. Atlas led the Titans against Zeus and the new gods of Olympus. When the Titans proved to be unsuccessful in their war, various punishments were meted out to them. Atlas, a giant, was condemned to hold up the heavens on his shoulders. This was supposed to have occurred near the place named after him, the Atlas Mountains, a range in northern Africa. The mountains were so high there they they seemed to be supporting the sky.

The use of the word *atlas* for a collection of maps or tables, charts, and graphs is said to date from the sixteenth century. Gerardus Mercator (1512–1594), Flemish mapmaker and geographer best known for the map projection that bears his name, designed and engraved a collection of maps which he called *Atlas, or Cosmographical Meditations on the Structure of the World.* Published by his son in 1595, it became extremely popular and influential not only in the Netherlands, where it was published, but also in England. The front matter of the work contained a representation of Atlas, a practice not uncommon to similar works of that period.

It is particularly appropriate that this new and different *Atlas of the United States* appears at the time when the bicentennial of the Constitution of the United States is about to be celebrated.

The American Constitution, as Richard B. Morris notes in *Witnesses at the Creation,* is the "one surviving symbol of that exceptionalism that sets off America from other nations. Above all, the Constitution is the mortar that binds the fifty-state edifice under the concept of federalism, the unifying symbol of a nation composed of many millions of people claiming different national origins, races and religions."

It is the similarities and the differences between the states which this atlas seeks to show first, followed by a section illustrating some of the exceptionalisms of America.

Alexander Hamilton got directly to the point in *The Federalist #1* when he said that ratification of the Constitution involved nothing less than "the existence of the Union, the safety and welfare of the parts of which it is composed, the fate of an empire in many respects the most interesting in the world." Four days later, John Jay reiterated the central question of "whether it would conduce more to the interest of the people of America that they should, to all general purposes, be one nation, under one federal government, or that they should divide themselves into separate confederacies, and give to the head of each the same kind of powers which they are advised to place in one national government."

The importance of this union of states is reflected in the mottoes of the District of Columbia: *E Pluribus Unum* (One out of many); Illinois: "State Sovereignty–National Union"; Kentucky: "United We Stand, Divided We Fall"; Louisiana: "Union, Justice, Confidence"; North Dakota: "Liberty and Union"; and Vermont: "Freedom and Unity."

This is an atlas in the broadest sense of the word. In addition to geographical features and numbers of population, it provides an array of sociological, economic, and scientific data. Each subject is treated on a two-page spread. On one page, a map—of the United States in the first half of the *Atlas,* and of the world in the second—shows distribution by state or by country, and on the facing page, diagrams, pie charts, and tables provide additional information. For example, the spread on Crop Production (pages 36–37) consists of a map showing distribution of major crops by state, while two diagrams give figures for the principal crops in the United States as a whole (Diagram A) and the value of the crops over an extended period (Diagram B). The accompanying text provides further information about trends and the causes of change.

The *Atlas* can, of course, also be used to study one state in depth. Students can collect all information on Nebraska, for instance, and draw a composite picture of the state's ethnographic, economic, and environmental characteristics. The same can be done for the United States as a whole in comparison with figures for the world as a whole.

Other areas of study easily suggest themselves. Students may want to establish a correlation, if any, between levels of literacy and mortality rates, or between population density and levels of industrialization.

It is fitting that one measure of a country's development—toward the end of the twentieth century—should be the number of television sets and radios per 1,000 of population (see World Communications, page 114). Just as a similar map a hundred years ago might have shown the number of pieces of mail or telegraph messages per 1,000 of population, so it is not inconceivable that an atlas published a hundred years hence—if indeed books will still be published then—will show the number of intergalactic radio stations per country. Such is the fascinating development of our technology.

Thirty-five of the sixty themes in this atlas refer to our union of states, illustrating, contrasting, and comparing states to each other. They show our growth from a country of 892,000 square miles and slightly less than 4 million people in 1790 to 3.6 million square miles and almost 239 million Americans in 1985. They show the wealth of our resources: the soil and the crops, the rivers and the forests, the rails and the roads, the minerals and the mountains.

The first part of this atlas criss-crosses the United States, from the easternmost point of Quoddy Head, Maine, to the islands of the Paradise of the Pacific, the fiftieth state in the union, from the northernmost tip of Point Barrow in the Frontier State to East Cape, Florida. From many different perspectives, this atlas allows us the opportunity to examine the rich diversity of our country from the heights of Mt. McKinley (20,320 feet) to Death Valley (282 feet below sea level).

The Atlas of the United States examines our richest resource, the people. Critical study will enable the reader to understand the transformation of the country from the small, homogeneous, rural, and agrarian society at the time of the Constitutional Convention, to the very opposite 200 years later. Readers will also see where Americans live, with special attention to the themes of age, economics, elections, education, health, crime, and other social issues.

The second half of this atlas examines the United States in relation to the rest of the world. The twenty-five themes in this part illustrate, as Hamilton said in *The Federalist #11,* "our intercourse with foreign countries." Hamilton noted in that paper that the adventurous commercial spirit of America "has already excited uneasy sensations in several of the maritime powers of Europe" and that these same countries were apprehensive of "what this country is capable of becoming."

This part of the atlas shows what this country has indeed become in just two centuries. In graphic terms, it shows that the dream of the Founding Fathers has come true and that the United States stands today as one of the most powerful countries in the world. We should reflect on the blessings showered upon us, however, and note the terrible inequities among the community of nations. These international themes illustrate—all too vividly—the poverty, starvation and malnutrition, illness, illiteracy, and overpopulation that exist.

The last spreads show a world preparing for its own destruction. They indicate that Harry Golden may have been right when he said that the reason that we have not yet had visitors from Outer Space is that they "are afraid they'll get killed the minute they set foot on this nervous, inhibited, frustrated, and trigger-happy little Earth." The author of *Only in America* concludes by saying: "Or maybe George Bernard Shaw was right. Maybe they all use Earth as a sort of interplanetary lunatic asylum."

It was the Pennsylvanian physician and signer of the Declaration of Independence, Benjamin Rush, who noted that there was common confusion between the terms American War and American Revolution. The former ended at Yorktown but the latter is a process that continues to unfold. The quest for "a more perfect Union" in the United States and throughout the world continues. The Revolution and the Constitution were only the opening acts of this drama.

CONTENTS

THE UNITED STATES

The United States is made up of fifty states and the District of Columbia, which contains the federal capital of Washington. These political units are not always convenient for economic, social, or other analyses, and the map shows larger units ("regions" and "divisions"), which are adopted on occasion in this atlas. (These larger units are also used by the Bureau of the Census and by other federal agencies concerned with national statistics.)

The four regions are the traditional ones of Northeast, South, Midwest, and West, which appear on the map as separate blocs. Each is further divided into two or three divisions, which are indicated on the map by color.

The capital city is shown for each state.

Alaska and Hawaii, geographically separated from the rest of the states, are included in the Pacific section of the Western bloc.

Source: U.S. Bureau of the Census

POPULATION AND AREA OF THE UNITED STATES BY REGION, DIVISION, AND STATE

Region, Division, and State	Population (1983) (thousands)*	Area (square miles)*	Region, Division, and State	Population (1983) (thousands)*	Area (square miles)*
NORTHEAST	**49,519**	**168,875**	**MIDWEST**	**58,953**	**766,365**
New England	**12,489**	**66,672**	**East North Central**	**41,531**	**248,540**
Maine	1,146	33,265	Ohio	10,746	41,330
New Hampshire	959	9,279	Indiana	5,479	36,185
Vermont	525	9,614	Illinois	11,486	56,345
Massachusetts	5,767	8,284	Michigan	9,069	58,527
Rhode Island	955	1,212	Wisconsin	4,751	56,153
Connecticut	3,138	5,018	**West North Central**	**17,422**	**517,825**
Middle Atlantic	**37,029**	**102,203**	Minnesota	4,144	84,402
New York	17,667	49,108	Iowa	2,905	56,275
New Jersey	7,468	7,787	Missouri	4,970	69,697
Pennsylvania	11,895	45,308	North Dakota	680	70,703
			South Dakota	700	77,116
SOUTH	**79,539**	**898,575**	Nebraska	1,597	77,355
South Atlantic	**38,805**	**278,927**	Kansas	2,425	82,277
Delaware	606	2,044			
Maryland	4,304	10,460	**WEST**	**45,970**	**1,784,955**
District of Columbia	623	69	**Mountain**	**12,331**	**863,563**
Virginia	5,550	40,767	Montana	817	147,046
West Virginia	1,965	24,231	Idaho	989	83,564
North Carolina	6,082	52,669	Wyoming	514	97,809
South Carolina	3,264	31,113	Colorado	3,139	104,091
Georgia	5,732	58,910	New Mexico	1,399	121,593
Florida	10,680	58,664	Arizona	2,963	114,000
East South Central	**14,946**	**181,947**	Utah	1,619	84,899
Kentucky	3,714	40,409	Nevada	891	110,561
Tennessee	4,685	42,144	**Pacific**	**33,639**	**921,392**
Alabama	3,959	51,705	Washington	4,300	68,138
Mississippi	2,587	47,689	Oregon	2,662	97,073
West South Central	**25,788**	**437,701**	California	25,174	158,706
Arkansas	2,328	53,187	Alaska	479	591,004
Louisiana	4,438	47,751	Hawaii	1,023	6,471
Oklahoma	3,298	69,956			
Texas	15,724	266,807	**United States**	**233,981**	**3,618,770**

* Rounding population figures to the nearest thousand and area figures to the nearest square mile means that state, division and region totals do not always agree exactly.

TOP TEN: LARGEST STATES BY POPULATION

1 California
2 New York
3 Texas
4 Pennsylvania
5 Illinois
6 Ohio
7 Florida
8 Michigan
9 New Jersey
10 North Carolina

TOP TEN: LARGEST STATES BY AREA

1 Alaska
2 Texas
3 California
4 Montana
5 New Mexico
6 Arizona
7 Nevada
8 Colorado
9 Wyoming
10 Oregon

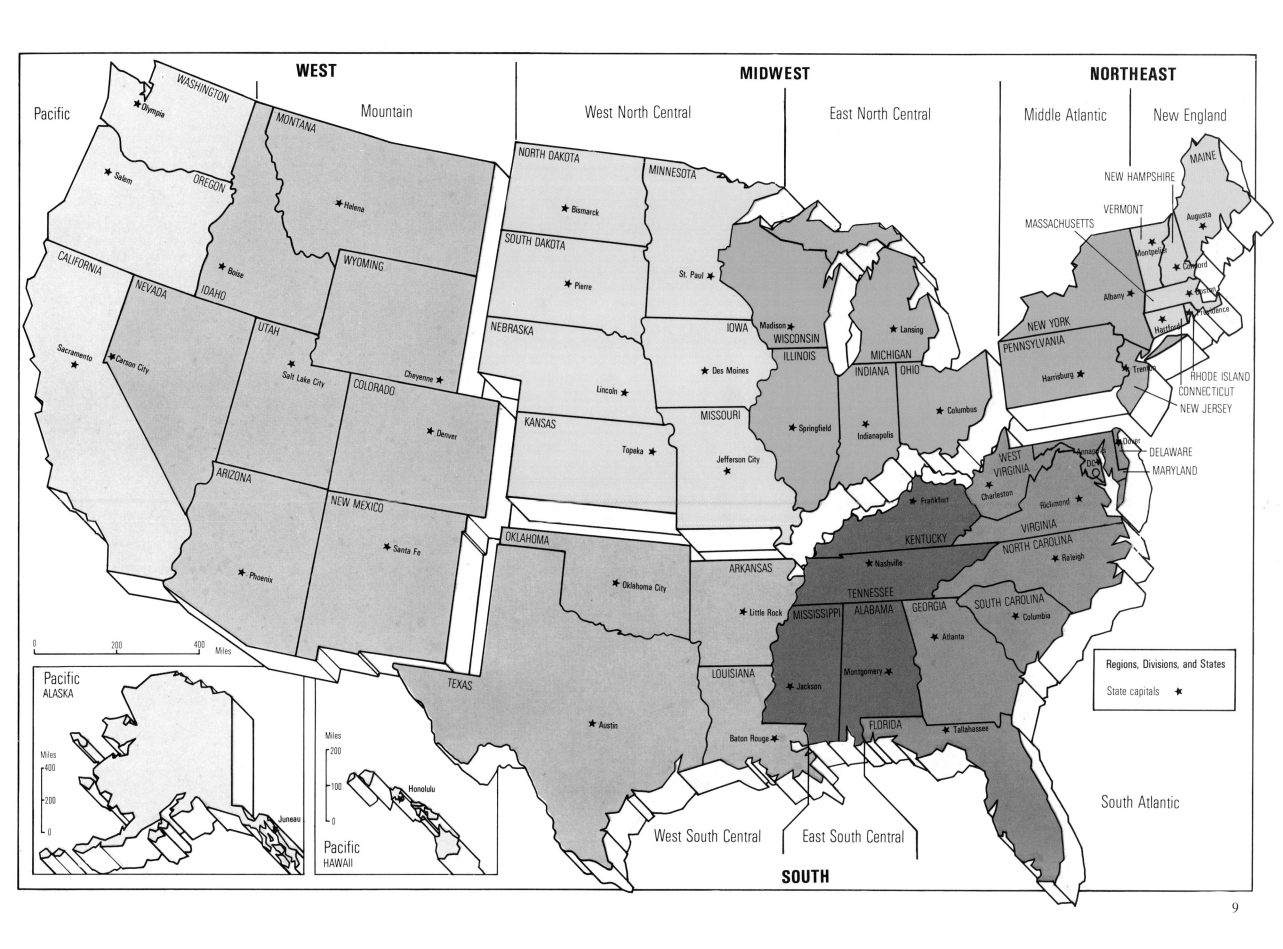

WEST

MIDWEST

NORTHEAST

Pacific

Mountain

West North Central

East North Central

Middle Atlantic

New England

WASHINGTON
★ Olympia

MONTANA
★ Helena

OREGON
★ Salem

IDAHO
★ Boise

WYOMING

NORTH DAKOTA
★ Bismarck

SOUTH DAKOTA
★ Pierre

MINNESOTA
★ St. Paul

MAINE
★ Augusta

NEW HAMPSHIRE

VERMONT
★ Montpelier

MASSACHUSETTS

★ Concord

★ Boston

CALIFORNIA

NEVADA

UTAH
★ Salt Lake City

COLORADO
★ Denver

NEBRASKA
★ Lincoln

IOWA
★ Des Moines

WISCONSIN
Madison ★

ILLINOIS
★ Springfield

MICHIGAN
★ Lansing

INDIANA
★ Indianapolis

OHIO
★ Columbus

Albany ★

NEW YORK

Hartford ★

★ Providence

RHODE ISLAND

CONNECTICUT

Sacramento ★
★ Carson City

★ Cheyenne

ARIZONA
★ Phoenix

NEW MEXICO
★ Santa Fe

KANSAS
Topeka ★

MISSOURI
★ Jefferson City

PENNSYLVANIA
★ Harrisburg

★ Trenton

NEW JERSEY

Annapolis ★ Dover

DELAWARE

★ DC
MARYLAND

OKLAHOMA
★ Oklahoma City

ARKANSAS
★ Little Rock

WEST VIRGINIA
★ Charleston

KENTUCKY
★ Frankfort

VIRGINIA
★ Richmond

NORTH CAROLINA
★ Raleigh

0   200   400
Miles

MISSISSIPPI
★ Jackson

TENNESSEE
★ Nashville

ALABAMA
★ Montgomery

GEORGIA
★ Atlanta

SOUTH CAROLINA
★ Columbia

Pacific
ALASKA

TEXAS
★ Austin

LOUISIANA
Baton Rouge ★

FLORIDA
★ Tallahassee

Regions, Divisions, and States

State capitals   ★

Miles
400
200
0

Juneau

Miles
200
100
0

Pacific
HAWAII

★ Honolulu

West South Central

East South Central

South Atlantic

SOUTH

9

THE SHAPE OF THE LAND

Diagram A: Natural regions of the United States

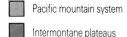

- Pacific mountain system
- Intermontane plateaus
- Rocky mountain system
- Interior plains
- Interior highlands
- Coastal plain
- Appalachian region
- Canadian shield
- Volcanic region

The terrain of the contiguous United States can be simply divided into three: two mountain chains running parallel with the coasts, with a large lowland plain between them. This is reflected in the map opposite which shows the mean elevation of the states.

The map below reveals that the layout of the land is more complicated. The mountains in the West are not a single range but a wide mountainous system consisting of three distinct, major regions: the Pacific mountain system, the intermontane plateaus, and the Rocky Mountains. These mountain systems in turn consist of series of associated ranges, such as the Sierra Nevada or the Cascades in the Pacific system. The whole region makes up about one-third of the area of the United States.

The Rocky Mountains, running through Canada, extend into Alaska and form the Aleutian island chain. There are two main mountain ranges in the north: the Alaskan and Brooks ranges. Between them lies the Yukon plateau, with the smaller Arctic plateau north of the Brooks range.

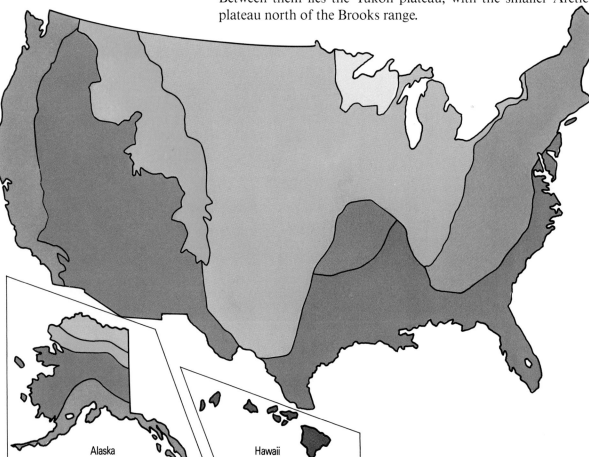

Alaska

Hawaii

The central lowland and plains region, east of the Rockies, contains the Great Plains and associated regions, including part of the Canadian Shield (an area of ancient rocks) and a number of upland areas. Though generally level, the Great Plains have an overall downward slope from west to east.

The Ozark plateau of southern Missouri and northwestern Arkansas forms an interior highland region separating the interior plains from the wide Atlantic plain of the South and East. Farther north, the Atlantic coastal plain is narrow or nonexistent.

Appalachia is the second major highland system, and, like the Rocky Mountains, it is made up of a series of ranges, including the Blue Ridge, Adirondack, Catskill, and Allegheny Mountains.

The islands of Hawaii are of volcanic origin, built up from the ocean floor by successive deposits of lava. On the larger islands, there are small plateaus between the volcanic peaks.

The map on the opposite page illustrates the main drainage basins. Much the largest is that of the Mississippi River and its tributaries. The Mississippi basin encompasses almost the entire region between the Rocky Mountains and the Appalachians, from the Canadian border down to the Gulf of Mexico. Areas that do not form part of the Mississippi system include a few small regions in the South, which are drained by rivers flowing directly into the Gulf, and the Great Lakes region in the Northeast, which belongs to the Canadian St. Lawrence River system.

East of the Appalachian region, the Hudson, Susquehanna, and many short streams cross the coastal plain to the Atlantic. In the West, the principal drainage basins are those of the Columbia system in the north, the Sacramento-San Joaquin system in the Central Valley of California, and the Colorado and the Rio Grande in the south.

The major part of the central plateau of Alaska is drained by the Yukon River.

The table gives the length of principal U.S. rivers. The St. Lawrence and other primarily Canadian rivers are not included. Measuring rivers is always controversial; rivers sometimes change course or have their courses altered, and the pinpointing of their source is often impossible. These figures, however, are the most reliable available.

The point of highest elevation above sea level in each state is also marked on the map. The highest point in the United States is Mount McKinley in Alaska, 20,320 feet. Highest in the contiguous United States is Mount Whitney in the Sierra Nevada, California, 14,494 feet. Less than 100 miles to the east is the lowest point in the United States, in Death Valley, 282 feet below sea level.

Source: U.S. Geological Survey

TOP TEN: LONGEST RIVERS
(in miles)

Mississippi/Missouri	3,710
Yukon	1,900
Rio Grande	1,885
Arkansas	1,459
Colorado	1,450
Ohio/Allegheny	1,306
Red (southern)	1,270
Columbia	1,243
Snake	1,038
Platte/North Platte	930

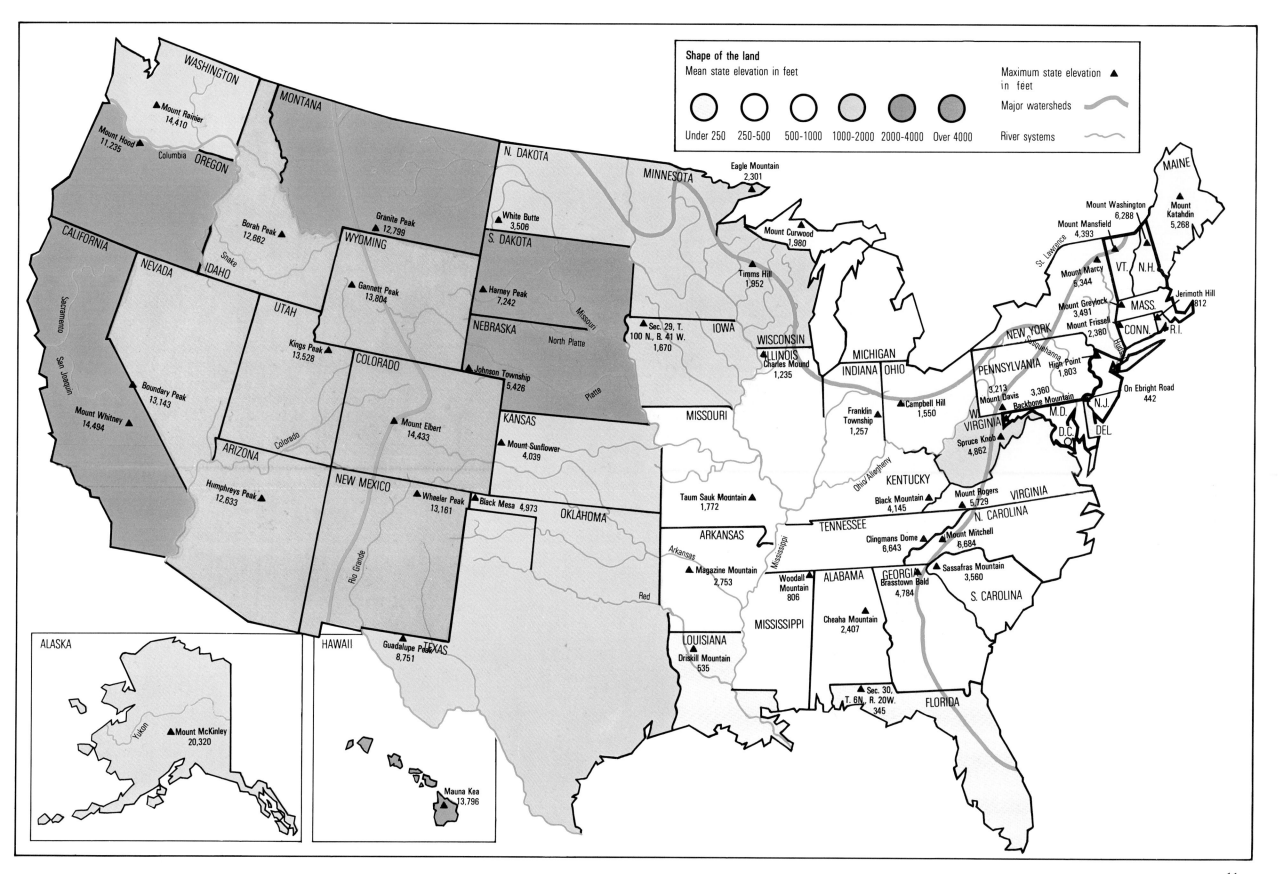

Shape of the land

Mean state elevation in feet

| Under 250 | 250-500 | 500-1000 | 1000-2000 | 2000-4000 | Over 4000 |

Maximum state elevation in feet ▲

Major watersheds

River systems

WASHINGTON

▲ Mount Rainier
14,410

Mount Hood ▲
11,235

Columbia   OREGON

MONTANA

Granite Peak ▲
12,799

N. DAKOTA

MINNESOTA

Eagle Mountain
2,301 ▲

Mount Curwood
1,980 ▲

MAINE

Mount Washington
6,288 ▲

Mount Mansfield
4,393 ▲

Mount Katahdin ▲
5,268

CALIFORNIA

NEVADA

IDAHO

Borah Peak ▲
12,662

Snake

WYOMING

▲ Gannett Peak
13,804

White Butte ▲
3,506

S. DAKOTA

▲ Harney Peak
7,242

Missouri

Mount Marcy
5,344

VT.   N.H.

Mount Greylock
3,491   MASS.

Mount Frissell
2,380   CONN.   R.I.

Jerimoth Hill
812

Sacramento

San Joaquin

UTAH

Kings Peak ▲
13,528

COLORADO

NEBRASKA

North Platte

▲ Sec. 29, T.
100 N., R. 41 W.
1,670

IOWA

Platte

WISCONSIN

Timms Hill
1,952 ▲

MICHIGAN

NEW YORK

Susquehanna

High Point
1,803

St. Lawrence

Hudson

N.J.

Boundary Peak ▲
13,143

Mount Whitney ▲
14,494

▲ Mount Elbert
14,433

Johnson Township ▲
5,426

KANSAS

ILLINOIS
Charles Mound
1,235 ▲

INDIANA   OHIO

PENNSYLVANIA

On Ebright Road
442

PA   3,213

Mount Davis
3,360

Backbone Mountain

M.D.

DEL

ARIZONA

Humphreys Peak ▲
12,633

NEW MEXICO

▲ Wheeler Peak
13,161

▲ Mount Sunflower
4,039

Black Mesa 4,973 ▲

Colorado

OKLAHOMA

MISSOURI

Franklin
Township
1,257 ▲

▲ Campbell Hill
1,550

W.
VIRGINIA

Spruce Knob
4,862 ▲

Ohio/Allegheny

KENTUCKY

D.C.

Rio Grande

Taum Sauk Mountain ▲
1,772

ARKANSAS

TENNESSEE

Black Mountain ▲
4,145

Mount Rogers
5,729 ▲

VIRGINIA

N. CAROLINA

Arkansas

Mississippi

Clingmans Dome
6,643 ▲

Mount Mitchell ▲
6,684

Red

▲ Magazine Mountain
2,753

Woodall
Mountain
806 ▲

ALABAMA

GEORGIA
Brasstown Bald
4,784 ▲

Sassafras Mountain ▲
3,560

S. CAROLINA

LOUISIANA

MISSISSIPPI

Cheaha Mountain ▲
2,407

ALASKA

▲ Mount McKinley
20,320

Yukon

HAWAII

Guadalupe Peak ▲
8,751   TEXAS

Driskill Mountain
535 ▲

▲ Sec. 30,
T. 6N., R. 20W.
345

FLORIDA

Mauna Kea ▲
13,796

WEATHER

Temperature and precipitation are the chief elements of weather. The map measures temperature nationwide in terms of degree days. Heating degree days (HDD) refers to the number of degrees the daily average temperature is below 65° Fahrenheit. Cooling degree days (CDD) refers to the number of degrees the daily average temperature is above 65° Fahrenheit. For example, on a day when the highest temperature is 69°F and the lowest is 51°F, the average is 60°F, resulting in 5 HDD.

In addition, the normal maximum temperature in January and July is shown at one or more weather stations (mainly airports near large cities) in each state, together with the average wind speed in miles per hour. The figures represent an average over a recorded period of, in most cases, more than 30 years.

The map shows clearly that temperature is largely governed by latitude: it is warmer in the south and cooler in the north. The map also shows two other factors affecting temperature: proximity to the sea and elevation. Coastal regions, especially near the Pacific, have warmer winters and cooler summers than inland places at the same latitude, while temperatures in general decrease with altitude. The moderating effect of the sea on temperatures can be clearly seen in Diagram A.

The figures enclosed in raindrops on the map represent the normal annual precipitation at selected stations.

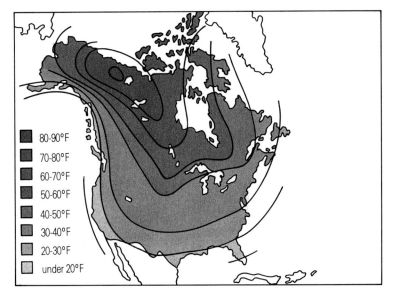

80-90°F
70-80°F
60-70°F
50-60°F
40-50°F
30-40°F
20-30°F
under 20°F

Diagram A: Mean annual range of temperature

The amount of precipitation is largely governed by two factors: the proximity of large bodies of water and the influence of mountain ranges. Areas near the sources of moisture and on windward slopes of mountains generally have the most precipitation.

The seasonal pattern of precipitation varies considerably. The diagram shows average precipitation in selected cities during the wettest and driest months of the year.

Sources: U.S. National Oceanic and Atmospheric Administration; U.S. Bureau of the Census

Diagram B: Seasonal precipitation of selected cities showing the wettest and driest months

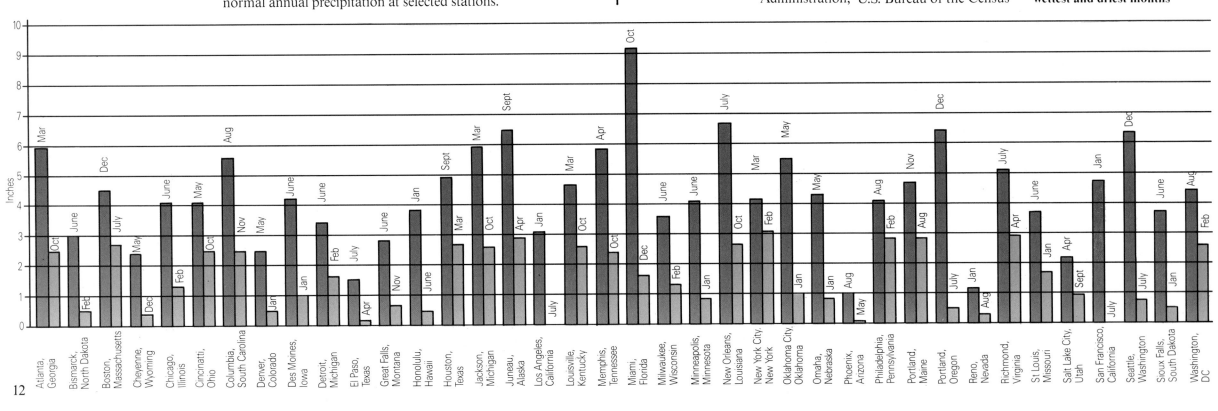

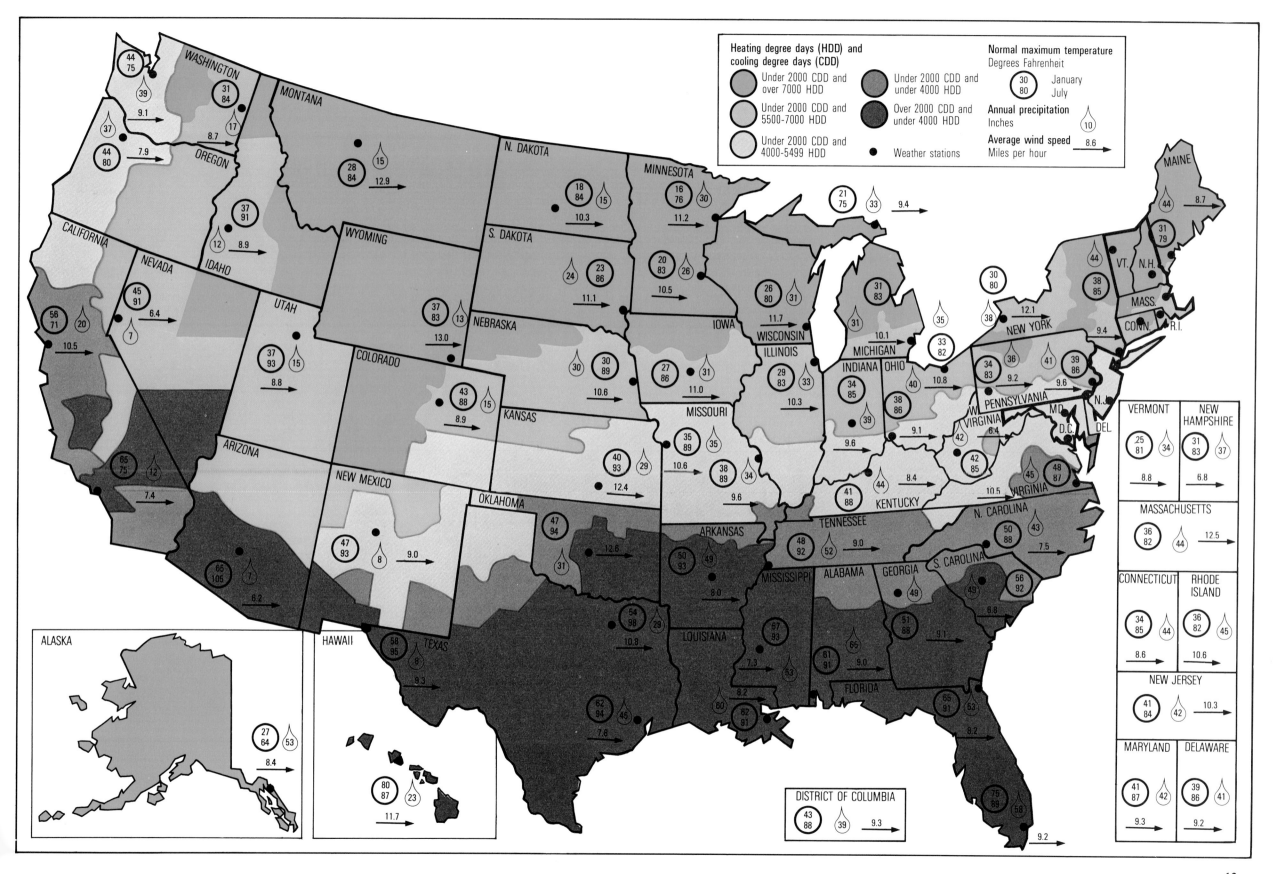

Heating degree days (HDD) and cooling degree days (CDD)

Under 2000 CDD and over 7000 HDD

Under 2000 CDD and 5500-7000 HDD

Under 2000 CDD and 4000-5499 HDD

Under 2000 CDD and under 4000 HDD

Over 2000 CDD and under 4000 HDD

● Weather stations

Normal maximum temperature
Degrees Fahrenheit

30 January
80 July

Annual precipitation
Inches

Average wind speed
Miles per hour

WASHINGTON
MONTANA
N. DAKOTA
MINNESOTA
MAINE
OREGON
IDAHO
WYOMING
S. DAKOTA
WISCONSIN
MICHIGAN
NEW YORK
VT. N.H.
MASS.
CALIFORNIA
NEVADA
UTAH
COLORADO
NEBRASKA
IOWA
ILLINOIS
INDIANA OHIO
PENNSYLVANIA
CONN. R.I.
N.J.
W. VIRGINIA
MD.
D.C. DEL
ARIZONA
NEW MEXICO
KANSAS
MISSOURI
KENTUCKY
VIRGINIA
OKLAHOMA
TENNESSEE
N. CAROLINA
ARKANSAS
S. CAROLINA
MISSISSIPPI ALABAMA GEORGIA
TEXAS
LOUISIANA
FLORIDA

ALASKA
HAWAII
DISTRICT OF COLUMBIA

VERMONT | NEW HAMPSHIRE
MASSACHUSETTS
CONNECTICUT | RHODE ISLAND
NEW JERSEY
MARYLAND | DELAWARE

13

SOILS AND VEGETATION

The United States is a land of great physical variety, and the variations of terrain and climate produce corresponding variations in soils and natural vegetation. There are more than 1,000 species or varieties of native forest trees and about 25,000 species of flowering plants (plus a great number introduced from other regions of the world).

In many regions, considerable differences in natural vegetation may occur within a small area; the map can show only the main divisions and approximate extents. Boundaries between zones are usually less sharp than they appear on the map, although abrupt changes do occur, particularly as a result of changes in altitude.

Natural vegetation consists generally of forest, grassland, or desert scrub. Alaska has a large area of Arctic tundra, which in the contiguous United States, is found only at high altitudes in the mountains.

Coniferous forests cover large parts of Alaska, occur in the Great Lakes region, the extreme Northeast, and the highest parts of Appalachia. Southwards the pines and spruces soon give way to a mixed forest and then to the true hardwood forest, which once extended uninterrupted from New England to Texas.

Southern pine forests grow in most of the coastal plain of the South and Southeast. In the southern mixed forest, the pines grow together with oaks, hickory, cedar, ash, and magnolia. The swamp forests contain the bald cypress as well as white cedar, tupelo gum, and brush vines.

Grassland is characteristic of the Great Plains, and it also occurs in large pockets among the Rocky Mountains. Mesquite grassland occurs in the dry Southwest.

The western forests contain a great variety of trees with different species dominating locally. The Pacific forest is limited to a narrow coastal belt where conditions are mild and humid. Chaparral is plentiful in California and scrub vegetation occurs in the arid basins and semidesert west of the Rocky Mountains. Sagebrush is the commonest plant in the northern areas and the thorny creosote bush in the southern areas. The desert, which stretches from southeastern California into Texas, is noted for the variety and abundance of cacti, notably the saguaro.

The United States has thousands of differently classified soils. The map on this page shows the main groups.

New England lost much topsoil to the glaciers which also deposited rocks so profusely. Patchy and often poor soils are characteristic of most of the Northeast.

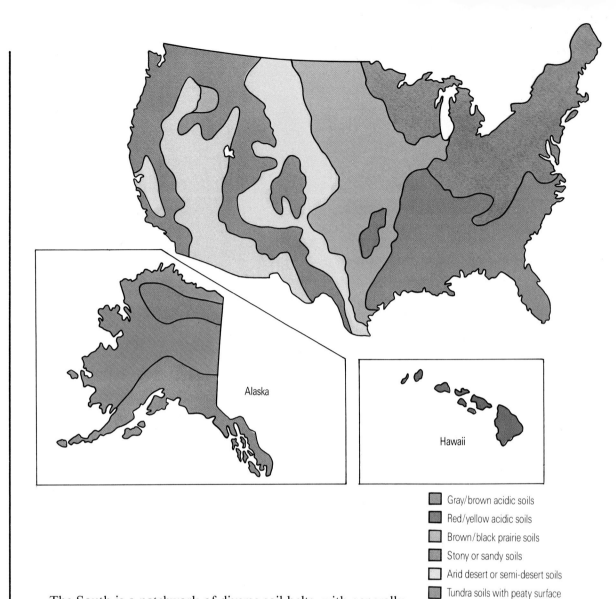

Gray/brown acidic soils
Red/yellow acidic soils
Brown/black prairie soils
Stony or sandy soils
Arid desert or semi-desert soils
Tundra soils with peaty surface
Volcanic soils

Diagram A: U.S. soils

The South is a patchwork of diverse soil belts, with generally low fertility. Along the coast and in much of Florida, the soil is sandy, with muddy flood plains and swamps. Alluvial soil makes an improvement in the Mississippi valley.

Farther west, in Texas and Oklahoma, many soils are too poor for anything but grazing, and drought is a constant problem. In the Ohio valley region, soils are much eroded, though there are better stretches in Kentucky and Tennessee. Extremely fertile, lime-rich soils are characteristic of the corn belt and the prairies but unreliability of water supply becomes a difficulty in the Great Plains.

The huge mountainous region of the West contains fertile soils in limited areas such as the Columbia plateau, but in general, soils are sparse, stony, or arid. The agricultural productivity of California, is largely dependent on irrigation.

Source: U.S. Dept. of Agriculture

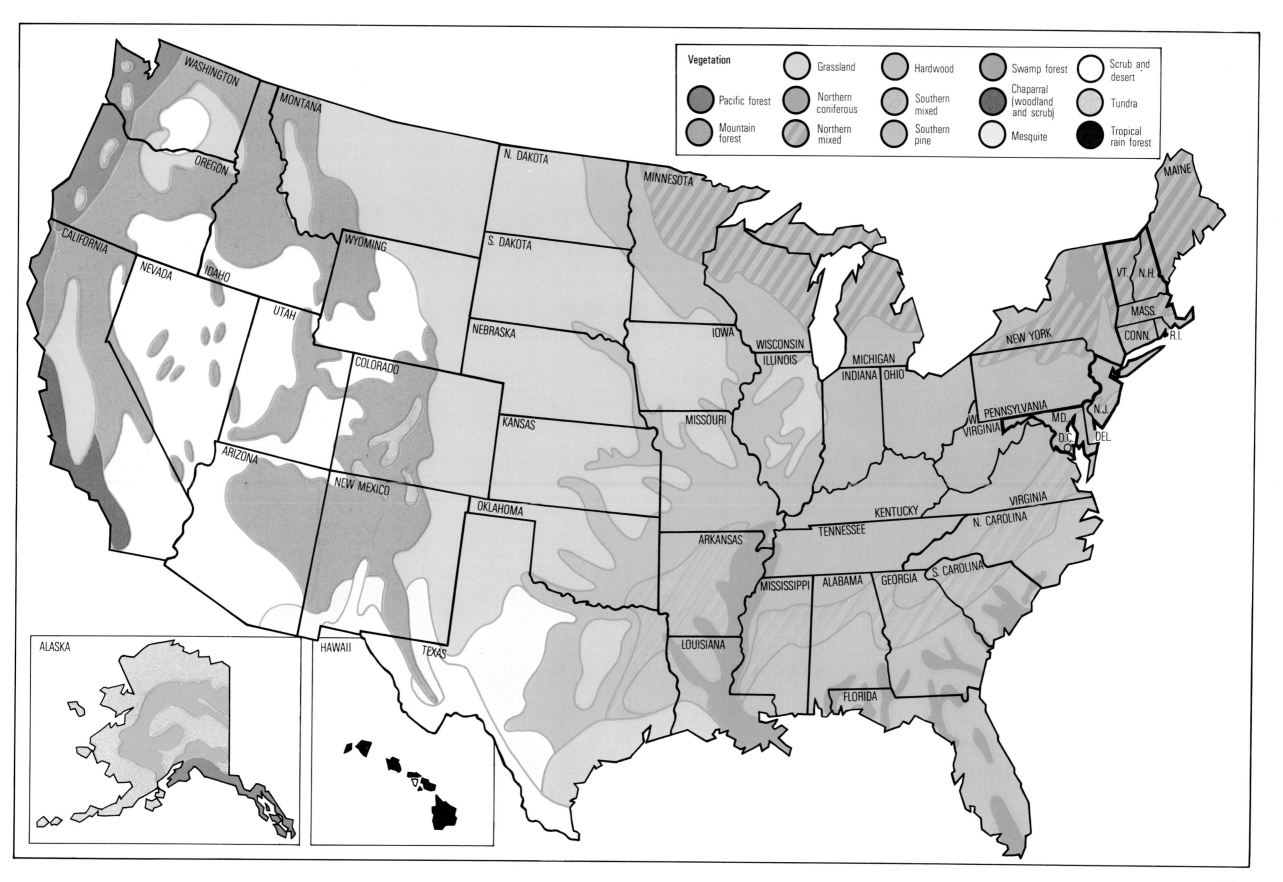

Vegetation

- Pacific forest
- Mountain forest
- Grassland
- Northern coniferous
- Northern mixed
- Hardwood
- Southern mixed
- Southern pine
- Swamp forest
- Chaparral (woodland and scrub)
- Mesquite
- Scrub and desert
- Tundra
- Tropical rain forest

WASHINGTON
MONTANA
OREGON
N. DAKOTA
MINNESOTA
MAINE
CALIFORNIA
IDAHO
WYOMING
S. DAKOTA
NEVADA
UTAH
NEBRASKA
IOWA
WISCONSIN
MICHIGAN
NEW YORK
VT. N.H.
MASS.
CONN. R.I.
COLORADO
ILLINOIS
INDIANA OHIO
PENNSYLVANIA
N.J.
W. VIRGINIA
MD.
D.C.
DEL
ARIZONA
KANSAS
MISSOURI
KENTUCKY
VIRGINIA
NEW MEXICO
OKLAHOMA
TENNESSEE
N. CAROLINA
ARKANSAS
S. CAROLINA
MISSISSIPPI
ALABAMA
GEORGIA
LOUISIANA
TEXAS
FLORIDA
ALASKA
HAWAII

NATIONAL PARKS

In 1872 President Ulysses S. Grant signed an act of Congress creating the Yellowstone National Park "as a pleasure ground for the benefit and enjoyment of the people". This marked the beginning of the concept of national parks under federal ownership. The protection of outstanding scenic areas, wildlife, and vegetation for posterity thus became part of national policy.

During the following decades the national park system grew, partly through the addition of huge natural areas, and partly through the acquisition of locations of historic interest. In 1916 an act of Congress established the National Park Service to administer the areas within the system. By 1983 the number of areas had grown to 335 and the total acreage to almost 75 million. The national parks are shown on the map.

Apart from the national parks themselves, there are many other protected areas within the national park system. National monuments include areas of scientific importance, such as the ecology of Death Valley and the rock arches of Utah. They also include remains of ancient Indian cultures and sites of importance in the development of the nation.

Other protected areas under the jurisdiction of the National Park Service include national parkways, trails, seashores and riverways, historical parks, and sites notable in the Revolutionary and Civil Wars.

The map also shows the extent of the national forest system in 1980. The dangers of forest clearance by settlers became obvious in the latter half of the nineteenth century and Congress passed legislation leading to the beginning of the national forest system in 1891. In 1983 this included a total of 230 million acres.

Source: U.S. National Park Service; National Association of State Park Directors; U.S. Forest Service

Diagram B: Acreage of National Park system (federal land only), 1960-1983. The leap in 1978 is accounted for by over 40 million acres of public domain land in Alaska being added to the system

Diagram A: Distribution of visitors to national parks compared to distribution of total acreage by division, 1983. Figures for visitors and acreage are in thousands

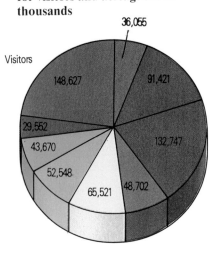

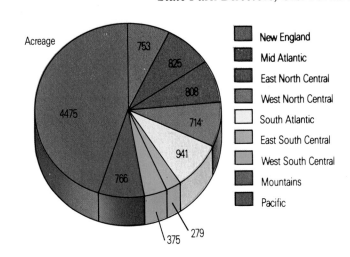

Legend:
- New England
- Mid Atlantic
- East North Central
- West North Central
- South Atlantic
- East South Central
- West South Central
- Mountains
- Pacific

NATIONAL PARKS (see map)

1 Olympic, Washington	25 Arches, Utah
2 Mount Rainier, Washington	26 Mesa Verde, Colorado
3 North Cascades, Washington	27 Rocky Mountain, Colorado
4 Glacier, Montana	28 Mammoth Cave, Kentucky
5 Theodore Roosevelt (North Unit), North Dakota	29 Shenandoah, Virginia
	30 Petrified Forest, Arizona
6 Theodore Roosevelt (South Unit), North Dakota	31 Carlsbad Caverns, New Mexico
7 Voyageurs, Minnesota	32 Hot Springs, Arkansas
8 Isle Royale, Michigan	33 Great Smoky Mountains, Tennessee
9 Acadia, Maine	
10 Crater Lake, Oregon	34 Guadalupe Mountains, Texas
11 Yellowstone, Wyoming	35 Big Bend, Texas
12 Grand Teton, Wyoming	36 Everglades, Florida
13 Wind Cave, South Dakota	37 Biscayne, Florida
14 Badlands, South Dakota	38 Kobuk Valley, Alaska
15 Redwood, California	39 Gates of Arctic, Alaska
16 Lassen Volcanic, California	40 Denali, Alaska
17 Yosemite, California	41 Katmai, Alaska
18 Kings Canyon, California	42 Lake Clark, Alaska
19 Sequoia, California	43 Kenai Fjords, Alaska
20 Channel Islands, California	44 Wrangell-St Elias, Alaska
21 Zion, Utah	45 Glacier Bay, Alaska
22 Bryce Canyon, Utah	46 Haleakala, Hawaii
23 Capitol Reef, Utah	47 Hawaii Volcanoes, Hawaii
24 Canyonlands, Utah	48 Grand Canyon, Arizona

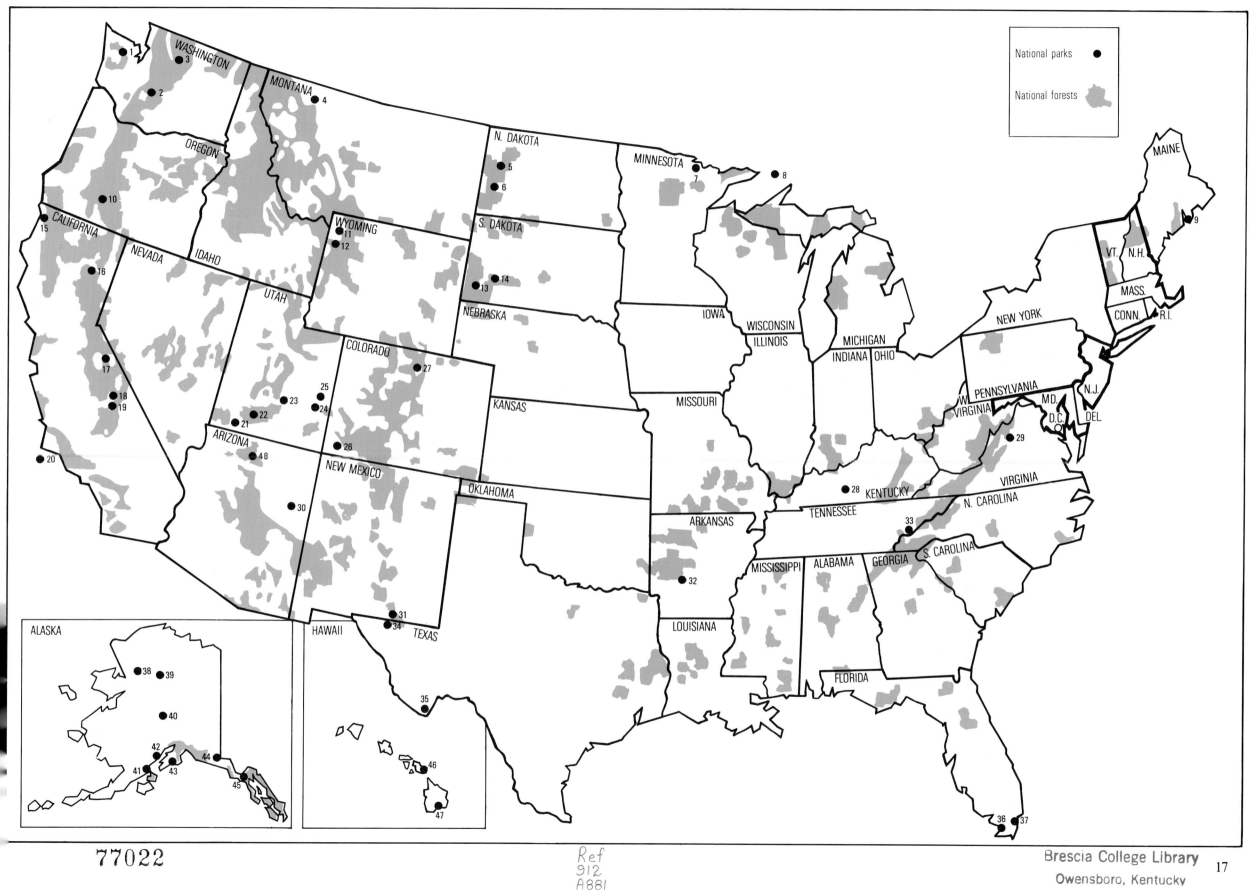

Ref
912
A881

17

RESIDENT POPULATION

A great mixture of ancestry groups makes up the resident population of the United States. The 1980 census classified people according to race, dividing them into "white," "black," "American Indian," several different Asian groups — Chinese, Filipino, Asian Indian, Korean, and Vietnamese — and "all other races." "American Indian" here includes Eskimo and Aleut people.

On the map, the states are colored according to the percentage of the population classified as "white." The District of Columbia shows the lowest percentage, having only 27 percent in this category. Hawaii also has a low percentage, 33. South Carolina and Louisiana come next, with 69 percent each. At the other extreme, Maine, New Hampshire, and Vermont have over 99 percent.

Each state also shows the percentage classified by the census as "of Spanish origin." These people, the Bureau of the Census explains, may be of any race. Not surprisingly, New Mexico shows the highest percentage, 36.6, followed by 19 percent for California.

In addition, the map gives a pie chart for each state, dividing the non-"white" population between "black," "American Indian,"

Diagram A: Population by main ancestry groups, 1980

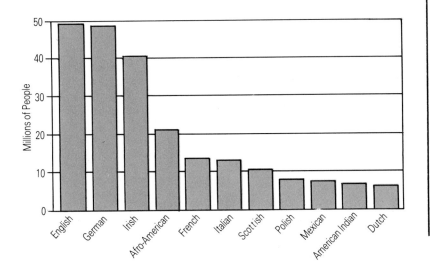

"Asian," and "all other." In most states "black" is by far the largest of these categories. The exceptions are North and South Dakota, Montana, and Alaska, where "American Indian" is the largest group, and New Mexico, where "all other" is the major group.

Because of the history of immigration into the United States from all over the world, people of similar ancestry groups have tended to settle in particular areas of the country. The 1980 census asked a sample of people about their ancestry. Those who answered either reported a single group, or gave multinational ancestry. Of those who gave "English" as their ancestry — either singly, or in combination with other nationalities — 40 percent live in the South; 41 percent of those who reported German ancestry live in the Midwest; 48 percent of those who said "Russian" are resident in the Northeast; and 53 percent of the group reporting Afro-American ancestry are in the South.

Remembering that multinational ancestry is common, we can use the same sample as a whole to estimate the numbers of people in the United States having foreign ancestry. See Diagram A.

The census also asked a sample of people whether they spoke a language other than English at home. It was estimated that, in 1980, there were 23 million such people. Diagram B gives the distribution of "foreign-speakers" omitting children aged less than 5 years. Spanish-speakers make up about 48 percent of the total, followed by Italian, French, and German, with about 7 percent each.

Source: U.S. Bureau of the Census

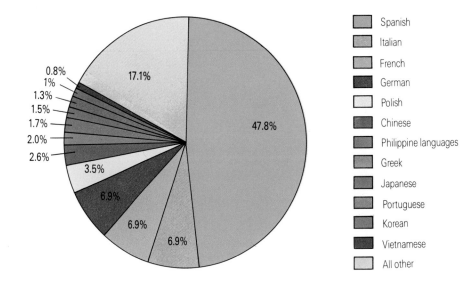

Spanish
Italian
French
German
Polish
Chinese
Philippine languages
Greek
Japanese
Portuguese
Korean
Vietnamese
All other

Diagram B: Percentage distribution of those aged 5 years and over, who currently speak a language at home other than English, by language

Note: Spanish origin — in the 1980 census, the Bureau of the Census collected data on the Spanish origin population in the United States by using a self-identification question. Persons of Spanish/Hispanic origin or descent are those who classified themselves in one of the specific Spanish origin categories listed on the questionnaire — Mexican, Puerto Rican, Cuban, or Other Spanish/Hispanic origin.

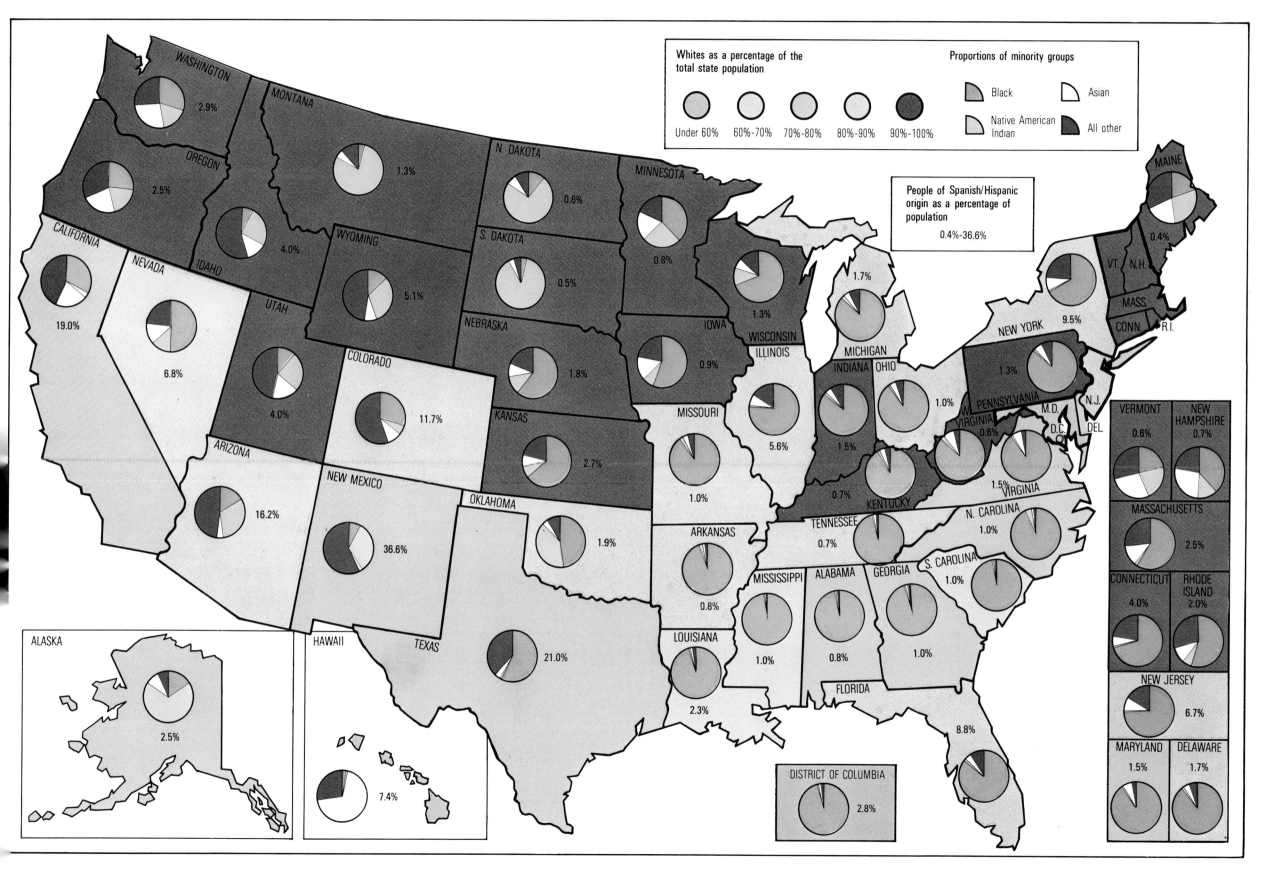

Whites as a percentage of the total state population

Under 60%   60%-70%   70%-80%   80%-90%   90%-100%

Proportions of minority groups

Black   Asian
Native American Indian   All other

People of Spanish/Hispanic origin as a percentage of population
0.4%-36.6%

WASHINGTON 2.9%
OREGON 2.5%
CALIFORNIA 19.0%
NEVADA 6.8%
IDAHO 4.0%
MONTANA 1.3%
WYOMING 5.1%
UTAH 4.0%
COLORADO 11.7%
ARIZONA 16.2%
NEW MEXICO 36.6%
N. DAKOTA 0.6%
S. DAKOTA 0.5%
NEBRASKA 1.8%
KANSAS 2.7%
OKLAHOMA 1.9%
MINNESOTA 0.8%
IOWA 0.9%
MISSOURI 1.0%
ARKANSAS 0.8%
WISCONSIN 1.3%
ILLINOIS 5.6%
MICHIGAN 1.7%
INDIANA 1.5%
OHIO 1.0%
KENTUCKY 0.7%
TENNESSEE 0.7%
MISSISSIPPI 1.0%
ALABAMA 0.8%
GEORGIA 1.0%
LOUISIANA 2.3%
TEXAS 21.0%
FLORIDA 8.8%
S. CAROLINA 1.0%
N. CAROLINA 1.0%
VIRGINIA 1.5%
W. VIRGINIA 0.6%
PENNSYLVANIA 1.3%
NEW YORK 9.5%
MAINE 0.4%

VERMONT 0.6%
NEW HAMPSHIRE 0.7%
MASSACHUSETTS 2.5%
CONNECTICUT 4.0%
RHODE ISLAND 2.0%
NEW JERSEY 6.7%
MARYLAND 1.5%
DELAWARE 1.7%

VT. N.H. MASS. CONN. R.I. M.D. N.J. DEL. D.C.

ALASKA 2.5%
HAWAII 7.4%
DISTRICT OF COLUMBIA 2.8%

19

AMERICAN INDIANS

The map shows the main culture areas, and major tribes of the American Indians in early colonial times, together with Indian reservations in 1982. (Many descendants of the original inhabitants of North America object to the name "Indian," which is based on a 500-year-old error, but, as for the Eskimo peoples, no fully satisfactory alternative has yet been devised; the term "Native Americans" is sometimes used but is open to misinterpretation.)

The federal government currently recognizes a special obligation to, and trust responsibility for, approximately 500 "Indian entities" in the contiguous United States and Alaska. These Indian entities include tribes, other groups, pueblos, and other villages, which are organizations approved and recognized by federal statutes, plus other Indian organizations of traditional structure, which may or may not have formal federal approval.

The term "tribe" can also be misleading. Originally, it was an approximate equivalent of the term "nation," and it is chiefly in this sense that the names of major tribes appear on the map. Nevertheless, "Seminole," for example, is a Creek word meaning "separatist," which came into use after 1775 to describe a group united primarily by hostility to the United States. Since the relegation of Indians to reservations, the word "tribe" has developed a variety of meanings. It may imply a group within an Indian community, the community itself, or a group of — sometimes separated — communities.

Indian-owned lands are known variously as reservations, communities, colonies, rancherias, pueblos, and so on, so that an exact accounting is difficult. In Oklahoma, where there is a high degree of assimilation with white culture, there are no reservations in the sense that the term is used in other parts of the United States. The map shows large reservations, such as the Navaho reservations in Arizona, New Mexico, and Utah, many of which have been enlarged by purchase to accommodate a growing population since the Indian Reorganization act of 1934.

The distribution of lands under the jurisdiction of the Bureau of Indian Affairs is shown in Diagram A. States containing less than 500,000 acres of land in this category have been excluded from the totals. The total for each region includes Trust allotted land (that is, landholdings of individuals), lands held by Indian tribes, and government-owned land. The amount of government-owned land is statistically insignificant except in the states of New Mexico (4.1 percent of the total), Indiana (3.9 percent), and Arizona (0.5 percent).

The proportion of lands held by tribes is 78.3 percent of all Indian lands in the United States as a whole. However, there are considerable variations from state to state. For example, in Alaska, the major part is held by individuals, and tribal lands account for only 18 percent of the state total. In South Dakota, tribal lands account for 52 percent of the total, in Montana, 56 percent. In Utah, on the other hand, the proportion of tribal land is 98 percent, and in New Mexico 91 percent (these figures exclude government-owned land).

The population of American Indians numbered 1,420,000 in 1980. The proportion of the total population in each region, is given in Diagram B.

Source: U.S. Bureau of Indian Affairs;
U.S. Bureau of the Census

Diagram A: Distribution of lands under the jurisdiction of the Bureau of Indian Affairs by region, 1982

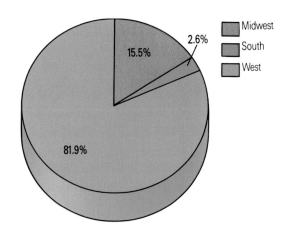

Diagram B: Distribution of American Indians by division, 1980

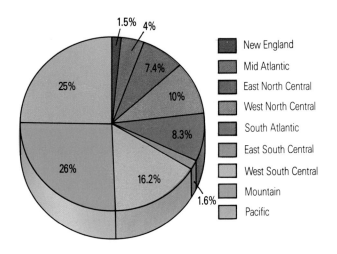

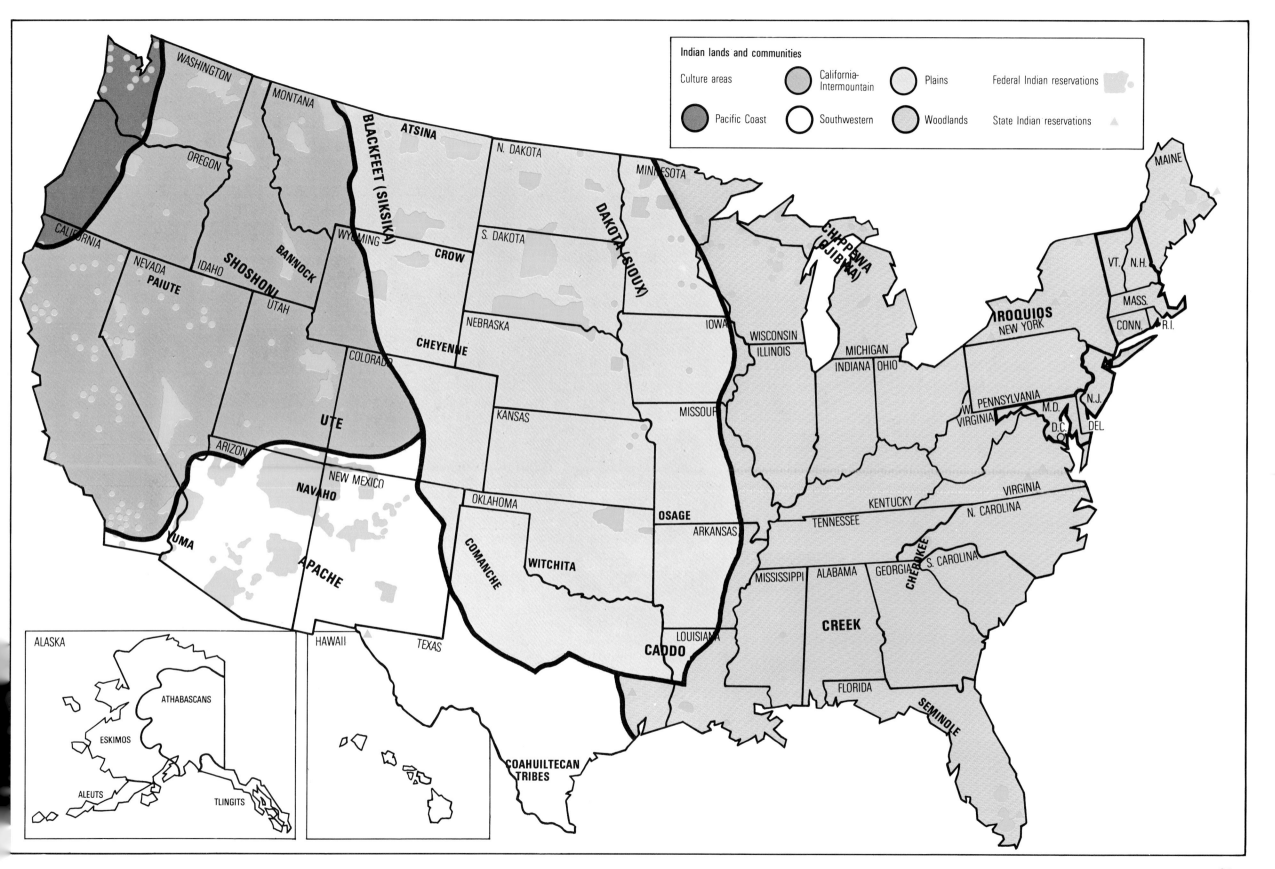

Indian lands and communities

Culture areas

Pacific Coast

California-Intermountain

Southwestern

Plains

Woodlands

Federal Indian reservations

State Indian reservations

WASHINGTON

OREGON

MONTANA

CALIFORNIA

NEVADA

IDAHO

SHOSHONI

BANNOCK

ATSINA

BLACKFEET (SIKSIKA)

CROW

N. DAKOTA

S. DAKOTA

DAKOTA (SIOUX)

MINNESOTA

CHIPPEWA (OJIBWA)

PAIUTE

UTAH

WYOMING

UTE

COLORADO

NEBRASKA

CHEYENNE

IOWA

WISCONSIN

ILLINOIS

MICHIGAN

INDIANA OHIO

IROQUIOS

NEW YORK

MAINE

VT. N.H.

MASS.

CONN. R.I.

ARIZONA

NEW MEXICO

NAVAHO

KANSAS

MISSOURI

PENNSYLVANIA

W. VIRGINIA

M.D.

D.C.

N.J.

DEL

YUMA

APACHE

OKLAHOMA

OSAGE

ARKANSAS

COMANCHE

WITCHITA

CADDO

LOUISIANA

KENTUCKY

VIRGINIA

TENNESSEE

N. CAROLINA

MISSISSIPPI

ALABAMA

GEORGIA

CHEROKEE

S. CAROLINA

CREEK

FLORIDA

SEMINOLE

ALASKA

ATHABASCANS

ESKIMOS

ALEUTS

TLINGITS

HAWAII

TEXAS

COAHUILTECAN TRIBES

YOUNG AND OLD

In 1983 26.7 percent of the population of the United States were aged under 18, while 11.7 percent were 65 or over. These two maps show the proportion of young people — under 18 years — and old people — 65 and over — in the different states.

There are wide variations between states. Utah, with 37.6 percent of its population under 18, stands out in the first map, along with Idaho (32.2 percent), Alaska (32.1), Wyoming (31.1), Mississippi (31.0), New Mexico (30.8), and Louisiana (30.6). Florida, with 23.0 percent aged under 18, has the lowest percentage of young people, followed by Rhode Island (23.8), and Massachusetts (23.9).

Florida shows the highest percentage of old people, 17.5 percent being aged 65 or more, followed by Arkansas, with 14.1 percent. Alaska, at the other extreme, has only 3 percent of people in this age group. Utah, with 7.6 percent, comes next.

Over the past few years, the age distribution for the United States as a whole has been shifting steadily toward the older age groups. In 1970, 9.8 percent of the population were aged 65 and over. In 1920, this percentage was only 4.6. The median age — the age at which exactly half the population is younger — has risen from 27.9 in 1970 to 30.9 in 1983.

These changes do not simply mean that people are living longer. The effect of the fall in fertility in the 1960s, which implied the fall in the numbers of young people later, is the major factor in the increase of the average age of the population.

Earlier in this century, falls in death rates did not have as great an effect on the proportion of old people as might have been expected, because of the decrease in mortality among younger age groups. In the future, however, this may not be the case, and future falls in death rates will make a greater difference to the proportion of people in the older groups. Demographers forecast that, by the end of the century, there will be nearly as many people aged over 75 as between 65 and 75 years old.

Even more striking than the tendency of the population to get older is the widening difference between the age distributions of the sexes. Women tend to live longer than men, and the gap is widening. Diagram A represents the age distributions for men and women in 1970, 1980, and 1983. While the percentage of men in the "65 and over" group went up from 8.5 in 1970 to 9.6 in 1983, the corresponding percentage for women rose from 11.1 to 13.6.

The median age for men has increased from 26.6 in 1970 to 29.6 in 1983. But that for women was 29.2 in 1970 and 32.2 in 1983. The "75 years and over" group is larger than it used to be and shows even more striking changes. In 1970, 3.0 percent of men were in this group, and 4.4 percent of women. In 1983, these percentages had risen to 3.4 percent for men and 5.9 percent for women.

Diagram B graphs the marked decline in the ratio of men to women in the "65 and over" group during the course of this century. In 1910, there were slightly more men than women. The numbers evened out by the early 1930s. Then, the longer lifespan of women began to show its effect: by 1983, there were only 67.1 men for every 100 women in this age group.

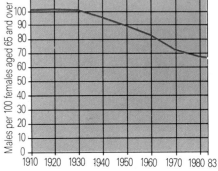

Diagram B: Number of men over 65 years old per 100 women over 65 years old, 1910-1983

Source: U.S. Bureau of the Census

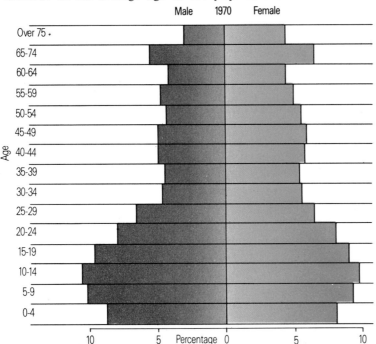

Diagram A: Age distributions, by sex, 1970, 1980, 1983

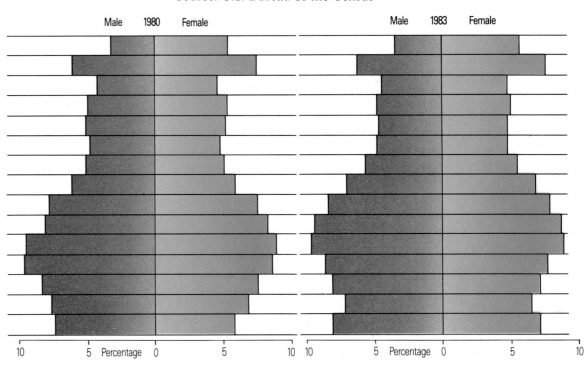

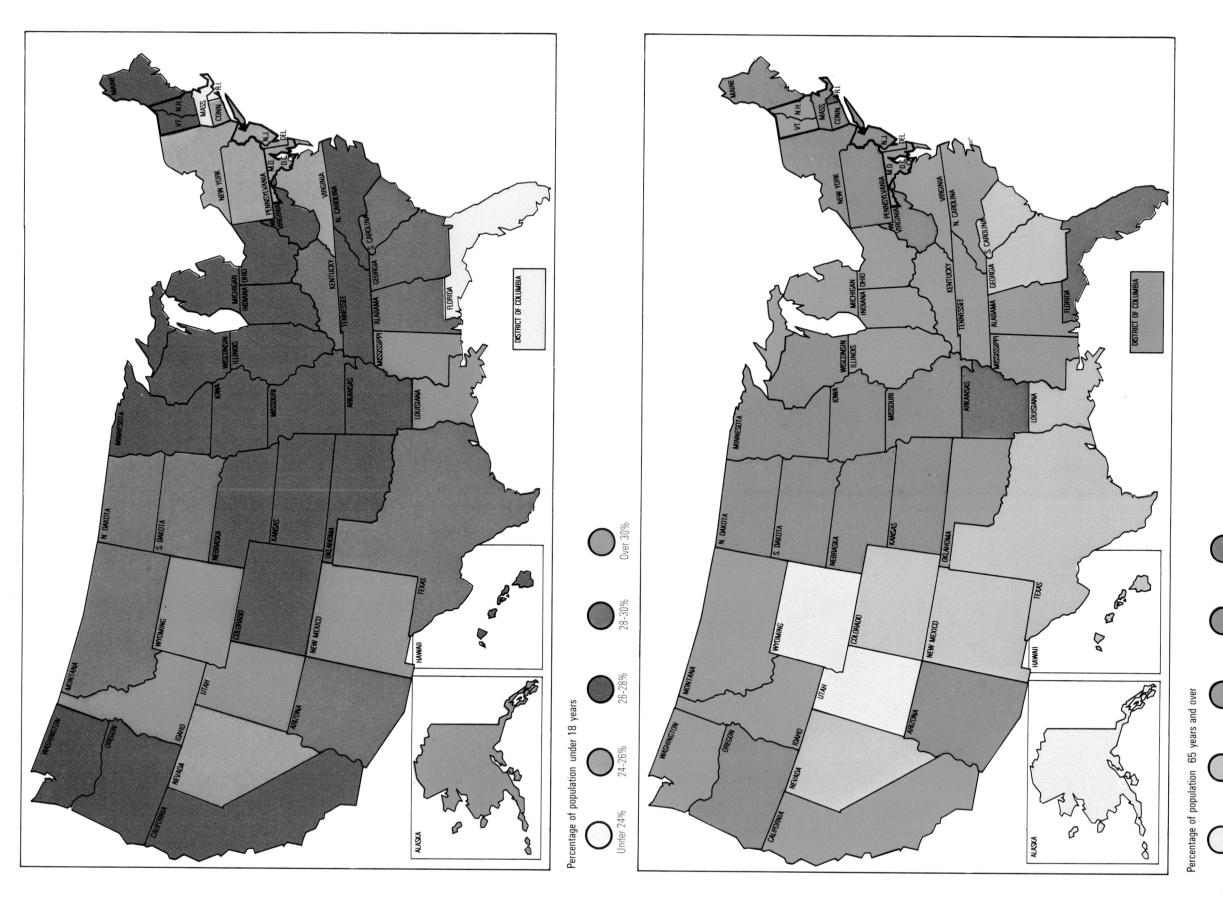

Percentage of population under 18 years

- Over 30%
- 28-30%
- 26-28%
- 24-26%
- Under 24%

DISTRICT OF COLUMBIA

Percentage of population 65 years and over

- Over 14%
- 12-14%
- 10-12%
- 8-10%
- Under 8%

DISTRICT OF COLUMBIA

23

POPULATION DENSITY

POPULATION DENSITY
(people per square mile, 1983)

1	Washington D.C.	9,891
2	New Jersey	1,000
3	Rhode I.	906
4	Massachusetts	737
5	Connecticut	644
6	Maryland	437
7	New York	373
8	Delaware	314
9	Pennsylvania	265
10	Ohio	262
11	Illinois	206
12	Florida	197
13	California	161
14	Michigan	159
15	Hawaii	159
16	Indiana	152
17	Virginia	140
18	N. Carolina	125
19	Tennessee	114
20	S. Carolina	108
21	New Hampshire	107
22	Louisiana	100
23	Georgia	99
24	Kentucky	94
25	Wisconsin	87
26	W. Virginia	81
27	Alabama	78
28	Missouri	72
29	Washington	65
30	Texas	60
31	Vermont	57
32	Mississippi	55
33	Minnesota	52
34	Iowa	52
35	Oklahoma	48
36	Arkansas	45
37	Maine	37
38	Kansas	30
39	Colorado	30
40	Oregon	28
41	Arizona	26
42	Nebraska	21
43	Utah	20
44	New Mexico	12
45	Idaho	12
46	N. Dakota	10
47	S. Dakota	9
48	Nevada	8
49	Montana	6
50	Wyoming	5
51	Alaska	1

About 234 million Americans occupy a total land area of 3.6 million square miles. So, on average, there are about 65 people for each square mile. But as you can see from this map there are considerable differences between the states.

The table (left) gives the average population densities (1983) of the states, in people per square mile, in descending order. As usual, the District of Columbia is exceptional, packing 623,000 people into 63 square miles to give an average density of almost 10,000. Of the states New Jersey heads the list with 1,000 people per square mile, followed by Rhode Island (906). Down at the bottom of the list are Wyoming, with 5 people to each square mile, and, not surprisingly, Alaska, with only one.

Obviously there are even greater variations within each state, urban areas carrying a far higher density of population. The map marks these centers of population, showing cities with over 100,000 people grouped into three bands according to size. The map also indicates the population of each state. California, with more than 25 million people, has over 10 percent of the total U.S. population, well ahead of New York (17.67 million) and Texas (15.72 million).

The differences between population densities of cities are also considerable. Using the figures for 1980, we find 23,455 residents for each square mile of New York City, rising to 64,337 in the borough of Manhattan. In comparison, the 1.2 million inhabitants of Houston, Texas, occupied 556 square miles — a density of 2,158. In Los Angeles, California, the density of population in 1980 was 6,384, in Detroit, Michigan, 8,874, in Chicago, Illinois, 13,174 and in San Francisco, California, 14,633. At the other extreme, there were only 101 people for every square mile in Anchorage, Alaska.

Diagram A is a pie chart showing how the total U.S. population is distributed among the nine divisions of the country. The Atlantic Seaboard — East North Central, Middle Atlantic, and South Atlantic — accounts for about half of the total, each division being about one-sixth. The Pacific division approaches the same proportion. This leaves the remaining five divisions accounting for one-third of the total.

Diagram B shows how the population density of the United States has increased over the last 200 years as the country has gradually expanded its territory. The five small maps show the area occupied by the United States in 1790, 1840, 1890, 1940 and 1980. The area of the square beneath each map is proportional to the area shaded on the map. Each dot in a square represents one

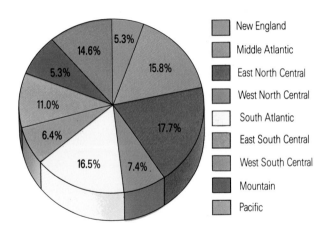

New England
Middle Atlantic
East North Central
West North Central
South Atlantic
East South Central
West South Central
Mountain
Pacific

Diagram A: Distribution of total population by division

POPULATION DENSITY BY DIVISION

The average population densities of the divisions in 1980 were as follows:

New England	196
Middle Atlantic	369
East North Central	171
West North Central	34
South Atlantic	138
East South Central	82
West South Central	56
Mountain	13
Pacific	36

However, it is important to recognize that this pattern is changing. During the past half century, population densities in the Northeast and Midwest have risen by about 50 percent, and those in the South by 100 percent, but in the West they have risen by approximately 35 percent.

Diagram B: Population density, 1790-1980. The area of each square is proportional to the area shaded on the small map above. Each dot represents one million people

million people living in the area at the time. Below each square is the corresponding population density.

The first settlements on the Atlantic coast had grown by the time of the first census in 1790 to a density of 4.5 people per square mile. Between then and 1840 the area of settlement increased by almost 70 percent. Yet, despite this massive increase in territory, a major influx of immigrants in the early nineteenth century pushed the density up to 9.8. Again the territory expanded and again an even greater flood of immigrants in the middle of the century had more than doubled the density by 1890, to give 21.2 people per square mile. By the start of World War II the density had doubled once more, though this time the increase was not accompanied by an expansion of territory. By 1980, both Alaska and Hawaii had become states and the density had risen a further 70 percent.

Source: U.S. Bureau of the Census, 1980

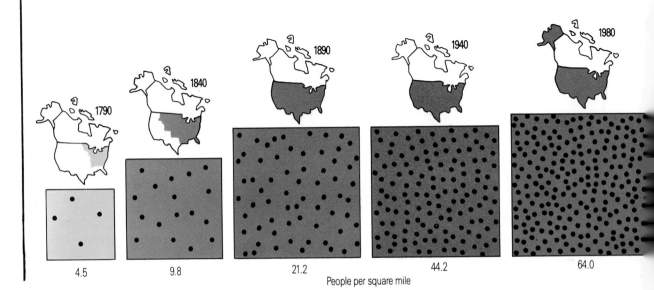

| 4.5 | 9.8 | 21.2 | 44.2 | 64.0 |

People per square mile

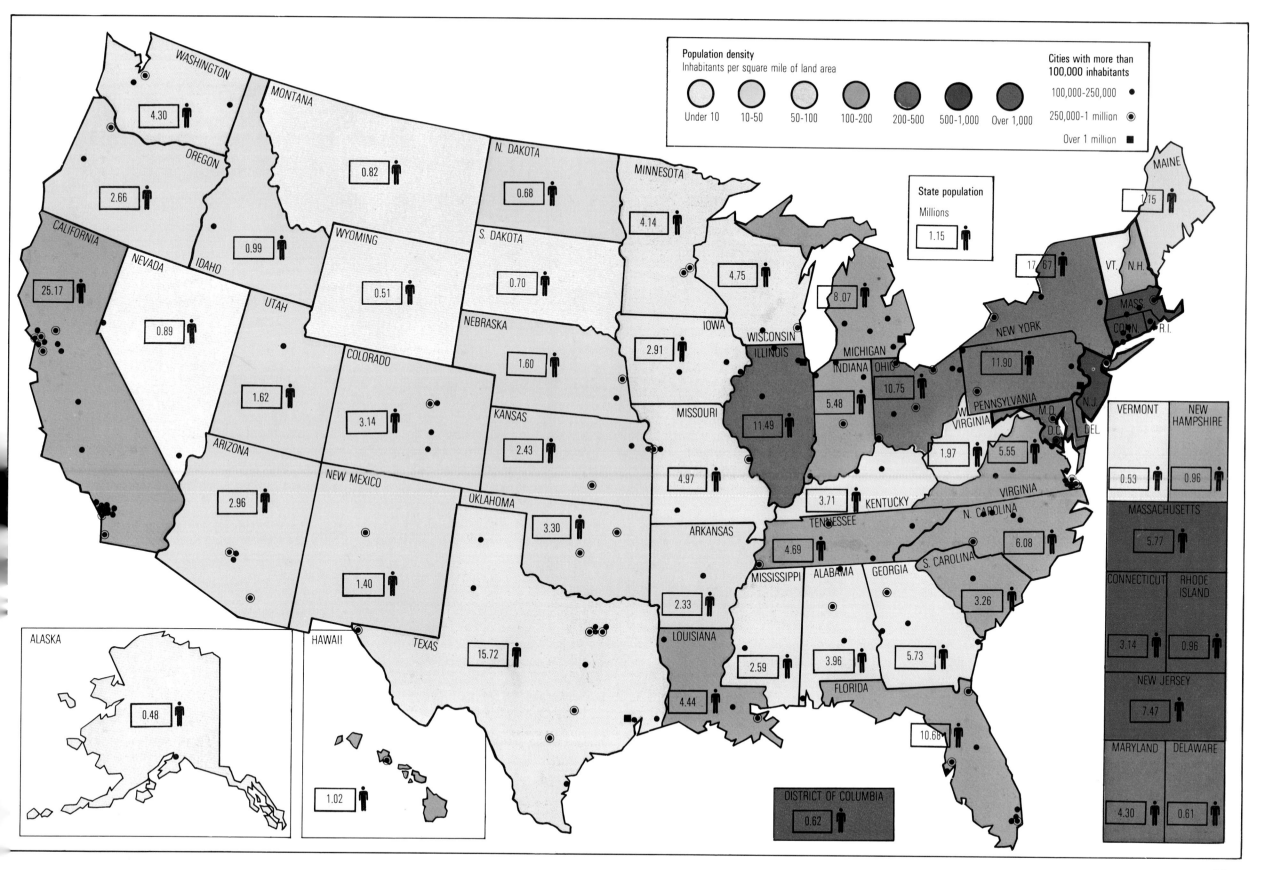

Population density
Inhabitants per square mile of land area

Under 10 | 10-50 | 50-100 | 100-200 | 200-500 | 500-1,000 | Over 1,000

Cities with more than 100,000 inhabitants

· 100,000-250,000
⊙ 250,000-1 million
■ Over 1 million

State population

Millions

1.15

WASHINGTON 4.30

OREGON 2.66

MONTANA 0.82

N. DAKOTA 0.68

MINNESOTA 4.14

MAINE 1.15

IDAHO 0.99

WYOMING 0.51

S. DAKOTA 0.70

WISCONSIN 4.75

CALIFORNIA 25.17

NEVADA 0.89

UTAH 1.62

COLORADO 3.14

NEBRASKA 1.60

IOWA 2.91

ILLINOIS 11.49

MICHIGAN 8.07

INDIANA 5.48

OHIO 10.75

NEW YORK 17.67

PENNSYLVANIA 11.90

ARIZONA 2.96

NEW MEXICO 1.40

KANSAS 2.43

OKLAHOMA 3.30

MISSOURI 4.97

KENTUCKY 3.71

W. VIRGINIA 1.97

VIRGINIA 5.55

ARKANSAS 2.33

TENNESSEE 4.69

N. CAROLINA 6.08

S. CAROLINA 3.26

TEXAS 15.72

LOUISIANA 4.44

MISSISSIPPI 2.59

ALABAMA 3.96

GEORGIA 5.73

FLORIDA 10.68

ALASKA 0.48

HAWAII 1.02

VERMONT 0.53

NEW HAMPSHIRE 0.96

MASSACHUSETTS 5.77

CONNECTICUT 3.14

RHODE ISLAND 0.96

NEW JERSEY 7.47

MARYLAND 4.30

DELAWARE 0.61

DISTRICT OF COLUMBIA 0.62

25

URBAN AND RURAL UNITED STATES

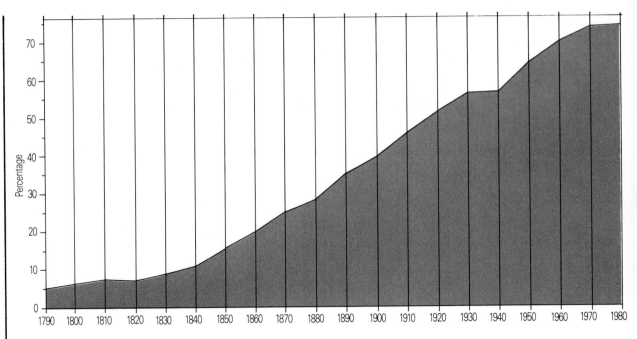

Nearly three-quarters of the population of the United States now live in urban areas. But, as the map shows, this proportion varies widely between different parts of the country. According to the 1980 census, while 9 out of 10 Californians live in urban areas, less than one-third of the people of Vermont do so.

The U.S. Bureau of the Census has a precise but involved definition of "urban". Basically, it includes (1) places with over 2,500 inhabitants, and (2) central cities that, together with "contiguous closely settled territory, have a total population of at least 50,000."

The map also indicates, for each state, the percentage of the area of the state considered to be urbanized. The Northeast region, as would be expected, shows the highest proportion of urban area, New Jersey heading the list with 29 percent. California also shows a fairly high proportion, with 4.2 percent of its area urbanized. Alaska, at the other extreme, has only 0.1 percent of its area classified as "urban." (The District of Columbia is not shown here, because it is classified as totally urban.)

It must be borne in mind that urbanized areas themselves will vary from small villages to massive industrialized regions. The map indicates this variation by showing the average density of population per acre in the urban areas of each state.

It is worth noting that in 1980, 28.4 million people — one-eighth of the population of the United States — lived in 22 cities of over 500,000 inhabitants. Since 1960, however, successive censuses have shown a decrease in the percentage of people who live in these large cities. In 1960, 16 percent lived in cities with over half a million

inhabitants, in 1970 15 percent, and in 1980 12.5 percent. On the other hand, the proportion of the population living in places with under 10,000 inhabitants has increased, from 25 percent in 1960, to 29 percent in 1970, and 30 percent in 1980.

A related process is revealed by the census breakdown of urban population into those living in "central cities" and those in the "urban fringe." In 1970, 54.5 million people were in this latter group, comprising 26.8 percent of the total population. By 1980, this figure had risen to 72.1 million, or 31.8 percent. In addition, the percentage of the population recorded as living in rural areas, but within what the Bureau of the Census calls "Metropolitan Statistical Areas", rose from 8.1 to 10.6 between 1970 and 1980. (A Metropolitan Statistical Area is defined as a large population nucleus together with adjacent associated communities.)

Diagram A is a pie chart showing the urban population of the nine divisions of the United States at the time of the 1980 census. Half of the urban population live in three divisions — Middle Atlantic, East North Central and South Atlantic, with the Pacific division accounting for another sixth.

Of the 59.5 million people classified by the 1980 census as living in rural areas, nearly one-quarter live in the East North Central division, and slightly more than a quarter in the South Atlantic division.

The movement from the countryside into the cities has gone on since the first settlements were established. Diagram B shows this process by graphing the percentage of the population considered to be urbanized for each census since 1790.

Source: U.S. Bureau of the Census

Diagram B: Percentage of total population living in urban areas, 1790-1980

Diagram A: Distribution of urban population by division, 1980

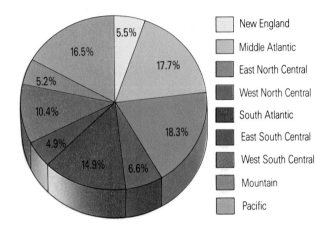

- New England — 5.5%
- Middle Atlantic — 17.7%
- East North Central — 18.3%
- West North Central — 6.6%
- South Atlantic — 14.9%
- East South Central — 4.9%
- West South Central — 10.4%
- Mountain — 5.2%
- Pacific — 16.5%

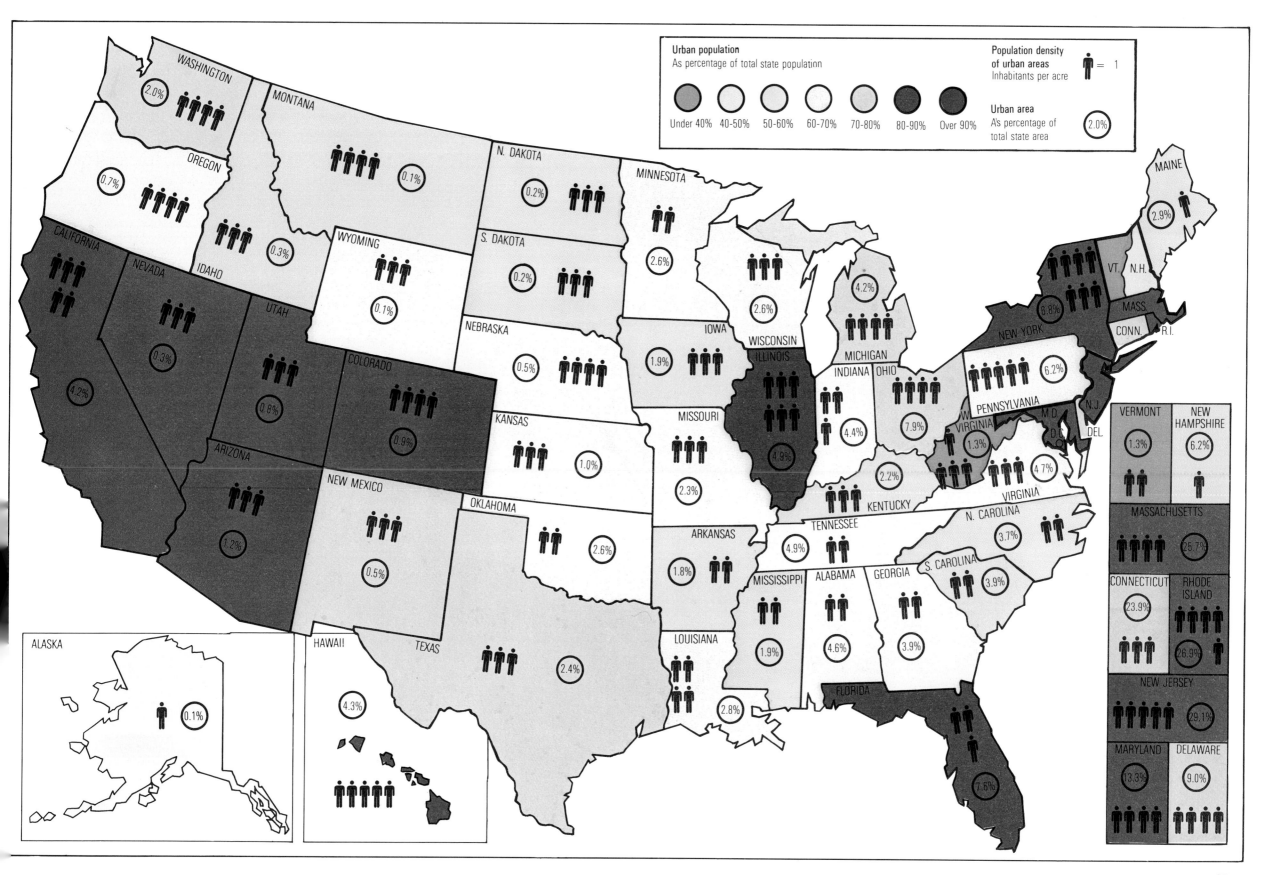

Urban population
As percentage of total state population

Under 40% | 40-50% | 50-60% | 60-70% | 70-80% | 80-90% | Over 90%

Population density of urban areas
Inhabitants per acre
👤 = 1

Urban area
As percentage of total state area
2.0%

27

AMERICANS ON THE MOVE

The migration of Americans has been from east to west. The map shows this tendency from several angles.

The Bureau of the Census has computed a "center of population" for each census since the first in 1790. It describes this as follows: "'center of population' is that point at which an imaginary flat, weightless, and rigid map of the United States would balance if weights of identical value were placed on it so that each weight represented the location of one person on the date of the census."

The map shows how this point has shifted from just east of Baltimore in 1790 to Jefferson County, Missouri, in 1980. Note how the rapid movement west after 1870 was followed by a much slower pace between 1890 and 1940, and then by a faster shift again during and after World War II.

The arrows on the map indicate net migration between the four regions, in the period 1975-1980. The main feature continued to be the movement out of the Northeast and Midwest, into the South and West.

Based on the results of the 1980 census, the Bureau of the Census worked out projections of population for the regions to the end of the century. The states are colored according to the percentage changes projected for the period 1980-2000. Most of the differences between states can be attributed to migration.

As would be expected, the biggest projected losses in population are to be found in the Northeast, and the biggest gains in the South and West. The District of Columbia is an exception. By the year 2000, its population is expected to fall to below 60 percent of its 1980 level. New York State comes next, with a projected drop of 14 percent.

Among the states with increasing populations, Nevada heads the list with an expected rise of 138 percent. It is followed by Wyoming with 113 percent, Arizona with 100 percent, and Florida with 75 percent. New Hampshire is the exception among the northeastern states, showing a projected rise in population of nearly 50 percent.

Diagram A traces the same process for the period 1950-1983, graphing the movement of regional populations, expressed as percentages of the total U.S. population. As will be seen, the West, which in 1950 held only one-eighth of the population, now accounts for one-fifth.

Diagram B gives a more detailed picture of movement. The 1980 census asked people where they had lived in 1975. The diagram ranks the states according to the percentage of those residents in 1980 who had lived in another state five years earlier. (This excludes those under five years old in 1980.) At the top we see that over 30 percent of Nevada residents in 1980 had moved there during the previous five years. At the bottom, we find that all but 4 percent of New York State residents in 1980 were already living there in 1975.

However, while all this information points to a continued trend of movement south and west, there are some indications that it has been slowing down. Some experts now think that the numbers of families moving out of the Northeast may have reached a peak around 1980, although the industrial Midwest is still losing people heavily.

During the 1970s the Northeast showed a net out migration averaging 289,000 per year. Between 1980 and 1983, however, this average dropped to about 85,000. The largest part of this change is accounted for by New York State, where an average loss due to migration of 182,000 per year in the 1970s was lowered to 45,000 in 1980-1983.

Source: U.S. Bureau of the Census

Diagram A: Percentage of total population resident in the regions, 1950-1983

- South
- North Central
- North East
- West

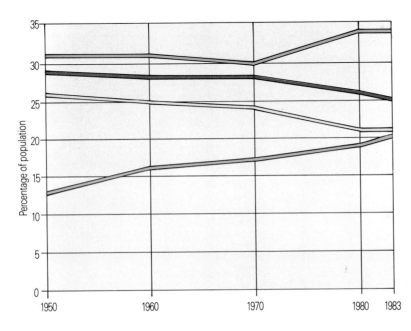

Diagram B: Percentage of 1980 resident population of each state (5 years of age and over) who lived in a different state in 1975

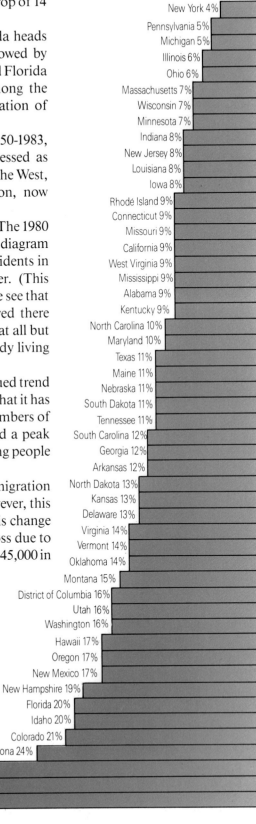

New York 4%
Pennsylvania 5%
Michigan 5%
Illinois 6%
Ohio 6%
Massachusetts 7%
Wisconsin 7%
Minnesota 7%
Indiana 8%
New Jersey 8%
Louisiana 8%
Iowa 8%
Rhode Island 9%
Connecticut 9%
Missouri 9%
California 9%
West Virginia 9%
Mississippi 9%
Alabama 9%
Kentucky 9%
North Carolina 10%
Maryland 10%
Texas 11%
Maine 11%
Nebraska 11%
South Dakota 11%
Tennessee 11%
South Carolina 12%
Georgia 12%
Arkansas 12%
North Dakota 13%
Kansas 13%
Delaware 13%
Virginia 14%
Vermont 14%
Oklahoma 14%
Montana 15%
District of Columbia 16%
Utah 16%
Washington 16%
Hawaii 17%
Oregon 17%
New Mexico 17%
New Hampshire 19%
Florida 20%
Idaho 20%
Colorado 21%
Arizona 24%
Wyoming 28%
Alaska 29%
Nevada 31.5%

MOBILITY

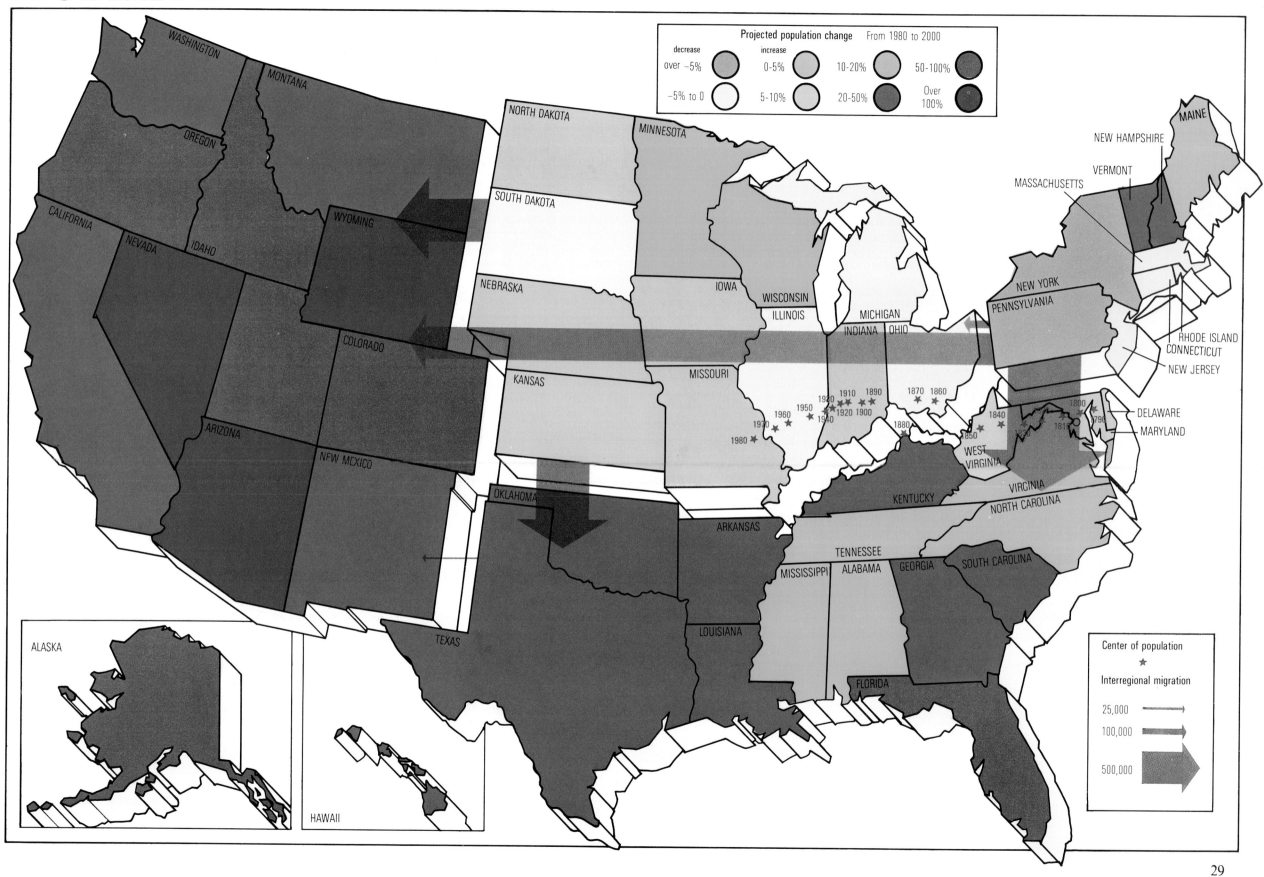

Projected population change — From 1980 to 2000

decrease		increase					
over −5%		0-5%		10-20%		50-100%	
−5% to 0		5-10%		20-50%		Over 100%	

WASHINGTON
MONTANA
OREGON
IDAHO
CALIFORNIA
NEVADA
WYOMING
UTAH
COLORADO
ARIZONA
NEW MEXICO

NORTH DAKOTA
SOUTH DAKOTA
MINNESOTA
NEBRASKA
IOWA
KANSAS
MISSOURI
OKLAHOMA
TEXAS
ARKANSAS
LOUISIANA

WISCONSIN
ILLINOIS
MICHIGAN
INDIANA
OHIO
KENTUCKY
TENNESSEE
MISSISSIPPI
ALABAMA
GEORGIA
FLORIDA
SOUTH CAROLINA
NORTH CAROLINA
VIRGINIA
WEST VIRGINIA

NEW YORK
PENNSYLVANIA
MAINE
NEW HAMPSHIRE
VERMONT
MASSACHUSETTS
RHODE ISLAND
CONNECTICUT
NEW JERSEY
DELAWARE
MARYLAND

1980 1970 1960 1950 1940 1920 1910 1890 1900 1930 1870 1860 1880 1850 1840 1810 1800 1790 1820

ALASKA

HAWAII

Center of population
★

Interregional migration

25,000
100,000
500,000

29

IMMIGRATION

Since 1820, over 50 million people have come to the United States to settle, and this map shows where they came from. The thickness of the arrows indicates how many immigrants there were in the period 1820-1980, the colors of the arrows corresponding to their continents of origin. The map also shows the numbers of immigrants from individual countries.

The earliest settlers on the northeastern coast were mainly from the British Isles, with a sprinkling of Germans and Dutch. In the eighteenth century, the largest influx consisted of people abducted from Africa as slaves — about half a million enforced "immigrants."

In the nineteenth century, however, many millions of immigrants arrived. Entry into the United States was almost entirely unrestricted at that time. It was only in 1819 that the numbers of immigrants even began to be recorded.

Diagram A graphs the annual rate of arrival since 1820. While immigration from Britain continued throughout the century, the steep rise in the total during the 1840s reflects two main factors. First, famine drove some 2 million Irish to make the Atlantic crossing. Second, after the political upheaval in Germany in 1848, many Germans immigrated to the United States, and they continued coming in great numbers until 1900.

During the Civil War, immigration fell off, but it resumed after 1865. The depression that began in 1872 also reduced the influx for a time, but it was followed by a rapid rise in immigration from southern and eastern Europe.

The tremendous expansion of U.S. industry then began to pull in huge masses of labor from Europe, with Italy and Russia making large contributions. In the 1880s, it was estimated that 28 percent of immigrants were German-speaking, while in 1901-1910, 23 percent were Italian-speaking.

Diagram A: Total annual immigration into the United States, 1820-1983

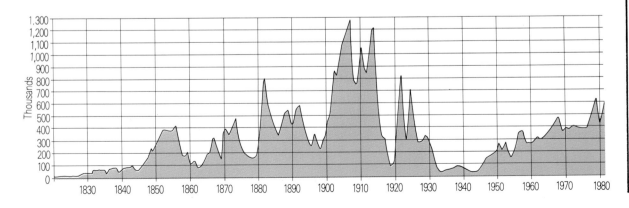

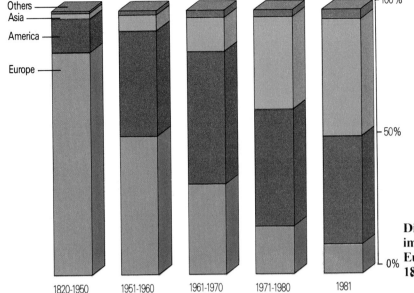

Diagram B: Percentage of immigrants from Asia, America, Europe and other countries, 1820-1981

Despite the first beginnings of legal restrictions on immigration, the curve moved up to record heights at the turn of the century. The all-time annual peak was reached in 1907, when nearly 1.3 million immigrants arrived in the United States.

After the disruption caused by World War I, the influx resumed, but it was now regulated by the Immigration Quota Acts of 1921 and 1924. The immigration of people from Asia had already been controlled under laws passed in 1882, 1907, and 1917. Now European immigration was also controlled, specific quotas being fixed for each country of origin. (This system continued until 1965.) The Great Depression of 1929-1934 brought the numbers of immigrants down to a fraction of their former levels. Then the war reduced the influx to a minimum.

Postwar immigration followed quite a different pattern from that of the previous century. Diagram B contrasts the proportions of immigrants from different parts of the world in the last few decades with the predominantly European origin of the earlier immigrations. It shows how Asia and Latin America have accounted for higher and higher proportions since World War II. In the 1960s and 1970s, about 30 percent of immigrants were from Spanish-speaking countries.

The social characteristics of the postwar immigrants are also quite different from those of their predecessors. In the 1820-1940 period, the typical immigrant was under 30 years old and from a peasant or laboring background. After World War II, many of the immigrants had professional or technical skills.

Sources: U.S. Immigration and Naturalization Service;
U.S. Bureau of the Census

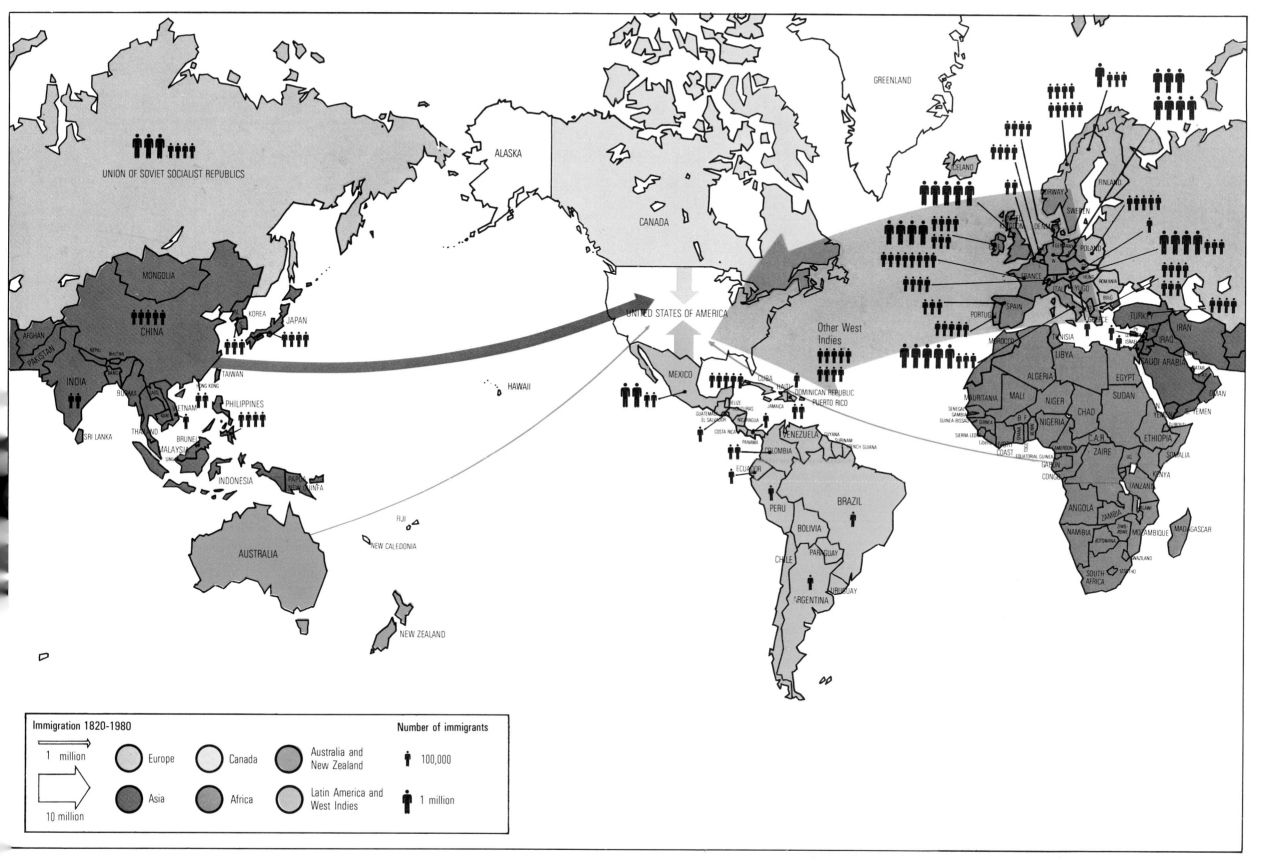

GREENLAND

ALASKA

CANADA

UNION OF SOVIET SOCIALIST REPUBLICS

MONGOLIA

KOREA
JAPAN

CHINA

AFGHAN

PAKISTAN

NEPAL BHUTAN
INDIA

BURMA

TAIWAN

HONG KONG

VIETNAM

PHILIPPINES

SRI LANKA

THAILAND

BRUNEI

MALAYSIA

INDONESIA

PAPUA
NEW GUINEA

HAWAII

FIJI

NEW CALEDONIA

AUSTRALIA

NEW ZEALAND

UNITED STATES OF AMERICA

MEXICO

CUBA
HAITI DOMINICAN REPUBLIC
PUERTO RICO

Other West
Indies

BELIZE
GUATEMALA HONDURAS
EL SALVADOR NICARAGUA
COSTA RICA
PANAMA

JAMAICA

VENEZUELA GUYANA
SURINAM
FRENCH GUIANA

COLOMBIA

ECUADOR

PERU

BOLIVIA

BRAZIL

PARAGUAY

CHILE

ARGENTINA

URUGUAY

ICELAND

NORWAY
FINLAND
SWEDEN

DENMARK
POLAND

FRANCE

GREECE
ITALY YUGO
BULG
ROMANIA

PORTUGAL
SPAIN

TURKEY
IRAN

MOROCCO
ISRAEL IRAQ

TUNISIA

ALGERIA
LIBYA
EGYPT

SAUDI ARABIA
QATAR
OMAN

MAURITANIA
MALI
NIGER
CHAD
SUDAN

YEMEN
S. YEMEN

SENEGAL
GAMBIA
GUINEA-BISSAU GUINEA
SIERRA LEONE
IVORY
COAST
GHANA
NIGERIA

LIBERIA

B.F.

BENIN

CAMEROON

EQUATORIAL GUINEA
GABON
CONGO

C.A.R.

ZAIRE

ETHIOPIA

SOMALIA

UGANDA
KENYA

TANZANIA

ANGOLA
ZAMBIA

ZIMBABWE

MALAWI

MOZAMBIQUE
MADAGASCAR

NAMIBIA
BOTSWANA

SWAZILAND
SOUTH
AFRICA
LESOTHO

Immigration 1820-1980				Number of immigrants	

1 million

10 million

Europe

Asia

Canada

Africa

Australia and
New Zealand

Latin America and
West Indies

100,000

1 million

TERRITORIAL EXPANSION

This map shows the territory of the United States of America, as it grew from the treaty of 1783 to the annexation of Hawaii in 1898. The map also shows the boundaries of each state, and the date on which it was admitted to the Union.

The territory of the "Original Thirteen" states, bounded by Canada in the north and Spanish-held Florida in the south, stretched from the Atlantic coast westward to the Mississippi River. It comprised 891,364 square miles, though many areas were subject to rival claims by France and Spain.

The Louisiana Purchase in 1803 was the most important territorial acquisition during the transcontinental development of the United States. Bought from France for $15 million, it almost doubled the area of the United States at one stroke and contained most of what is now the west-central section of the country. The Louisiana Purchase ensured the free navigation of the Mississippi River, and the elimination of France in the struggle for North America.

In 1819 Secretary of State John Quincy Adams succeeded in purchasing Florida from Spain for $5 million in return for abandoning U.S. claims to Texas. The same treaty (the Transcontinental Treaty) also recognized a U.S. boundary extending westward to the Pacific at the 42nd parallel. This strengthened the U.S. claim to the Pacific coast north of the 42nd parallel, an area which, by an 1818 agreement between the United States and Britain, was subject to joint occupation by the two countries.

At that time the only settlement in the region was a British Hudson's Bay Company post at Port Vancouver, but American settlers flocked to Oregon in the late 1830s and were soon petitioning for entry to the Union. In 1846 Britain acceded to U.S. claims in a treaty that continued the 49th parallel westward to the Pacific as a boundary between the two countries.

Diagram A: Growth of cities from 1790-1980. For each successive date shown, the size of city indicated on the map increases, from cities with over 10,000 inhabitants in 1790 to those with over half a million in 1980. Regions shaded blue indicate the extent of the contiguous United States at each date

TOP TEN: LARGEST U.S. CITIES

1790	1850	1900	1980
New York	New York	New York	New York
Philadelphia	Baltimore	Chicago	Chicago
Boston	Boston	Philadelphia	Los Angeles
Baltimore	Philadelphia	St Louis	Philadelphia
Richmond	New Orleans	Boston	Houston
Norfolk	Cincinnati	Baltimore	Detroit
Lexington-Fayette	St Louis	Cleveland	Dallas
Louisville	Pittsburgh	Buffalo	San Diego
——	Louisville	San Francisco	Phoenix
——	Buffalo	Cincinnati	Baltimore

In 1836 Texas declared its independence from Mexico and nine years later was annexed by the United States. This action worsened already bad relations between Mexico and the United States; and a boundary dispute in 1846 led to war between the two countries. The war was ended by treaty in 1848 in which Mexico ceded present-day Utah, Nevada, California, Arizona, Colorado, and New Mexico to the United States for $15 million. The border between the United States and Mexico was revised by the Gadsden Purchase of 1853.

In 1867 Alaska was purchased from Russia by Secretary of State William H Seward. The price was $7.2 million, about 2 cents per acre. Although many called this "Seward's Folly," the large natural resources and strategic location of "the last frontier" more than justified it. With 591,000 square miles, Alaska is one-fifth of the total area of the rest of the United States.

A brief war with Spain in 1898 gave the United States an overseas empire including Cuba, the Philippine Islands, Puerto Rico, and Guam. The first two later became independent nations but the latter two remain U.S. territories. During the war the United States annexed Hawaii.

Source: U.S. Bureau of the Census

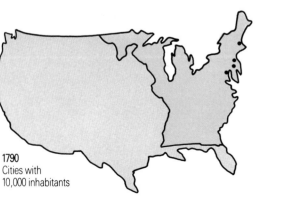

1790
Cities with
10,000 inhabitants

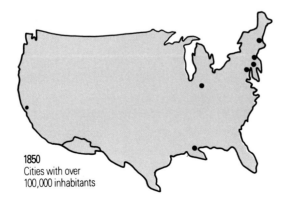

1850
Cities with over
100,000 inhabitants

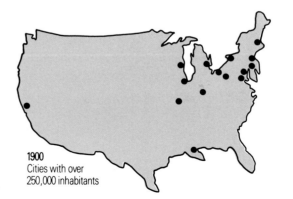

1900
Cities with over
250,000 inhabitants

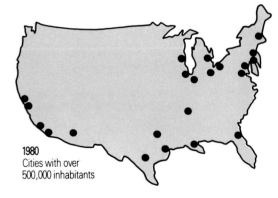

1980
Cities with over
500,000 inhabitants

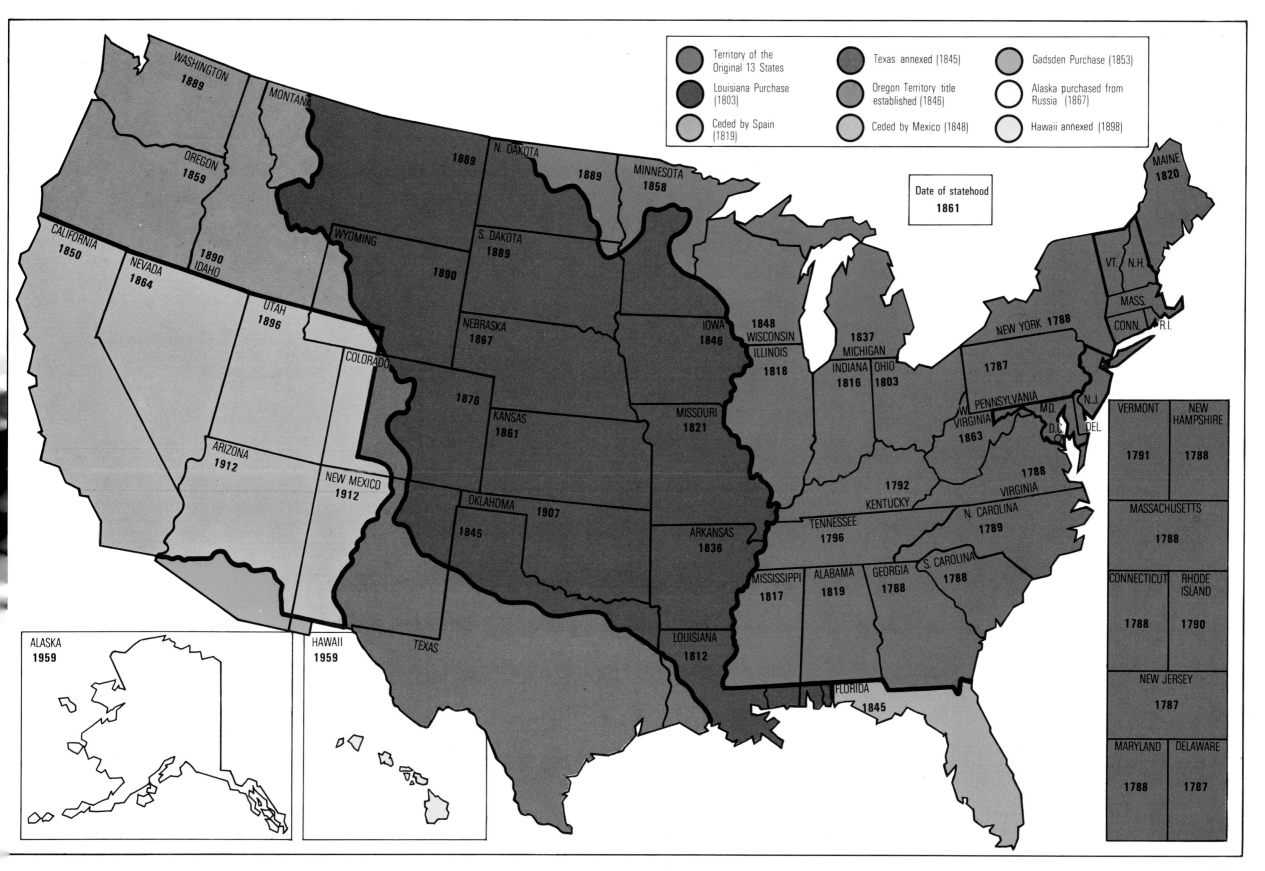

Territory of the Original 13 States

Louisiana Purchase (1803)

Ceded by Spain (1819)

Texas annexed (1845)

Oregon Territory title established (1846)

Ceded by Mexico (1848)

Gadsden Purchase (1853)

Alaska purchased from Russia (1867)

Hawaii annexed (1898)

Date of statehood
1861

WASHINGTON 1889

MONTANA

OREGON 1859

N. DAKOTA 1889

MINNESOTA 1858

MAINE 1820

CALIFORNIA 1850

NEVADA 1864

IDAHO 1890

WYOMING 1890

S. DAKOTA 1889

VT. N.H.

MASS.

UTAH 1896

COLORADO

NEBRASKA 1867

IOWA 1846

WISCONSIN 1848

NEW YORK 1788

CONN. R.I.

1876

MICHIGAN 1837

1787

ILLINOIS 1818

INDIANA OHIO 1816 1803

ARIZONA 1912

NEW MEXICO 1912

KANSAS 1861

MISSOURI 1821

W. VIRGINIA 1863

PENNSYLVANIA

MD.

N.J.

D.C. DEL

OKLAHOMA 1907

1845

KENTUCKY 1792

TENNESSEE 1796

VIRGINIA

N. CAROLINA 1789

1788

ARKANSAS 1836

MISSISSIPPI 1817

ALABAMA 1819

GEORGIA 1788

S. CAROLINA 1788

TEXAS

LOUISIANA 1812

FLORIDA 1845

ALASKA 1959

HAWAII 1959

VERMONT 1791	NEW HAMPSHIRE 1788
MASSACHUSETTS 1788	
CONNECTICUT 1788	RHODE ISLAND 1790
NEW JERSEY 1787	
MARYLAND 1788	DELAWARE 1787

FARMLANDS

As in other industrial countries, the number of people working on farms and the relative contribution of agriculture to the national income have declined in recent decades. This does not mean that agriculture is less important in the economic sector generally. If anything, it has become more important. U.S. farmers must satisfy a growing population demanding a greater variety of food. They have succeeded to such an extent that the main problem of agriculture in the United States is not shortages but surpluses, which require government intervention to regulate prices and buy up superfluous product.

Farmland in the contiguous United States amounts to about 64 percent of the total area, excluding federally-owned land. The map shows the area of farmland as a proportion of the total area in each state. It also shows the amount of farmland in each state divided into three types: cropland, pasture, and rangeland. (Areas of less than 1 million acres have been omitted.) Rangeland is confined almost entirely to the western half of the country, whereas pasture and cropland are more evenly spread, with only a few of the most arid western states failing to register in all three categories.

The absence of symbols for some small northeastern states means that none of the categories of farmland attains an area of 1 million acres.

Diagram B: Farmland by type as a percentage of total non-federally owned land, 1982

- Rangeland — 27%
- Pastureland — 8.8%
- Cropland — 28%
- Other — 36.2%

The decline in the number of workers employed on farms (see Diagram A) has been rapid since World War II. Agrarian economists have referred to "a new agriculture" in this period, in which, despite the sharp decline in farmworkers, output increased at a rate faster than demand from an ever-growing population.

In terms of productivity, this is a remarkable success story, based mainly on the effects of applying science and technology to agricultural functions. The total area of cropland did not change significantly in the period 1950-1980, though there were marked regional variations (for example, cropland in the South declined by 46 percent between 1939 and 1974). But with capital, in the shape of machines, chemicals, etc., replacing labor in food production, today's farms are generally much larger while employing far fewer workers.

An associated feature is the rise of "agribusiness," a term implying an industrial-type operation that manages every stage of food production, "from seed to supermarket."

Between 1940 and 1980 the number of farms fell from 6.4 million to 2.4 million, and the average size increased from 167 acres to 430 acres. Large farms are characteristic of the West rather than the East or South, but the trend toward fewer and larger farms, involving the rise of farming corporations and the decline of family farms, is nationwide.

Sources: U.S. Dept. of Agriculture;
U.S. Bureau of Labor Statistics

Diagram A: Number of farmworkers, 1820-1983. Pie charts show farmworkers as a percentage of population

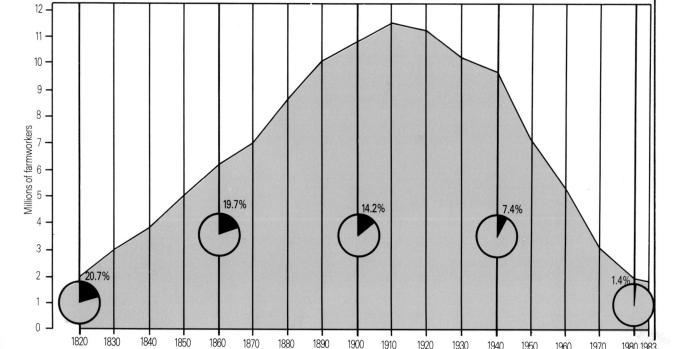

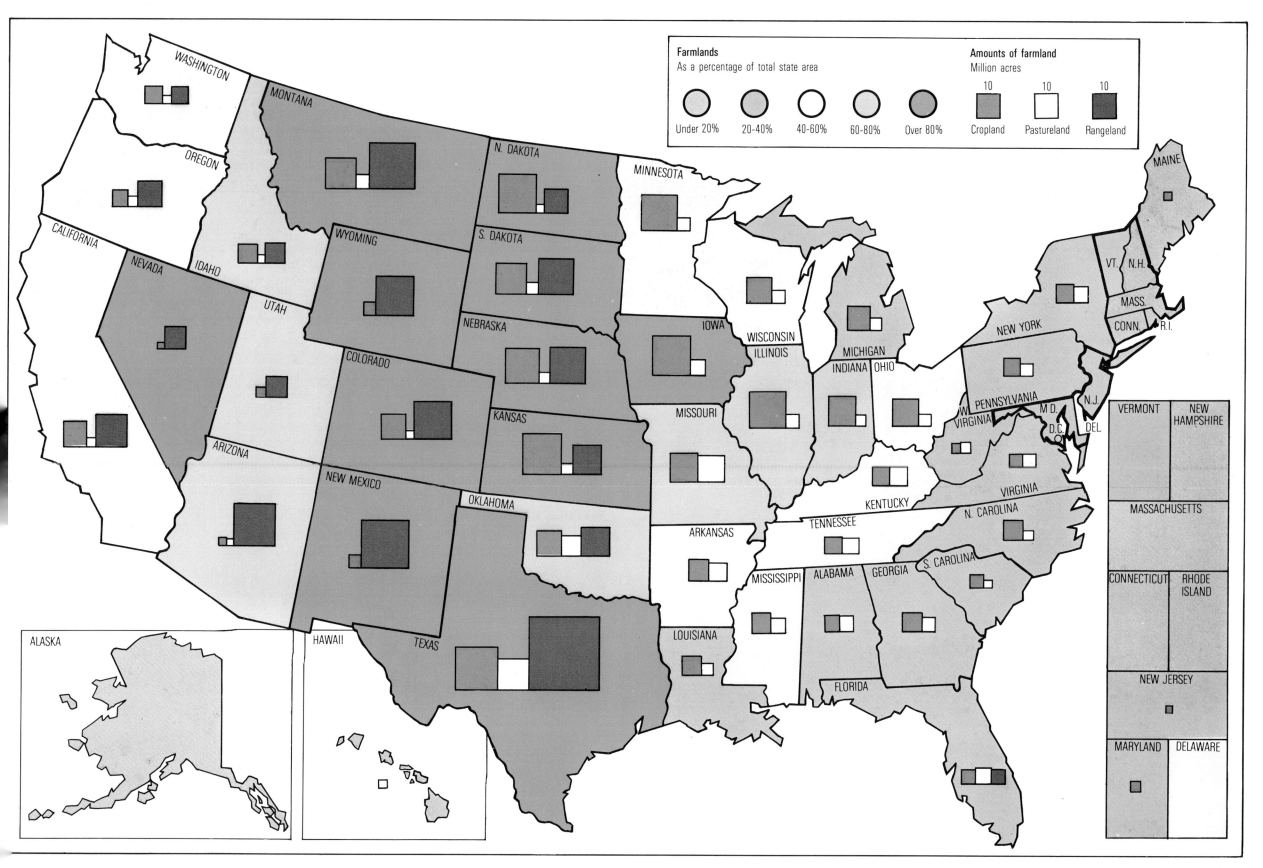

Farmlands
As a percentage of total state area

Under 20%   20-40%   40-60%   60-80%   Over 80%

Amounts of farmland
Million acres

10 Cropland   10 Pastureland   10 Rangeland

WASHINGTON

OREGON

CALIFORNIA

NEVADA

IDAHO

UTAH

ARIZONA

MONTANA

WYOMING

COLORADO

NEW MEXICO

N. DAKOTA

S. DAKOTA

NEBRASKA

KANSAS

OKLAHOMA

TEXAS

MINNESOTA

IOWA

MISSOURI

ARKANSAS

LOUISIANA

WISCONSIN

ILLINOIS

MICHIGAN

INDIANA   OHIO

KENTUCKY

TENNESSEE

MISSISSIPPI   ALABAMA   GEORGIA

FLORIDA

NEW YORK

PENNSYLVANIA

W. VIRGINIA   M D.   N.J.

D.C.   DEL

VIRGINIA

N. CAROLINA

S. CAROLINA

MAINE

VT.   N.H.

MASS.

CONN.   R.I.

VERMONT   NEW HAMPSHIRE

MASSACHUSETTS

CONNECTICUT   RHODE ISLAND

NEW JERSEY

MARYLAND   DELAWARE

ALASKA

HAWAII

CROP PRODUCTION

The United States is not only self-sufficient in most crops (though not tropical produce), it is a net exporter of many, notably of grains and cereals. This fact is of more than economic importance. Grain exports may be used as an instrument of foreign policy, as President Carter demonstrated when he imposed a grain embargo on the Soviet Union in 1979.

The map shows the production in each state of the five largest U.S. crops expressed as a proportion of the national total. Where the total state production of any crop is less than 1 percent of the national total, it has been omitted. These minor producers contribute to the national total as follows: corn 9.5 percent; wheat 6.4 percent; soybeans 3.6 percent; tobacco 1.7 percent; cotton 1.1 percent.

The map is based on production figures for 1983. For most crops, notably corn and cotton but also many lesser crops such as sorghum, rice, oats, and sugar beets, 1983 production was low by comparison with the annual average during the preceding decade (see Diagram B). Nevertheless, production far outweighed domestic consumption, and exports, even of corn and cotton, were larger than in the previous year.

Diagram A: Principal crops by value, 1983, in billions of dollars

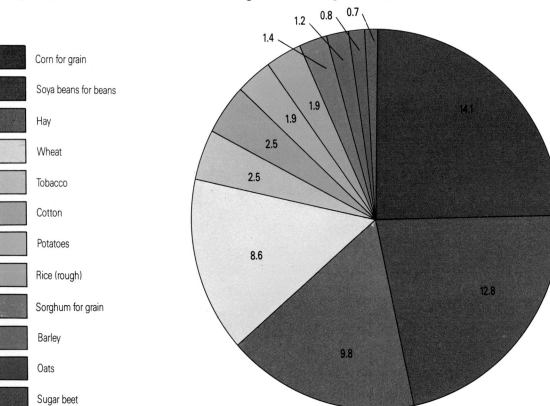

- Corn for grain
- Soya beans for beans
- Hay
- Wheat
- Tobacco
- Cotton
- Potatoes
- Rice (rough)
- Sorghum for grain
- Barley
- Oats
- Sugar beet

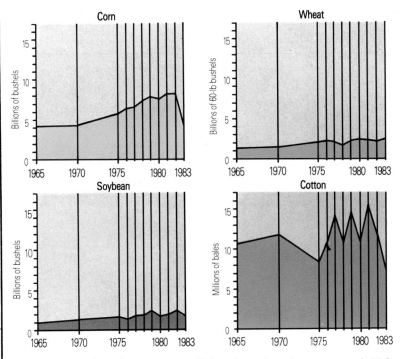

Diagram B: Production of leading crops, 1965-1983

The map reflects the traditional regional pattern of U.S. agriculture: the massive grain harvests of the corn belt, which stretches from Ohio to Nebraska and from Minnesota to Missouri, and the cotton belt of the South, which stretches from South Carolina to Texas. It also reflects the substantial changes in crop distribution that have occurred in recent years.

The increase in soybeans, corn, wheat and rice and the reduction in the area under tobacco, cotton, oats, and hay have changed the character of the main crop-producing regions. Cotton has moved increasingly to the Southwest, with Texas and California together producing more than half the national total — much of it under irrigation.

Among the major crops, output of cotton and tobacco decreased slightly between 1960 and 1980. By contrast, output of food grains increased by 80 percent. Wheat production roughly doubled, while the increase for corn was about 60 percent. These production figures are all the more remarkable considering that the area of cropland in use increased by less than 10 percent during the same period.

Increased productivity is largely the result of new strains of plants and new fertilizers, pesticides, etc. Between 1950 and 1980, the use of agricultural chemicals increased by a factor of six. Machines such as harvesters, balers, etc., did not increase significantly in number, but they did increase considerably in individual size and performance. In addition, irrigation has been a major factor in the Southwest, a region highly favorable to agriculture save for its natural aridity.

Source: U.S. Dept. of Agriculture

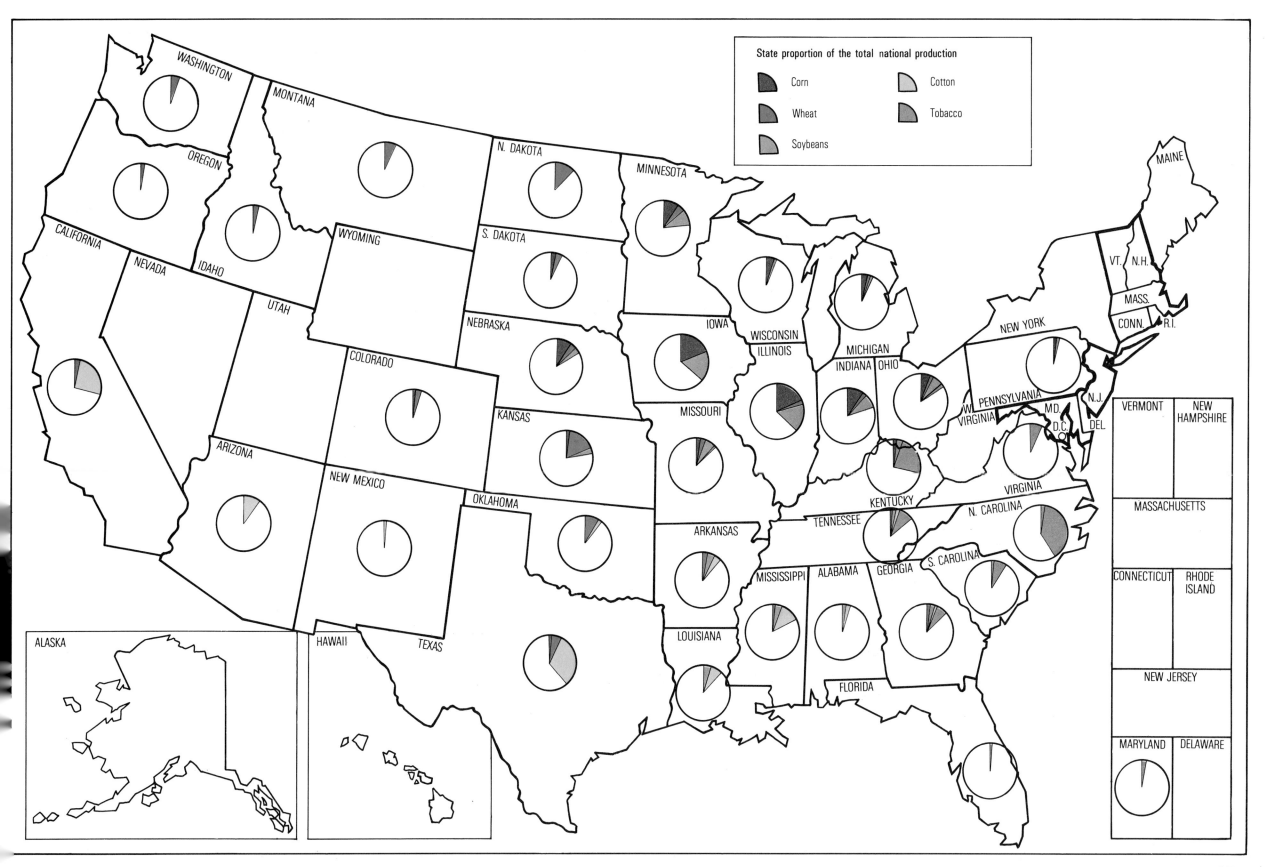

State proportion of the total national production

- Corn
- Wheat
- Soybeans
- Cotton
- Tobacco

LIVESTOCK PRODUCTION

The remarkable increase in productivity that has characterized U.S. agriculture since World War II is no less evident in livestock than in crop production. All categories increased, though by varying proportions. The growth in poultry and egg output was especially notable.

The map shows the number of cattle, milk cows, sheep and hogs in each state expressed as a proportion of the national total. Where the state proportion is less than 1 percent of the national total it has been omitted.

It can be seen from the map that the traditional, regional pattern of livestock farming still holds, despite the changes of recent years. Dairy farming predominates in the Northeast, and dairy products contribute the largest share of cash receipts of farms in New England and in states such as New York, Pennsylvania, and Wisconsin.

The map also confirms that the corn belt is a misleading term for that rich agricultural area of the Midwest, where farm prosperity has always rested on a wider basis. A considerable proportion of the crop is fed to livestock which is subsequently marketed in the form of top-quality beef and pork. Livestock sales generally contribute a larger share than corn to farmers' incomes in this region.

In any state-oriented study, it is easy to be misled by scale. California and Texas are the leading states in terms of total farm products, but that is largely a result of their size; figures adjusted to take account of this would show more clearly the contribution of the corn/meat belt states of Iowa, Illinois, Indiana, and Ohio. Moreover, in terms of the value of farm sales per acre, neither Texas, which is more remarkable for sheer acreage than productivity, nor California feature prominently: the leading state, due to its intensive poultry farming, is Delaware. Yet Delaware does not appear among the leading states for poultry production simply because it is so small.

The poultry production figures show that production of chickens (and eggs) is spread relatively evenly across the country by comparison with broilers (young birds bred exclusively for meat) and turkeys. The figures relate to chickens and turkeys produced during 1983. The *total number* of birds on farms is of course considerably higher.

The table shows the leading states in livestock production at the end of 1983. As on the map, "cattle" means all cattle on farms;

TOP TEN: STATES WITH GREATEST NUMBER OF LIVESTOCK, 1983

Cattle		(Thousands)	Milk cows		(Thousands)
1	Texas	15,000	1	Wisconsin	1,840
2	Nebraska	7,200	2	California	940
3	Iowa	6,450	3	New York	935
4	Kansas	5,750	4	Minnesota	890
5	Missouri	5,500	5	Pennsylvania	738
6	Oklahoma	5,350	6	Michigan	400
7	California	4,900	7	Ohio	393
8	Wisconsin	4,400	8	Iowa	386
9	South Dakota	4,060	9	Texas	385
10	Minnesota	3,610	10	Missouri	252

Sheep		(Thousands)	Hogs		(Thousands)
1	Texas	2,225	1	Iowa	14,800
2	California	1,115	2	Illinois	5,400
3	Wyoming	1,060	3	Minnesota	4,270
4	Colorado	750	4	Indiana	4,200
5	South Dakota	680	5	Nebraska	3,900
6	New Mexico	610	6	Missouri	3,550
7	Utah	590	7	North Carolina	2,300
8	Montana	560	8	Ohio	2,100
9	Oregon	515	9	South Dakota	1,650
10	Iowa	457	10	Kansas	1,600

"milk cows" represents cows and heifers that have calved and are kept for milk; "sheep" includes lambs.

In most cases, it is not a very close race at the top of the table. For instance, Texas has more than twice as many sheep and nearly twice as many cattle as its nearest rivals (California and Nebraska respectively). Wisconsin has twice as many milk cows as the second state, California. Most remarkable of all, the state of Iowa contains three times as many hogs as Illinois (second in the table), and more than one-quarter of the national total. Iowa is also the only state to feature in the "top ten" of all four main livestock categories.

Source: U.S. Dept. of Agriculture

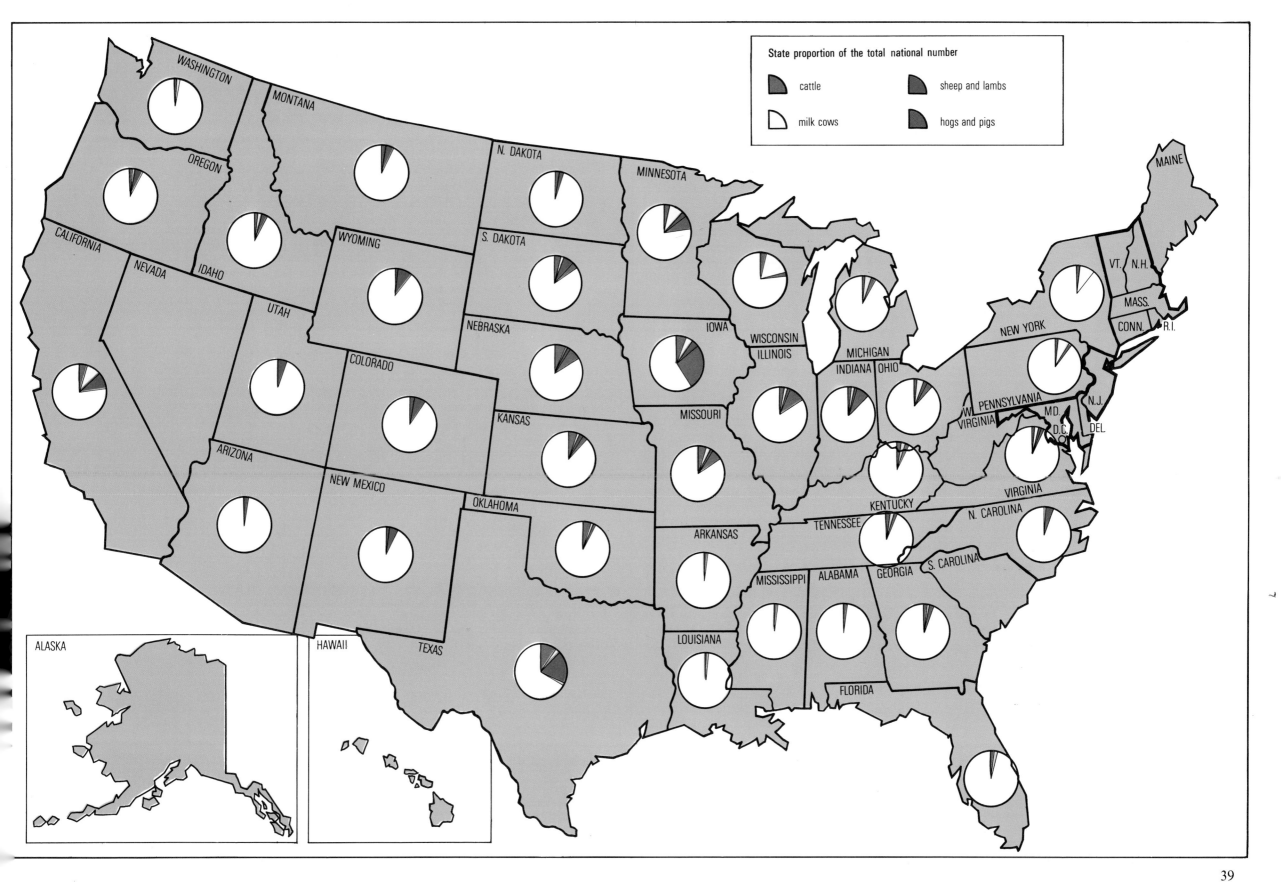

State proportion of the total national number

- cattle
- milk cows
- sheep and lambs
- hogs and pigs

FARM ECONOMICS

The map shows the average value of farmland and farm buildings by state in 1984. New Jersey leads, with an average of $3,148 per acre, followed by Rhode Island at $3,046. However, it should be pointed out that neither of these states has a great deal of farmland. Wyoming has the lowest value per acre, $165. The average for the whole of the United States is $739.

The map also shows the average value of farm marketings in 1983, in dollars per acre. On average, U.S. farm marketings were worth $137 per acre. State averages varied from $622 per acre in Massachusetts, down to $16 in Wyoming, and $12 in Alaska.

Diagram A shows the decline in the number of U.S. farms since 1950, and Diagram B the corresponding rise in the average size of a farm. In 1950, there were 5.65 million farms in the United States. By 1982, the number had halved. By 1983, it had fallen to 2.37 million. The 1984 figure was 2.33 million.

In 1983 the 25 farms whose sales valued $500,000 or over made up 1 percent of the total number of U.S. farms. They accounted for 10 percent of the total assets of farms and earned between them 48 percent of the total net income. At the opposite end of the scale, farms whose sales amounted to less than $20,000 made up 60 percent of all farms and together registered a net *loss* of $500 million in 1983.

Another consequence of large-scale farming is the increased use of machinery. This can be measured by the value of machinery per man-hour of labor employed. Diagram D graphs this indicator between 1960 and 1983. In 1960 it stood at $2.30 per man-hour of labor employed; by 1970 it had risen to $5.50; and in 1983 it reached $30.

Diagram E graphs the net income of farm operators from farming, expressed in constant (1967) dollars. This reached an all-time peak of $34.4 billion in current dollars in 1973. By 1983 it had fallen to $16.1 billion in current dollars. Taking account of inflation, the graph illustrates how large a decline this reflects in real terms.

In 1970, the per capita disposable income of the farm population was estimated to be $2,421, compared with $3,439 for the nonfarm population. In 1973, these figures were $4,401 for the farm population, and $4,311 for the rest. In 1983, the position had changed drastically: farm population, $6,917; non-farm, $10,057.

Sources: U.S. Bureau of the Census; U.S. Dept. of Agriculture, Economic Research Service

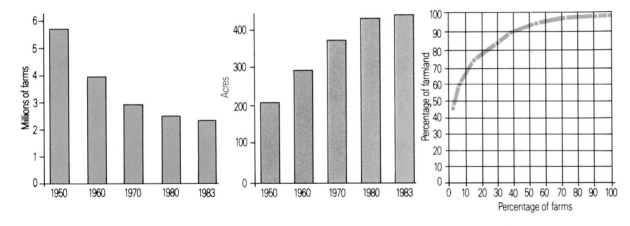

Diagram A: Numbers of U.S. farms, 1950-1983

Diagram B: Average farm size, 1950-1983

Diagram C: Concentration of U.S. farmland, 1982

Over the same period, the total acreage of farms fell only slightly, from 1,202 million acres, to 1,020 million acres. So the average farm size has more than doubled, from 213 acres in 1950, to 432 acres in 1983. (By 1984, it was 437.)

This concentration of farmland into large farms is illustrated in Diagram C, where it can be seen that the leading 3 percent of farms in terms of size contain almost half the total farmland, while the leading 17 percent account for over 75 percent of the total.

The economic results of the decrease in the number of farms and the increase in size are even more dramatic.

Diagram D: Capital intensity of U.S. farms by value of machinery in dollars per hour of labor, 1960-1983

Diagram E: Net income of farm operators from farming, in constant (1967) dollars, 1970-1983

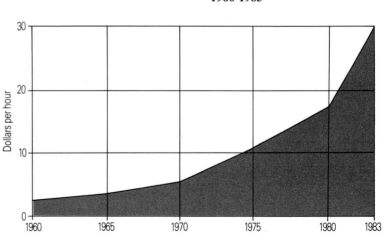

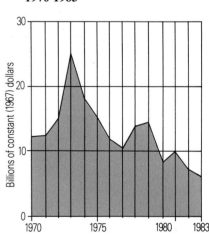

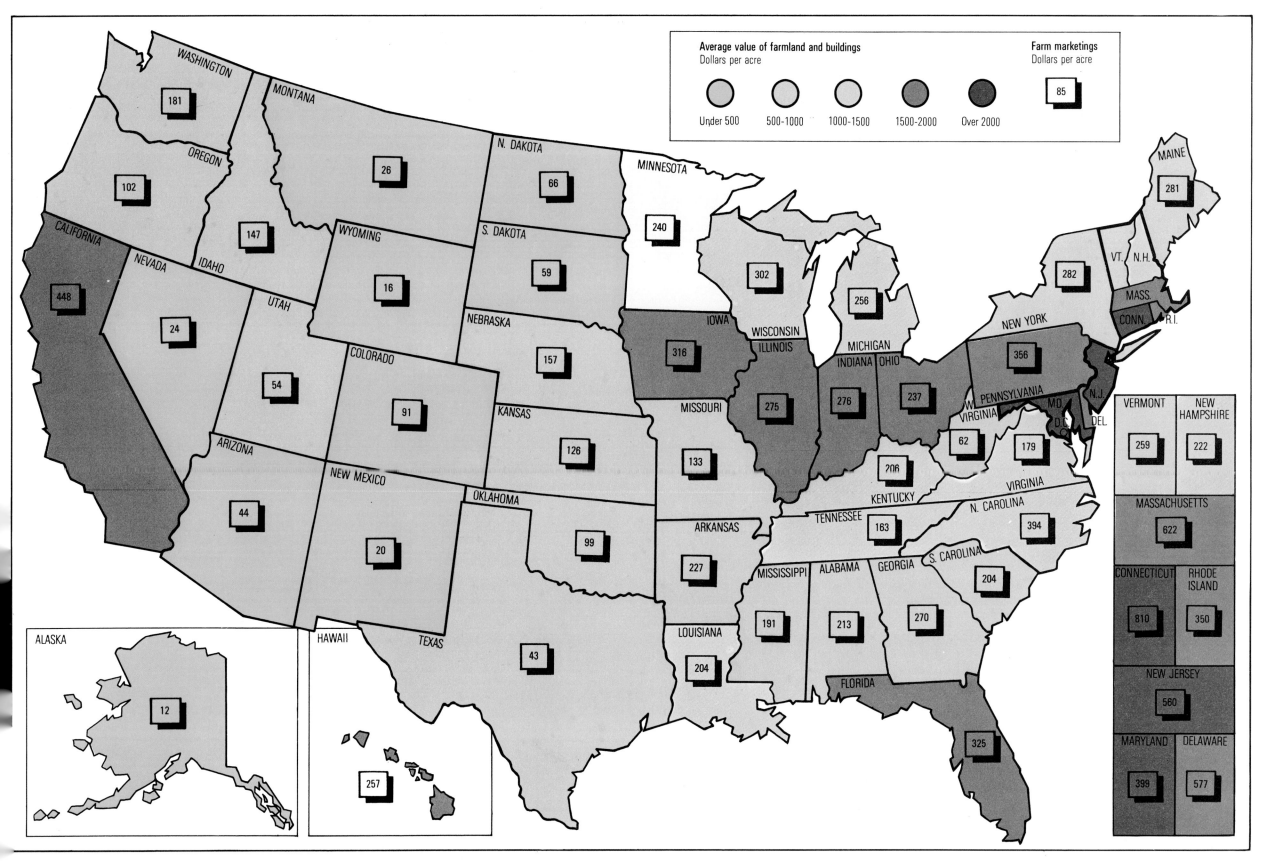

Average value of farmland and buildings
Dollars per acre

Under 500   500-1000   1000-1500   1500-2000   Over 2000

Farm marketings
Dollars per acre

85

WASHINGTON 181
MONTANA 26
N. DAKOTA 66
MINNESOTA 240
MAINE 281
OREGON 102
IDAHO 147
WYOMING 16
S. DAKOTA 59
WISCONSIN 302
MICHIGAN 256
NEW YORK 282
VT. N.H.
MASS.
CONN. R.I.
CALIFORNIA 448
NEVADA 24
UTAH 54
COLORADO 91
NEBRASKA 157
IOWA 316
ILLINOIS 275
INDIANA 276
OHIO 237
PENNSYLVANIA 356
N.J.
MD. DEL
D.C.
ARIZONA 44
NEW MEXICO 20
KANSAS 126
MISSOURI 133
KENTUCKY 206
W. VIRGINIA 62
VIRGINIA 179
OKLAHOMA 99
ARKANSAS 227
TENNESSEE 163
N. CAROLINA 394
S. CAROLINA 204
TEXAS 43
LOUISIANA 204
MISSISSIPPI 191
ALABAMA 213
GEORGIA 270
FLORIDA 325

ALASKA 12
HAWAII 257

VERMONT 259
NEW HAMPSHIRE 222
MASSACHUSETTS 622
CONNECTICUT 810
RHODE ISLAND 350
NEW JERSEY 560
MARYLAND 399
DELAWARE 577

FORESTRY

Approximately one-third of the total land area of the United States is forested. This is a small area compared with the unending virgin forests that confronted the first European settlers, but it is still substantial.

Of the total forested land, about 65 percent is classed as commercial timberland, and this area contains, according to the estimate of the U.S. Forest Service, approximately 2.6 trillion board feet of sawtimber, which is enough to rehouse the entire population.

Nevertheless, it is barely sufficient to meet the total current demands for timber and timber products. The balance between annual estimated growth and annual volume cut is a delicate one, and, although there has been a small growth in supply since about 1975, consumption has consistently exceeded production, and imports of timber and timber products such as newsprint have risen.

The map illustrates the highly regional nature of the timber industry. Production of softwood, which represents about 80 percent of total timber production, is concentrated in the states of the Pacific Northwest. Four states (Alaska, California, Oregon, and Washington) contain 56 percent of all commercially available softwood, and if Idaho and Montana are included the contribution of the Northwest rises to 67 percent.

In Oregon, which contains the largest body of standing timber in the United States, lumbering is the state's largest industry, and timber products make up more than half the total value of manufactures.

The plains of the Midwest have relatively few trees, but Texas has about 23 million acres of forest, about half of which grows commercial timber.

The main timber-producing region after the Northwest is the South. Here hardwood, insignificant in the Northwest, forms a high proportion of total timber resources. Just over half the national stock of hardwood grows in the southern states.

It is in the East that the virgin forest has been most severely depleted. The demands of agriculture, housing, industry and transport have reduced the forests by an estimated 75 percent. Nevertheless, considerable forestland remains, especially in the northeastern corner. Table A shows that this is still the most heavily forested region of the country, with Maine heading the list.

Diagram A reveals the enormous potential, in terms of volume of sawtimber, in the quick-growing forests of Oregon compared with those of Maine. Of course, a direct comparison is almost meaningless, as the nature of the industry is entirely different in those two states. For example, Maine's timber resources include a high proportion of hardwood.

Diagram B shows the main types of commercial timber currently grown. Douglas fir and southern yellow pine together provide a high percentage of the standing sawtimber in the United States. The Douglas fir is predominant in Washington and Oregon, where it grows to a height of 200 feet, with a trunk diameter of up to six feet. Symmetrical saplings are often sold as Christmas trees.

Southern yellow pine, as the name suggests, is cut primarily in the South, especially in Alabama, Georgia, Louisiana, and Mississippi. Ponderosa pine is second only to Douglas fir in the Northwest. Eastern white pine, which was the chief lumber-producing tree in the nineteenth century, is now of far less significance.

The United States contains nearly 100 species of oak, but only about one-quarter of these are of commercial significance. Together, they form by far the largest source of hardwood.

Sources: U.S. Forest Service; U.S. Bureau of the Census

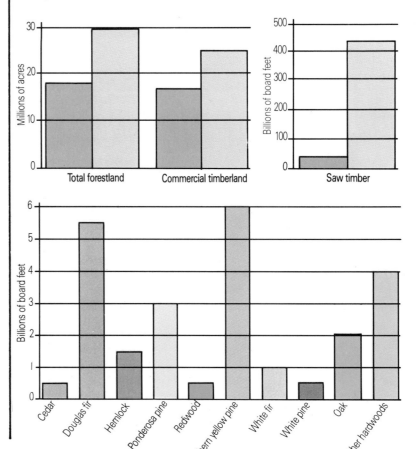

Diagram A: Comparison of total forestland and volume of sawtimber in Maine and Oregon

Diagram B: Lumber production by type of wood, 1981

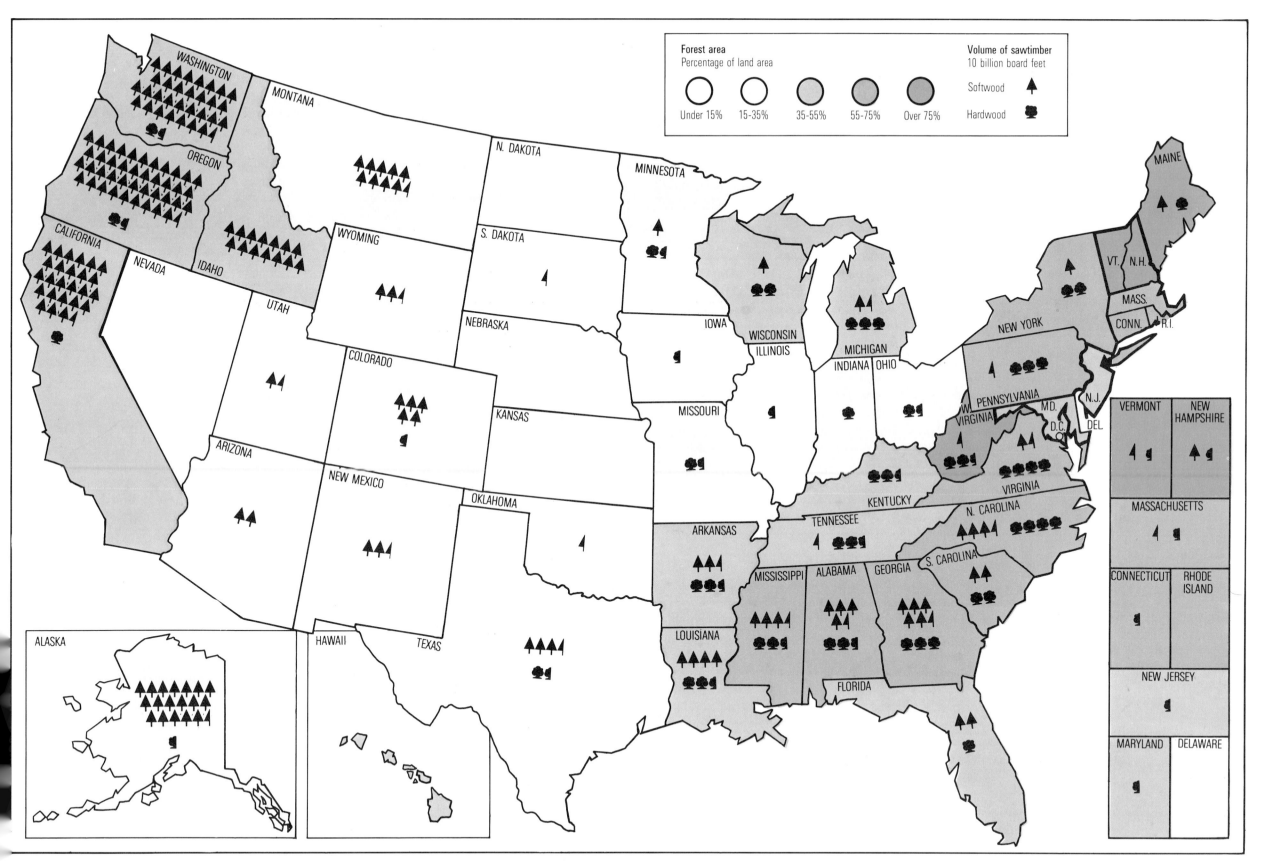

43

MINERAL RESOURCES

The United States was richly endowed by nature with mineral resources, but high rates of production and the efforts of two world wars made severe inroads into that inheritance. After World War II, the United States became an importer of many metallic minerals that it had formerly exported.

Supplies of nearly 90 percent of the most essential minerals in use in the 1980s depended in part on imports. Some minerals, such as manganese ore and chromite (both vital in the steel industry), were wholly imported. The dependence on other nations, sometimes nations of doubtful political stability, for supplies of vital raw materials has been a cause of concern for the U.S. government in recent years. (The main suppliers of chromite are South Africa and the Soviet Union.)

One result of the rapid depletion of traditional mineral resources has been a concern to explore and exploit new resources. The oceans, which have already proved a fruitful provider of fossil fuels, also contain vast mineral supplies. Several U.S. enterprises have shown interest in developing techniques to recover in particular manganese nodules, which also contain copper, nickel and cobalt, from the ocean floor.

The map shows the value of total annual mineral production by state (including fossil fuels), together with the leading state producers of important minerals.

Mining altogether contributes less than 2 percent of the national income, and if oil, gas, and coal extraction are subtracted, the figure slumps to about 0.2 percent. Nevertheless, metallic minerals alone represent approximately $5.5 billion. Moreover, the fundamental, historical importance of the exploitation of natural resources in the development of industrial prosperity has given the mining industry in general a special significance as an indicator of the material wellbeing of the nation.

After fossil fuels — petroleum, natural gas, and coal — which are considered separately on the next page, the most valuable group are the nonmetallic, nonfuel minerals. These include the materials used primarily in the construction industry — stone, sand, and gravel, which are the most valuable mineral resources in a majority of the states — as well as gypsum, clays, sulfur, fluorspar, phosphate rock (for fertilizers), potassium salts, asbestos, and common salt. Most of these, especially the products of the stone and gravel quarries, are widely available. Production of others is more localized; for instance, sulfur comes from the coastal region of Louisiana and Texas. But supplies are large: U.S. production of sulfur is about 20 percent of annual world production.

Metals are the third most valuable group of mineral resources. The map displays the predominance of the West in the production of metallic minerals, while Diagram A illustrates the main components of the group on a national basis.

The main exception to western predominance is iron ore, which is the leading metallic mineral in terms of both volume and value. Historically, the main center of iron ore production has been the Great Lakes region, but by the 1980s these supplies had been severely depleted. Although Minnesota and Michigan remain the chief producers, third and fourth places are occupied by California and Wyoming.

Mining of copper, second in importance to iron, has also declined in the Lakes region, having ceased almost completely in Michigan. The main copper producers in the early 1980s were Arizona, Montana, Nevada, New Mexico, and Utah.

Bauxite, the main ore of aluminum, is an example of a metallic ore of which production (mainly in Arkansas) has dwindled to relatively insignificant amounts within recent years. As a result, it is one of the leading imported minerals (see Diagram B).

Lead and zinc are reasonably widespread in the East, Midwest, and Rocky Mountain regions. In recent years, mines in southern Missouri have maintained national production figures, especially of lead.

Sources: U.S. Bureau of Economic Analysis;
U.S. Bureau of Mines

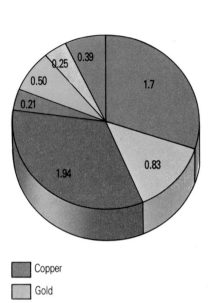

Diagram A: Value of U.S. production of metallic minerals (recoverable content of ore), 1983 in billions of dollars

Copper
Gold
Iron ore
Lead
Silver
Zinc
Other

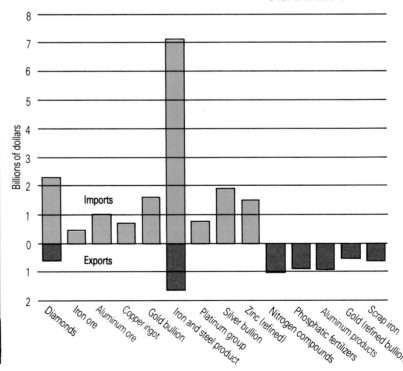

Diagram B: U.S. imports and exports of selected minerals, 1983

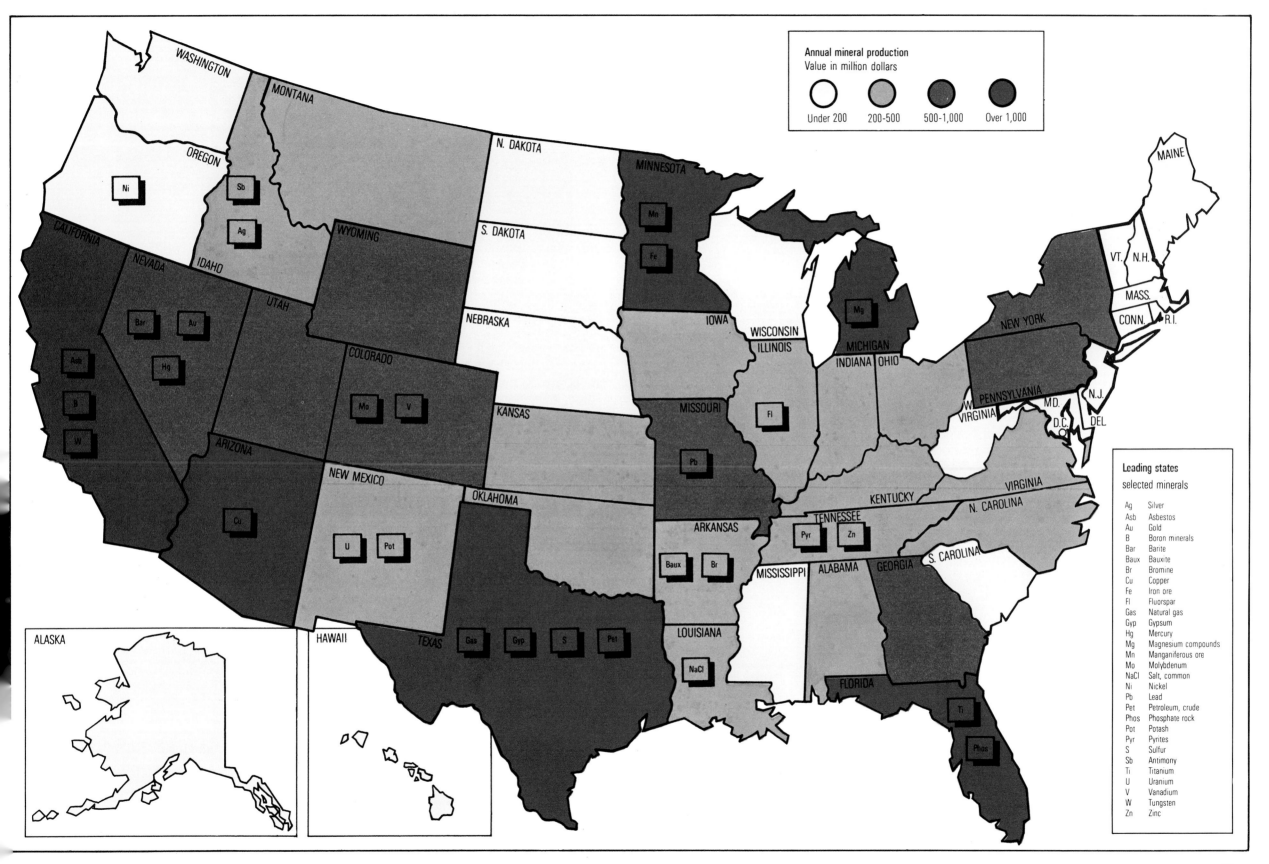

Annual mineral production
Value in million dollars

○ Under 200　◐ 200-500　● 500-1,000　● Over 1,000

Leading states
selected minerals

Ag	Silver
Asb	Asbestos
Au	Gold
B	Boron minerals
Bar	Barite
Baux	Bauxite
Br	Bromine
Cu	Copper
Fe	Iron ore
Fl	Fluorspar
Gas	Natural gas
Gyp	Gypsum
Hg	Mercury
Mg	Magnesium compounds
Mn	Manganiferous ore
Mo	Molybdenum
NaCl	Salt, common
Ni	Nickel
Pb	Lead
Pet	Petroleum, crude
Phos	Phosphate rock
Pot	Potash
Pyr	Pyrites
S	Sulfur
Sb	Antimony
Ti	Titanium
U	Uranium
V	Vanadium
W	Tungsten
Zn	Zinc

FOSSIL FUELS

When the Arab nations imposed an embargo on oil exports to the United States in 1973, many people were surprised to discover that the country is not self-sufficient in fossil fuels (coal, oil, and natural gas). Moreover, as Diagram A illustrates, imports of crude petroleum increased dramatically during the 1970s.

The map shows total production of fossil fuels by states. The most productive region for oil and natural gas is the Gulf — mainly the offshore wells of Louisiana and Texas — and the inshore fields of Texas, Oklahoma, and California. Lesser amounts are produced in many other states, especially in the South and West.

The main addition to these resources in recent years has come from Alaska, where oil production began in 1959. By 1961 oil was already the state's most important mineral, with over 6 million barrels produced that year. By 1984 annual production had reached 630 million barrels, making Alaska the largest oil producer after Texas. Natural gas exceeded 260 billion cubic feet, and the combined value of the two fuels represented the majority of state revenue. Nevertheless, while the Alaska pipeline greatly improved national oil production figures, total supplies still fell far short of total consumption.

The intense public concern over diminishing supplies of fossil fuels — particularly oil — in the 1970s abated considerably during the early 1980s, when an economic recession combined with widespread energy conservation led to a decline in the import of

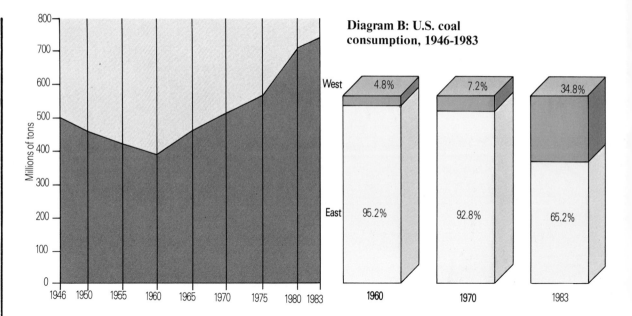

Diagram B: U.S. coal consumption, 1946-1983

Diagram C: Regional change in coal production, 1960-1983

crude petroleum. But, with total consumption of oil and natural gas outstripping total discoveries each year, proved reserves continue to fall. They are currently equivalent to about 10 years' production.

By contrast, there is no worry about running out of coal. There is enough coal in the ground to last, at current rates of consumption, for several hundred years.

Coal consumption entered a period of decline after World War II, but experienced a revival during the 1960s, and accelerated in the following decade as a result of the oil crisis — and consequent rising oil prices (see Diagram B).

In 1960, nearly all coal mining was in the East (see Diagram C), particularly Appalachia. Eastern coal, however, is high in sulfur and thus environmentally objectionable. The rise in production of western coal, which has a low sulfur content, was also assisted in the 1970s by the rising price, which helped to compensate for high transportation costs.

The main coal-mining state in the West is Wyoming, where production — negligible before the 1970s — rose to nearly 15 percent of the national total by 1980. Wyoming is also a major producer of crude petroleum and natural gas. Its total output of fossil fuels reached $6.0 billion in 1984.

Sources: U.S. Bureau of Mines;
U.S. Energy Information Administration

Diagram A: Total petroleum output compared with imports of crude oil and refined petroleum products, 1950-1983

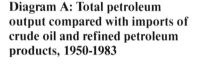

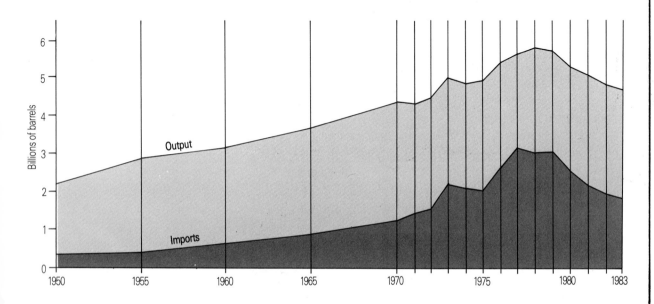

Note: Various energy sources are converted from original units (e.g., short tons, cubic feet, barrels, kilowatt-hours) to the thermal equivalent using British thermal units (Btu). A Btu is the amount of energy required to raise the temperature of 1 pound of water 1 degree Fahrenheit at or near 39.2 degrees F.

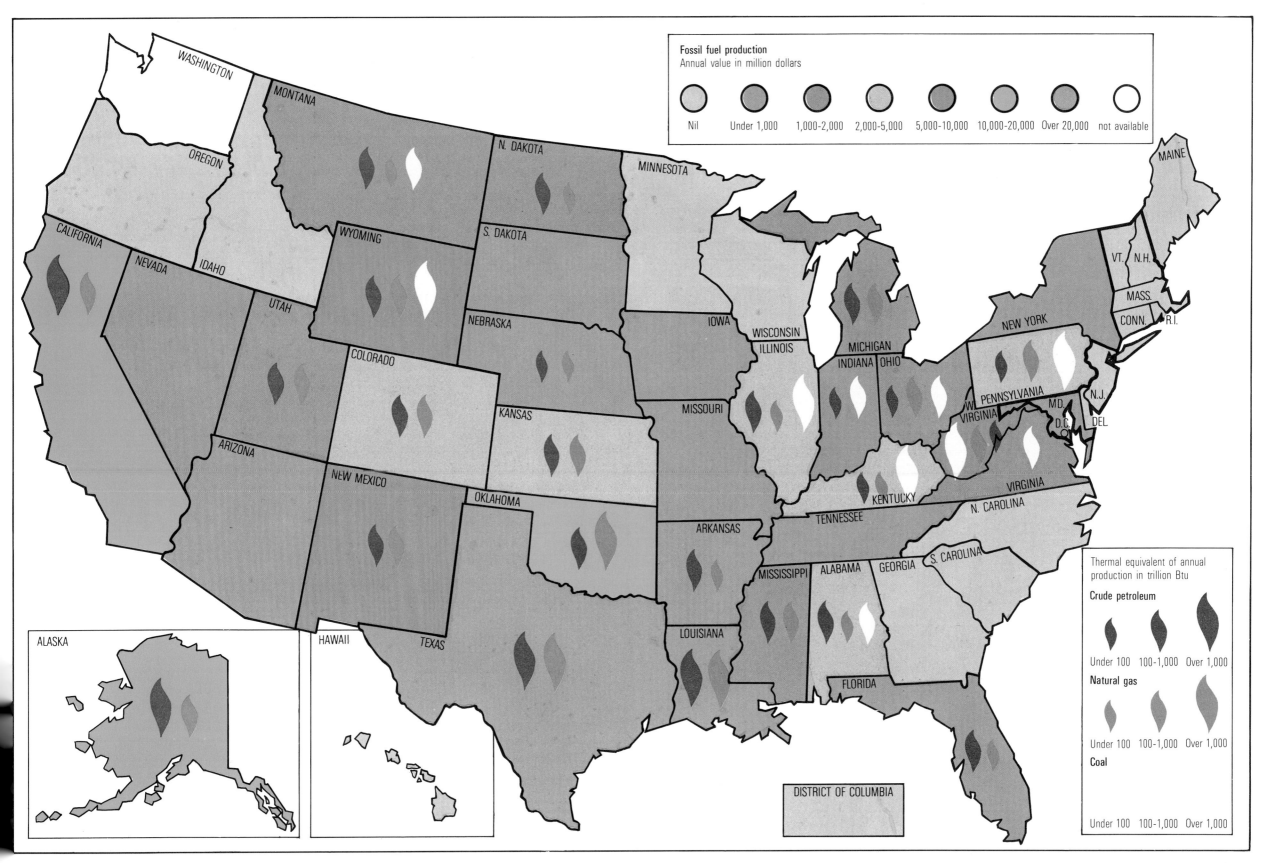

Fossil fuel production
Annual value in million dollars

Nil   Under 1,000   1,000-2,000   2,000-5,000   5,000-10,000   10,000-20,000   Over 20,000   not available

WASHINGTON
MONTANA
N. DAKOTA
MINNESOTA
MAINE
OREGON
IDAHO
WYOMING
S. DAKOTA
WISCONSIN
VT.   N.H.
CALIFORNIA
NEVADA
UTAH
NEBRASKA
IOWA
MICHIGAN
NEW YORK
MASS.
CONN.   R.I.
COLORADO
KANSAS
MISSOURI
ILLINOIS
INDIANA   OHIO
PENNSYLVANIA
N.J.
ARIZONA
NEW MEXICO
OKLAHOMA
W. VIRGINIA
MD.
D.C.   DEL.
KENTUCKY
VIRGINIA
TENNESSEE
N. CAROLINA
ARKANSAS
MISSISSIPPI   ALABAMA   GEORGIA   S. CAROLINA
TEXAS
LOUISIANA
FLORIDA

ALASKA

HAWAII

DISTRICT OF COLUMBIA

Thermal equivalent of annual
production in trillion Btu

Crude petroleum

Under 100   100-1,000   Over 1,000

Natural gas

Under 100   100-1,000   Over 1,000

Coal

Under 100   100-1,000   Over 1,000

ENERGY

The subject of energy consumption might not have featured in an atlas of the United States twenty years ago, but since the oil crisis of the 1970s it has become a subject of major importance.

The map illustrates the consumption of energy by state, in two aspects: (1) consumption per capita, and (2) total energy consumption. The figures are given in Btu (British thermal units). This is a useful overall indication of energy consumption, which avoids the difficulty of comparison between (for example) a barrel of petroleum, a ton of coal, and a cubic foot of gas. One Btu is the amount of energy required to raise the temperature of one pound of water by one degree Fahrenheit at its maximum density. Sample conversions are as follows:

1 barrel of petroleum	=	5.41 million Btu
1 cubic foot of natural gas	=	1.03 thousand Btu
1 short ton of coal	=	21.55 million Btu

There is in general no significant relationship between total energy consumption and consumption per capita; the crucial sector is not the domestic but the industrial sector. Nationwide, the industrial sector accounts for more than one-third of total consumption, which can be broken down as follows:

Industrial	37 percent
Transportation	27 percent
Residential	21 percent
Commercial	15 percent

In a highly industrialized state such as Ohio, industrial consumption is over 42 percent of the total, whereas in Arizona, industry accounts for less than 27 percent of total energy consumption.

The predominance of petroleum as a source of energy is shown in Diagram A. Natural gas and coal are the other main sources. The smallest slice of the pie, "Others," includes hydropower, nuclear power, and geothermal power, as well as such statistically insignificant contributors as windmills.

Considerable changes have taken place in the composition of energy supply since World War II. Between 1950 and 1960, the contribution of coal declined from 38 percent of the national total to 22 percent. It continued to decline, though at a slower rate, until the oil crisis of the early 1970s. By 1983 coal consumption had regained the level of 1960. Petroleum and natural gas production increased during the same period, although since the 1950s the United States has become steadily more dependent on oil imports.

The energy crisis of the 1970s is shown in the movement of fossil fuel prices in Diagram B. The figures represent prices in real terms (based on 1972 values). During the decade 1960-1970, prices were more or less steady (discounting inflation), and the sharp increase between 1970 and 1975 reflects the rocketing international price of oil. That affected other fuels, and indeed prices generally. The trend continued until halted in 1980-1981 by a combination of reduced demand and increased supplies.

Source: U.S. Energy Information Administration

Diagram A: Major sources of energy consumption

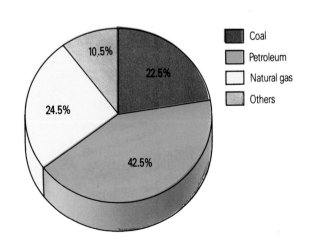

- Coal
- Petroleum
- Natural gas
- Others

Diagram B: Fossil fuel prices, 1960-1983

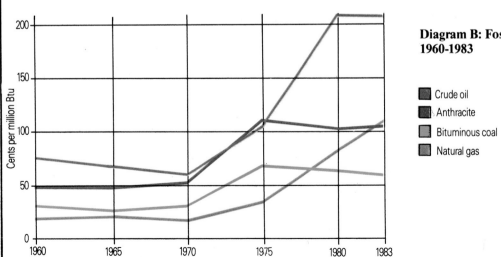

- Crude oil
- Anthracite
- Bituminous coal
- Natural gas

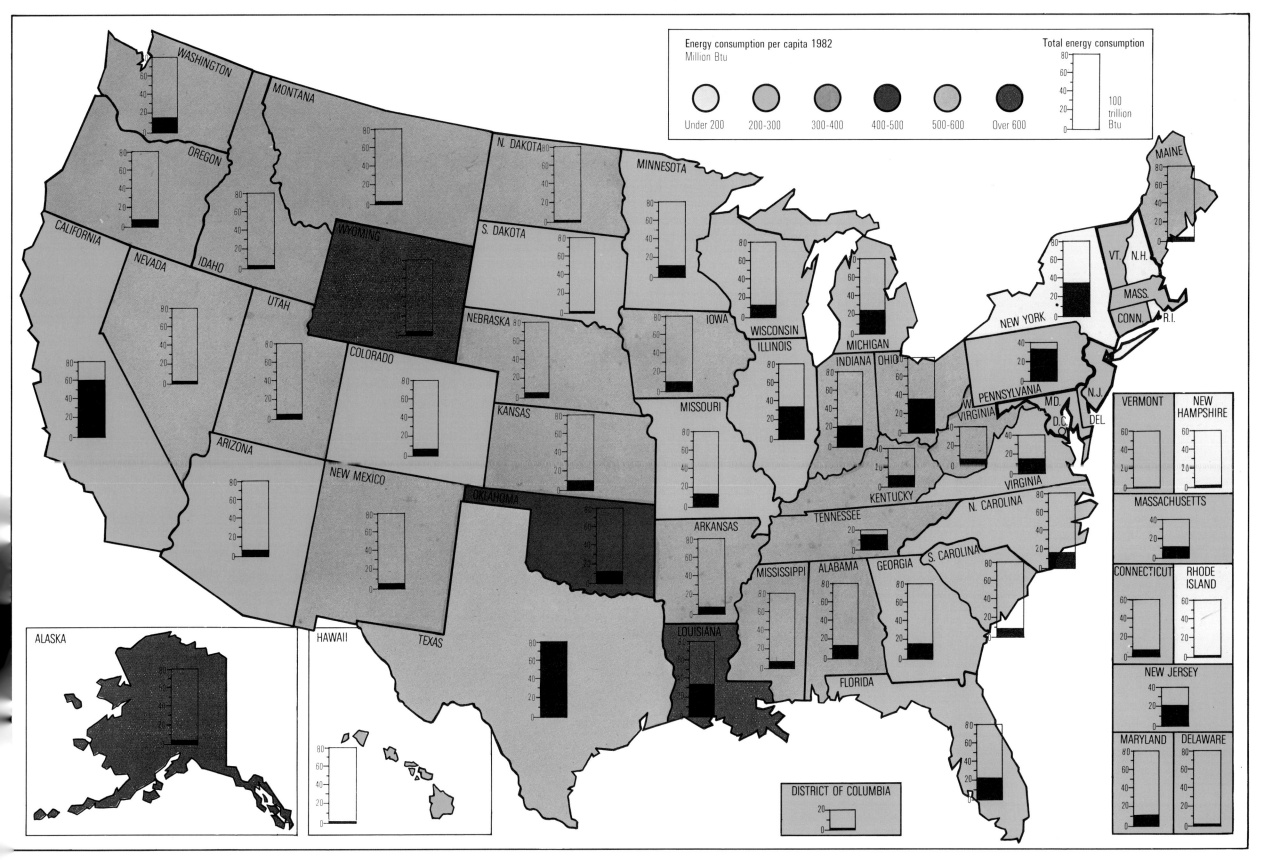

Energy consumption per capita 1982
Million Btu

Under 200   200-300   300-400   400-500   500-600   Over 600

Total energy consumption

100 trillion Btu

WASHINGTON
MONTANA
OREGON
N. DAKOTA
MINNESOTA
MAINE
CALIFORNIA
IDAHO
S. DAKOTA
WISCONSIN
VT.   N.H.
MASS.
CONN.   R.I.
NEW YORK
NEVADA
WYOMING
NEBRASKA
IOWA
MICHIGAN
UTAH
COLORADO
ILLINOIS
INDIANA   OHIO
PENNSYLVANIA   MD.   N.J.
W. VIRGINIA   DEL
D.C.
ARIZONA
KANSAS
MISSOURI
KENTUCKY
VIRGINIA
NEW MEXICO
OKLAHOMA
ARKANSAS
TENNESSEE
N. CAROLINA
MISSISSIPPI   ALABAMA   GEORGIA   S. CAROLINA
TEXAS
LOUISIANA
FLORIDA

ALASKA

HAWAII

DISTRICT OF COLUMBIA

VERMONT   NEW HAMPSHIRE

MASSACHUSETTS

CONNECTICUT   RHODE ISLAND

NEW JERSEY

MARYLAND   DELAWARE

MANUFACTURING

The United States ranks first in the world as a manufacturing nation in terms of both total value and output per capita. It achieved this enviable position through a combination of advantageous circumstances, chief of which was the rich abundance of raw materials. A large, flexible, and intelligent labor supply, the early development of mass-production methods and transportation networks, a substantial and prosperous domestic market — these have all contributed, along with such immeasurable factors as the individual pursuit of profit and traditional American enterprise.

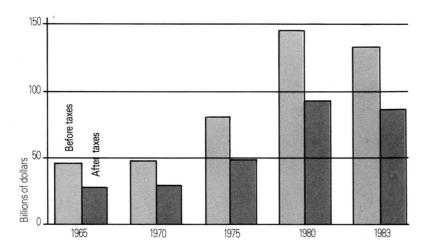

Diagram A: Net profits of U.S. manufacturing corporations, 1965-1983

Manufacturing has become the single largest sector of the economy, providing over one-third of all wages and salaries. The proportion of the national income derived from manufactures is 22 percent (about $580 billion), and although the percentage has declined during recent years (in 1963 it was 29 percent), manufacturing remains perhaps the single most vital indicator of the national economic performance.

The map illustrates the value of manufacturing output by state and the number of people employed in manufacturing industries in 1981. Measurement by shipment is the most reliable overall indicator of value, for although it includes some duplication as a result of shipments between two establishments within the same general industry, that has little effect on the relative performance of each state. The number of employees given includes administrative, clerical, and other staff, as well as production workers.

Recent trends in the manufacturing industry are obvious. The same map compiled thirty years ago would look rather different,

with the Northeast more dominant by comparison with both West and South. Even now it may surprise some of us to find California so far ahead in terms of manufacturing employees. California is also the leader in total value of shipments.

Diagram A indicates the profitability of manufacturing business. This has shown an upward progression ever since the Depression of the 1930s with no serious interruption. Even the recession of the late 1970s made a comparatively minor impact (though its effect was greater than the figures suggest, taking inflation into account), and the upward trend was resumed by 1983.

The percentage of net profits paid in taxation registered a small but steady decline, from about 40 percent in 1965 to about 35 percent in 1983.

The varying contributions of the main sectors of the manufacturing industry are shown in Diagram B. The figures here are for "value added," which is, broadly, the value of the finished product less the value of raw materials. The largest item is "food," which includes everything from chocolate bars to diet cola. In general, this table should be interpreted flexibly, as it is difficult to group tens of thousands of different forms of manufacturers in ten categories. The extra category, "Others," includes tobacco products, rubber and many plastic products, leather goods, glass, pottery, and numerous miscellaneous items (the *Census of Manufactures* lists, for example, "guided missiles" and "costume jewelry and notions;" moreover, the latter category is considerably the larger of the two in terms of value added!).

Sources: U.S. Bureau of the Census;
U.S. Federal Trade Commission

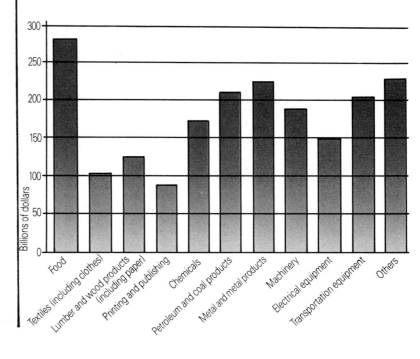

Diagram B: Value of major manufactures, 1982

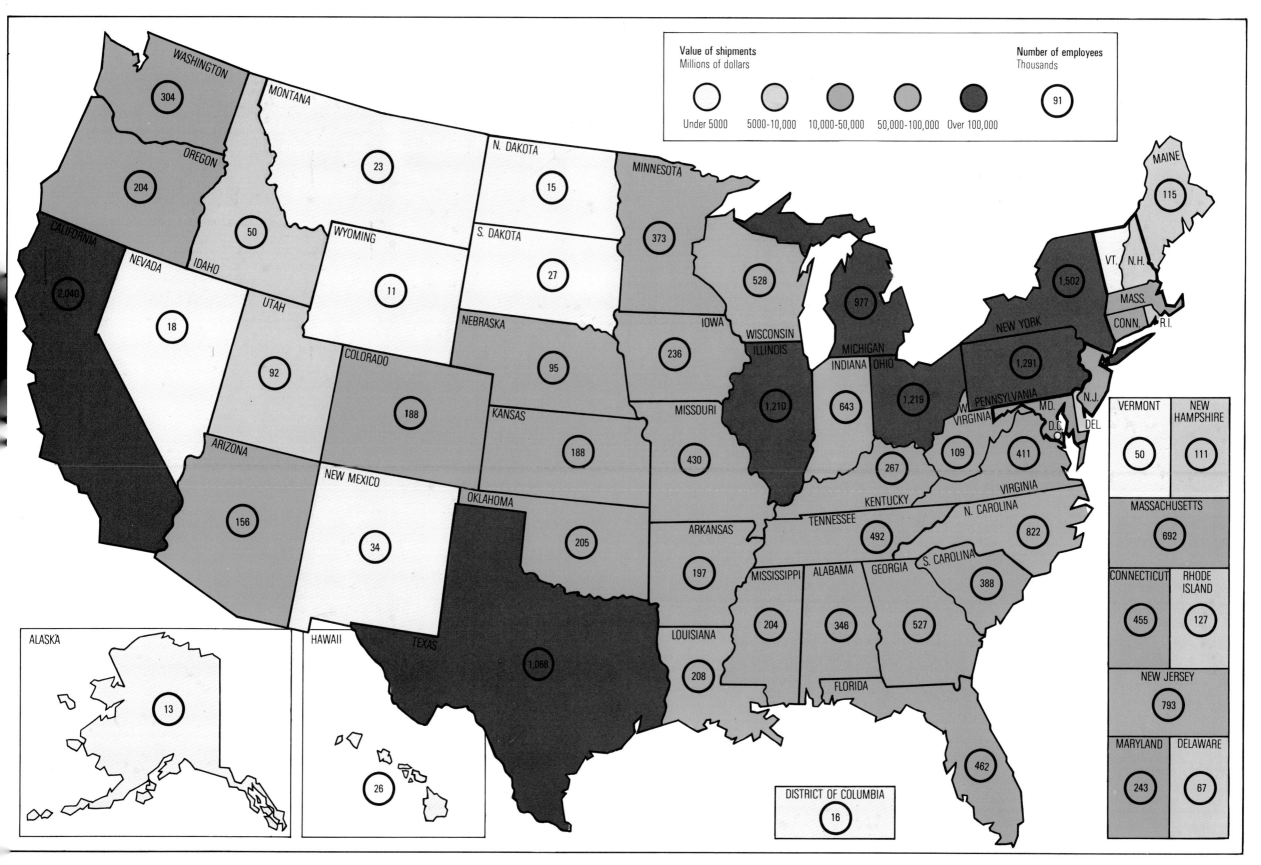

Value of shipments
Millions of dollars

Under 5000　5000-10,000　10,000-50,000　50,000-100,000　Over 100,000

Number of employees
Thousands

91

WASHINGTON 304

MONTANA 23

OREGON 204

IDAHO 50

CALIFORNIA 2,040

NEVADA 18

UTAH 92

WYOMING 11

COLORADO 188

N. DAKOTA 15

S. DAKOTA 27

MINNESOTA 373

WISCONSIN 528

MICHIGAN 977

NEW YORK 1,502

MAINE 115

VT. N.H.

MASS.

CONN. R.I.

ARIZONA 156

NEW MEXICO 34

NEBRASKA 95

KANSAS 188

IOWA 236

ILLINOIS 1,210

INDIANA 643

OHIO 1,219

PENNSYLVANIA 1,291

W. VIRGINIA 109

MD.

D.C.

DEL

N.J.

MISSOURI 430

KENTUCKY 267

VIRGINIA 411

OKLAHOMA 205

ARKANSAS 197

TENNESSEE 492

N. CAROLINA 822

S. CAROLINA 388

ALASKA 13

HAWAII 26

TEXAS 1,068

LOUISIANA 208

MISSISSIPPI 204

ALABAMA 346

GEORGIA 527

FLORIDA 462

DISTRICT OF COLUMBIA 16

VERMONT 50

NEW HAMPSHIRE 111

MASSACHUSETTS 692

CONNECTICUT 455

RHODE ISLAND 127

NEW JERSEY 793

MARYLAND 243

DELAWARE 67

51

EMPLOYMENT

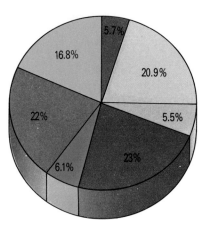

- Construction and mining
- Manufacturing
- Transport and public utilities
- Wholesale and retail trade
- Finance and insurance
- Services
- Government

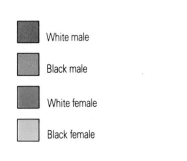

- White male
- Black male
- White female
- Black female

Diagram B: Percentage rate of unemployment, 1982, by sex, age, and race

The map illustrates two aspects of socioeconomic life: the percentage of civilian population aged 16 and over employed in 1983, and the average percentage of the labor force unemployed during the same year.

The Current Population Survey, from which these data are obtained, uses a monthly household survey to gather its information. People are classified as being employed, unemployed, or not in the labor force.

Several factors must be remembered in considering these data. Most important is sex, since women enter or leave the labor force with more frequency than do men, and this plays a major role in the calculation. The age structure of the population is also significant, and so are educational levels.

There is a great variation between different parts of the country. West Virginia has the lowest percentage of the population employed, 43 percent, and the lowest proportion of women who are classified as being in the labor force. It also has the highest rate of unemployment, 18 percent. As with some other southern states, this is associated with the decline in agricultural employment due to mechanization.

At the opposite end of the scale is New Hampshire, with 65 percent of the adult population employed, and only 5.4 percent of the labor force unemployed. However, the two percentages — employment and unemployment — are not always inversely related. Nevada and Alaska combine high percentages of the population employed with fairly high rates of unemployment. New York State and Florida, on the other hand, show fairly low percentages of employment and only moderate unemployment rates.

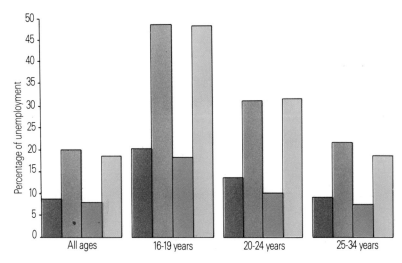

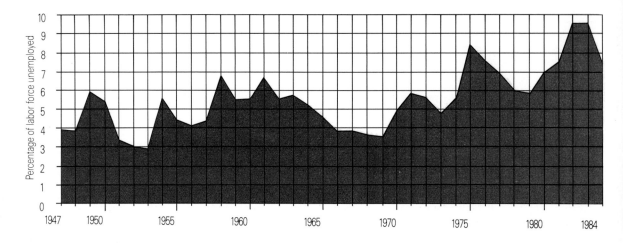

Diagram C: Percentage unemployment, 1947-1984

Diagram A shows the nonagricultural labor force divided into its main sectors. Wholesale and retail trade is the largest single category, just ahead of services and manufacturing. Government accounts for 17.6 percent of the total, although this proportion varies widely among the states.

Diagram B examines the rate of unemployment in relation to age, sex, and race. Its message is only too clear. The burden of unemployment falls most heavily on blacks, by a ratio of over 2 to 1. For both black and white groups, it is the youngest people who are affected most.

Diagram C traces the trend of unemployment since the end of World War II. The peak years — 1950, 1954, 1958, 1962, 1975 and 1982 — show a rising trend. It is more difficult to continue the picture back to earlier times, since methods of gathering and classifying data have changed too much to make direct comparison meaningful.

During the time period covered by Diagram C, another aspect of employment also changed considerably: the participation of women in the labor force. In 1950, only 34 percent of women aged 16 and over were included in the labor force. By 1960, this figure had risen to 38 percent, and this included over 30 percent of married women in the 20-34 age group. In 1984, these figures had risen to 53 percent of all women, and 64 percent of women aged 20-34.

Source: U.S. Bureau of Labor Statistics

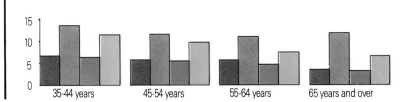

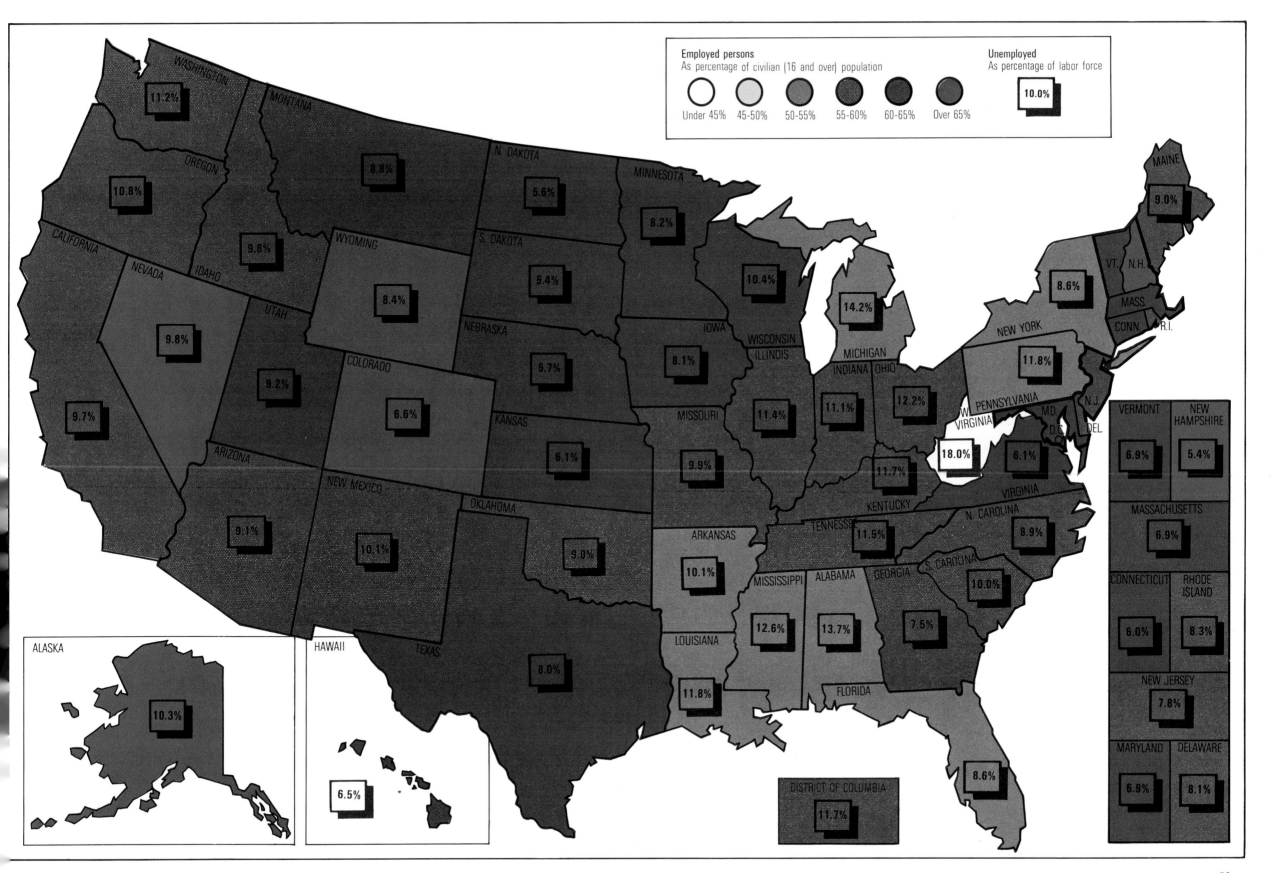

Employed persons
As percentage of civilian (16 and over) population

| Under 45% | 45-50% | 50-55% | 55-60% | 60-65% | Over 65% |

Unemployed
As percentage of labor force

10.0%

WASHINGTON 11.2%
MONTANA 8.8%
OREGON 10.8%
IDAHO 9.8%
N. DAKOTA 5.6%
MINNESOTA 8.2%
MAINE 9.0%
CALIFORNIA 9.7%
NEVADA 9.8%
UTAH 9.2%
WYOMING 8.4%
S. DAKOTA 5.4%
WISCONSIN 10.4%
MICHIGAN 14.2%
NEW YORK 11.8%
VT. N.H.
COLORADO 6.6%
NEBRASKA 5.7%
IOWA 8.1%
ILLINOIS 11.4%
INDIANA 11.1%
OHIO 12.2%
PENNSYLVANIA
N.J.
ARIZONA 9.1%
NEW MEXICO 10.1%
KANSAS 6.1%
MISSOURI 9.9%
KENTUCKY 11.7%
W. VIRGINIA 18.0%
VIRGINIA 6.1%
OKLAHOMA 9.0%
ARKANSAS 10.1%
TENNESSEE 11.5%
N. CAROLINA 8.9%
S. CAROLINA 10.0%
MISSISSIPPI 12.6%
ALABAMA 13.7%
GEORGIA 7.5%
TEXAS 8.0%
LOUISIANA 11.8%
FLORIDA 8.6%

VERMONT 6.9%
NEW HAMPSHIRE 5.4%
MASSACHUSETTS 6.9%
CONNECTICUT 6.0%
RHODE ISLAND 8.3%
NEW JERSEY 7.8%
MARYLAND 6.9%
DELAWARE 8.1%

ALASKA 10.3%
HAWAII 6.5%
DISTRICT OF COLUMBIA 11.7%

53

DIRECTION OF U.S. TRADE

This map shows the destination of the exports of the United States, and the origin of its imports in 1983. The thickness of the arrows represents the relative value of the trade with different parts of the world.

The European Economic Community received 22 percent of U.S. exports, Canada 19 percent, East and South Asia 13 percent, and Japan 11 percent.

Turning to the pattern of U.S. imports, over 20 percent came from Canada and 15 percent from the EEC, but Japan accounted for a significant 16 percent.

In 1984 the picture remained about the same. Taking Europe as a whole, it received over 29 percent of the exports of the United States, and Asia nearly 30 percent. Japan alone accounted for 23.6 percent of the total, and the United Kingdom accounted for 12.2 percent. Asia supplied 37 percent of the imports of the United States, Japan's share amounting to 17.5 percent.

Diagram A looks at the tendencies in U.S. exports and imports in the period 1955-1983. Values of annual trade are here expressed in terms of constant (1967) dollars. The tremendous rise in the total real value of U.S. foreign trade is clear in both graphs, reaching a peak in 1980. Over this quarter of a century, there was a fivefold rise in U.S. exports, and nearly an eightfold rise in imports.

Within these totals, there have been some significant changes. Canada has come to account for a larger share of U.S. exports, and the EEC countries for a smaller one. Canadian exports to the United States, however, have tended to be less important, while Japan has obtained an increasingly larger share.

Diagram B looks at the types of commodity that made up U.S. exports and imports in 1983. The largest single group of goods by value in U.S. exports comprised machinery and transport equipment. Such items made up 45 percent of the total, while "other manufactured goods" amounted to another 15 percent.

The other pie chart in Diagram B shows that machinery and transport equipment also made up a large part of U.S. imports. Together with "other manufactured goods," these commodities accounted for 60 percent of U.S. imports in 1983.

It is interesting to contrast these features of U.S. trade in the 1980s with the pattern found in the past. In the last century, the United States received about 55 percent of its imports from Europe, and sent some 70 percent of its exports there. As noted above, finished manufactured goods account for a large part of both imports and exports these days. In former times, the picture was very different.

Thus, in 1930, such items made up 50 percent of U.S. exports; in 1900, 25 percent; in 1870, 15 percent. The trend in the importance of manufactured goods in imports is less simple. The percentages represented by them in U.S. imports was as follows: 1840, 45; 1870, 40; 1900, 21; 1930, 25; 1970, 55.

Sources: *Government Finance Statistics Yearbook, 1985; Survey of Current Business, 1985; Historical Statistics of the United States, Colonial Times to 1970, Volume II*

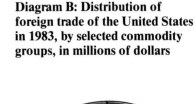

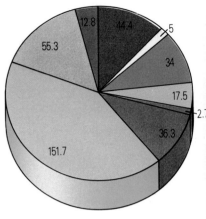

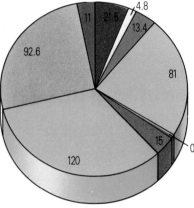

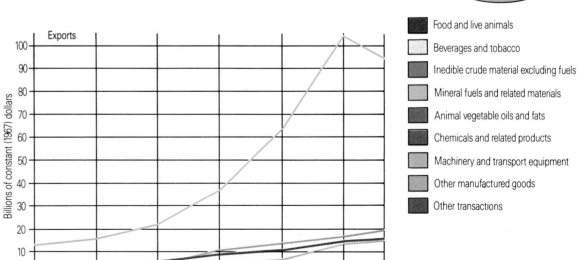

- Food and live animals
- Beverages and tobacco
- Inedible crude material excluding fuels
- Mineral fuels and related materials
- Animal vegetable oils and fats
- Chemicals and related products
- Machinery and transport equipment
- Other manufactured goods
- Other transactions

Diagram A: U.S. trade in billions of constant (1967) dollars, 1955-1983

- Total
- EEC
- Canada
- Japan

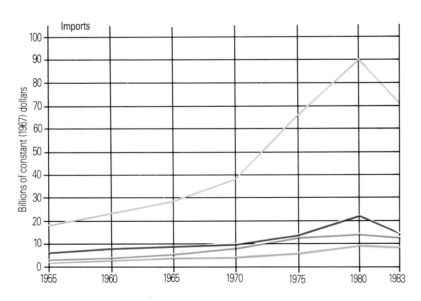

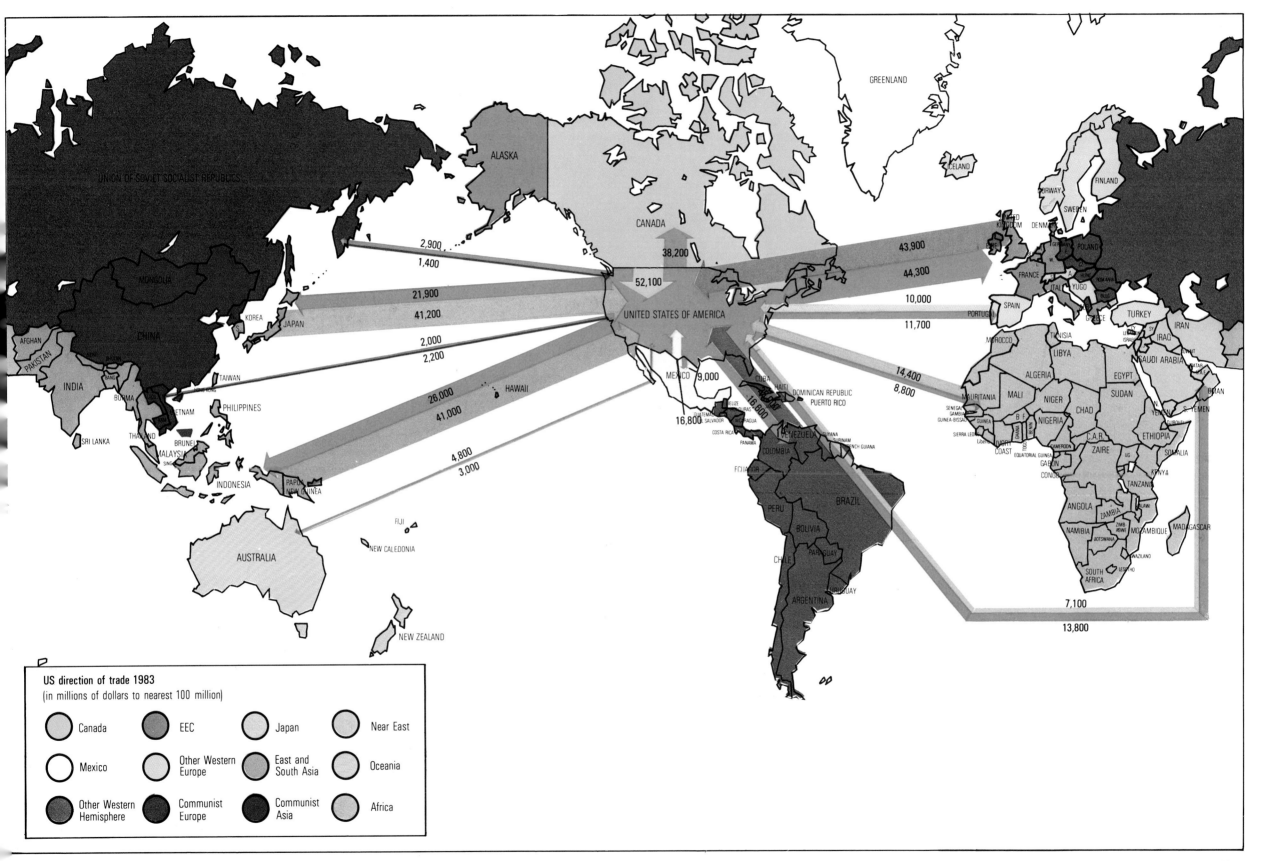

GREENLAND

UNION OF SOVIET SOCIALIST REPUBLICS

ALASKA

MONGOLIA

CANADA

ICELAND

NORWAY   SWEDEN   FINLAND

UNITED
KINGDOM   DENMARK
                     POLAND

AFGHAN   KOREA   JAPAN
                              FRANCE   ITALY   YUGO   ROMANIA

CHINA   SPAIN   GREECE   TURKEY   IRAN
PAKISTAN   IRAQ

INDIA   BURMA   TAIWAN   MOROCCO   TUNISIA   LIBYA   EGYPT   SAUDI ARABIA   QATAR

SRI LANKA   VIETNAM   PHILIPPINES
                                        MEXICO   CUBA   HAITI   DOMINICAN REPUBLIC   MAURITANIA   MALI   NIGER   CHAD   SUDAN   YEMEN
THAILAND   BRUNEI   PUERTO RICO   S. YEMEN
MALAYSIA   BELIZE   GUATEMALA   HONDURAS   SENEGAL   GAMBIA   GUINEA
                                        SALVADOR   NICARAGUA   GUINEA-BISSAU   NIGERIA   C.A.R.   ETHIOPIA
                                        COSTA RICA   SIERRA LEONE   IVORY   GHANA   SOMALIA
INDONESIA   PAPUA   PANAMA   VENEZUELA   GUYANA   COAST   CAMEROON   EQUATORIAL GUINEA   GABON   ZAIRE   KENYA
             NEW GUINEA   COLOMBIA   SURINAM   CONGO   TANZANIA
                                        ECUADOR   FRENCH GUIANA
                        FIJI   ANGOLA   ZAMBIA   MALAWI
             NEW CALEDONIA   PERU   BRAZIL   NAMIBIA   ZIMBABWE   MOZAMBIQUE   MADAGASCAR
                                                        BOLIVIA   BOTSWANA   SWAZILAND
AUSTRALIA   CHILE   PARAGUAY   SOUTH   LESOTHO
                                                                                                AFRICA
             NEW ZEALAND   URUGUAY
                                                ARGENTINA

UNITED STATES OF AMERICA

2,900
1,400

21,900
41,200

2,000
2,200

26,000
41,000

4,800
3,000

38,200

52,100

9,000

16,800

16,600

43,900
44,300

10,000

11,700

14,400
8,800

7,100

13,800

US direction of trade 1983
(in millions of dollars to nearest 100 million)

- Canada
- Mexico
- Other Western Hemisphere
- EEC
- Other Western Europe
- Communist Europe
- Japan
- East and South Asia
- Communist Asia
- Near East
- Oceania
- Africa

ROAD AND RAIL TRANSPORT

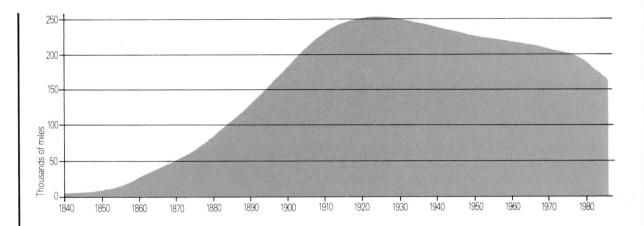

The map indicates the degree of utilization of road and rail transportation in the United States. States are colored according to the density of roads, expressed in miles of urban and rural road per thousand square miles of territory. The map shows interstate and toll highways. The symbols give the number of motor vehicles (in thousands) registered in each state.

The densest road system is to be found in the District of Columbia, which packs 1,100 miles of road into its 64 square miles. At the other extreme, Alaska's 591,000 square miles contain only 10,000 miles of road. While there are 34 registered vehicles for every mile of road in Alaska, the equivalent number in D.C. is 200.

Part of the price paid for the ability to move large numbers of people along our roads at high speed includes the heavy toll in road

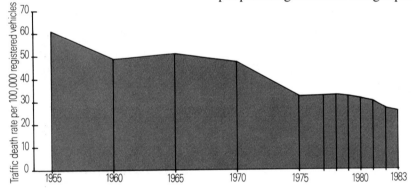

Diagram A: Traffic death rates per 100,000 registered vehicles, 1955-1983

Diagram B: Fuel consumption by cars and trucks, 1970-1982. "Cars" includes taxicabs and motorcycles

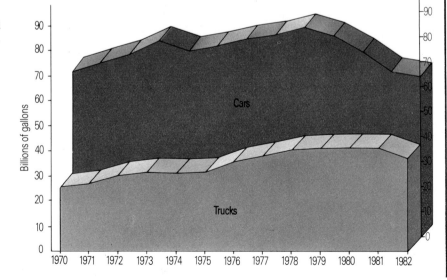

accidents. It is interesting to see the effects of the attention paid to road safety in the numbers of traffic deaths recorded per 100,000 registered vehicles. Graphed in Diagram A, this shows a marked fall in fatalities since 1965.

The intense use of road transport — over 85 percent of eligible Americans hold driver licenses — is reflected in the figures for fuel consumption, graphed in Diagram B. Fuel consumption by cars, climbing steadily in the early 1970s, fell back in 1974 as the rise in fuel costs led to the use of vehicles with more efficient gas consumption. On the other hand, fuel consumption by trucks continued to rise almost without pause. The total amount of travel by trucks is now estimated to be well over 400 billion vehicle-miles per year, while passenger cars travel over 1,100 billion vehicle-miles.

Diagram C graphs the rise and decline of the railroads of the United States. The laying of thousands of miles of railroad track was a major feature of the transcontinental expansion in the period 1860-1920. As the diagram shows, this process of expansion reached its peak just before the Great Depression of the early 1930s. Although the U.S. railroad system played a vital part during World War II, it has shared the financial difficulties of railways in general since then.

In 1983, private automobiles accounted for by far the greatest proportion of intercity passenger traffic, 83 percent of the total in terms of passenger-miles. Bus and rail transportation accounted for only 1.6 and 0.7 percent respectively. In intercity freight transportation, however, railroads played a leading role, accounting for 36 percent of the total ton-mileage. Motor vehicles accounted for 24 percent.

Sources: U.S. Dept. of Transportation; U.S. Federal Highway Administration

Diagram C: Mileage of railroad line, 1840-1980

Note: A ton-mile is the movement of 1 ton (2,000 pounds) of freight for the distance of 1 mile. A passenger-mile is the movement of 1 passenger for the distance of 1 mile.

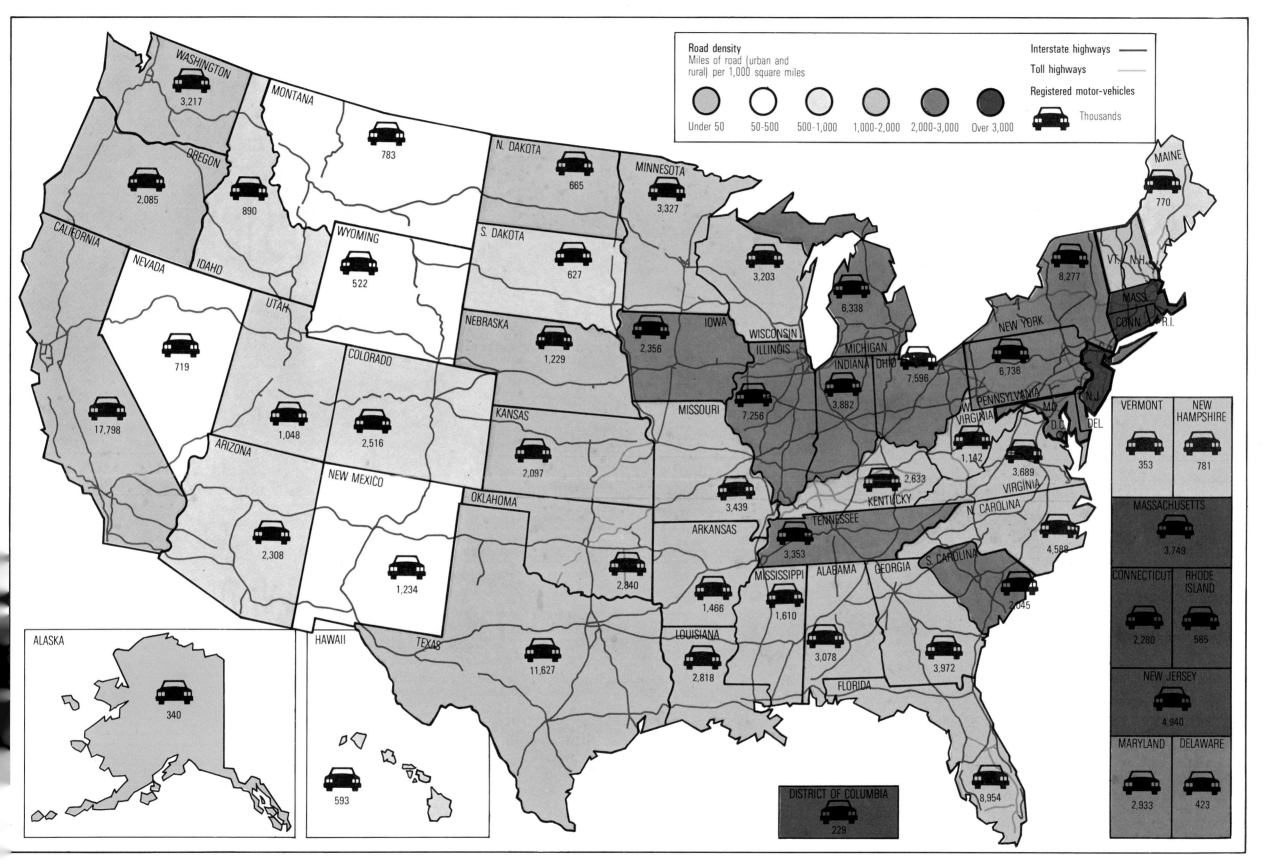

Road density
Miles of road (urban and rural) per 1,000 square miles

| Under 50 | 50-500 | 500-1,000 | 1,000-2,000 | 2,000-3,000 | Over 3,000 |

Interstate highways
Toll highways
Registered motor-vehicles
Thousands

WASHINGTON 3,217
MONTANA 783
N. DAKOTA 665
MINNESOTA 3,327
MAINE 770
OREGON 2,085
890
WYOMING 522
S. DAKOTA 627
3,203
6,338
8,277
NEW YORK
CALIFORNIA
NEVADA
IDAHO
UTAH 719
COLORADO
NEBRASKA 1,229
IOWA 2,356
WISCONSIN
MICHIGAN
ILLINOIS INDIANA OHIO
7,596
6,736
VT. N.H.
MASS.
CONN. R.I.
17,798
1,048
2,516
KANSAS
MISSOURI 7,256
3,882
PENNSYLVANIA
W. VIRGINIA
MD. N.J.
D.C. DEL.
ARIZONA
NEW MEXICO
2,097
OKLAHOMA 3,439
2,633
KENTUCKY
VIRGINIA
1,142
3,689
N. CAROLINA
4,588
2,308
1,234
ARKANSAS
TENNESSEE 3,353
2,840
MISSISSIPPI ALABAMA GEORGIA
S. CAROLINA
2,045
1,466
1,610
TEXAS 11,627
LOUISIANA 2,818
3,078
3,972
FLORIDA 8,954

VERMONT 353
NEW HAMPSHIRE 781
MASSACHUSETTS 3,749
CONNECTICUT 2,280
RHODE ISLAND 585
NEW JERSEY 4,940
MARYLAND 2,933
DELAWARE 423

ALASKA 340
HAWAII 593
DISTRICT OF COLUMBIA 229

57

AIR AND WATER TRANSPORT

There were 16,029 civil airports in the United States in 1983, including heliports, seaplane bases, and military airports with joint civil and military use. The majority of flights, however, were from airports making up the large air-traffic hubs. An "air-traffic hub" is a city or metropolitan area requiring aviation services. A large air-traffic hub is defined as one responsible for at least 1 percent of the total number of revenue passengers using U.S. certificated route air carriers (often referred to as "scheduled airlines"). In 1983 these large air-traffic hubs numbered 26. They included 40 airports and accounted for 220 billion passengers. The 26 large air-traffic hubs are shown on the map, together with the number of aircraft departures from each in 1983.

The expansion of domestic air travel has been a major feature of U.S. transportation since World War II. One of the graphs on Diagram A shows the number of passenger-miles flown on domestic routes between 1970 and 1983. During that period, this number more than doubled, although there was a significant dip between 1979 and 1982.

The other graph on this diagram shows the average rate charged for these flights, expressed in constant (1983) dollars per passenger-mile. In general, the rate has fallen as the number of passenger-miles has increased.

Diagram A: Domestic passenger traffic, 1970-1983, showing passenger-miles flown, and rates in constant (1983) dollars per passenger-mile

Diagram B: Domestic air freight, 1970-1983, showing ton-miles flown, and rates in constant (1983) dollars per ton-mile

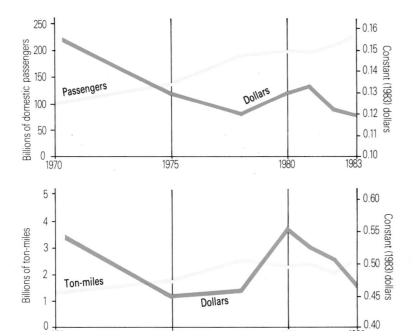

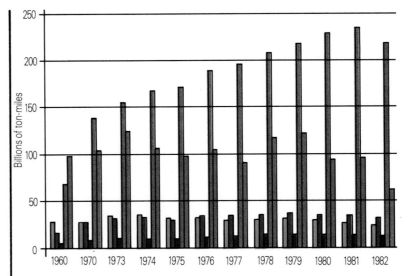

Diagram C: Freight carried on inland waterways, by system, 1960-1982

Domestic air flights have also carried an increasing amount of freight and mail over the same period. Diagram B graphs the domestic freight carried between 1970 and 1983, in ton-miles. This rose sharply until 1979, remaining relatively constant thereafter. The diagram also shows the average rate charged for this freight, in constant (1983) dollars per ton-mile. The rate fell strikingly from 1970 to 1979.

The volume of freight carried on U.S. domestic flights is considerable, but it is insignificant compared with the volume carried on the inland waterways. In 1982, this totaled 351 billion ton-miles.

Diagram C graphs the freight traffic on inland waterways, by system, between 1970 and 1982. The expansion of the Mississippi River system is particularly notable.

Inland waterborne traffic played a major part in the opening up of the interior of the continent in the nineteenth century. In the 1830s and 1840s, a considerable amount of capital was invested in canals. One major undertaking was the construction of the Illinois-Michigan Canal connecting the Mississippi and its tributaries with the Great Lakes, and, incidentally, leading to the expansion of Chicago from a small village to a major industrial center.

Over a century later, the history of the U.S. inland waterways took another leap forward, when agreement between the U.S. and Canadian governments made possible the opening of the St. Lawrence Seaway in 1959. This opened the Great Lakes to ocean-going vessels.

Sources: United States Federal Aviation Administration; U.S. Corps of Engineers

Note: A ton-mile is the movement of 1 ton (2,000 pounds) of freight for the distance of 1 mile. A passenger-mile is the movement of 1 passenger for the distance of 1 mile.

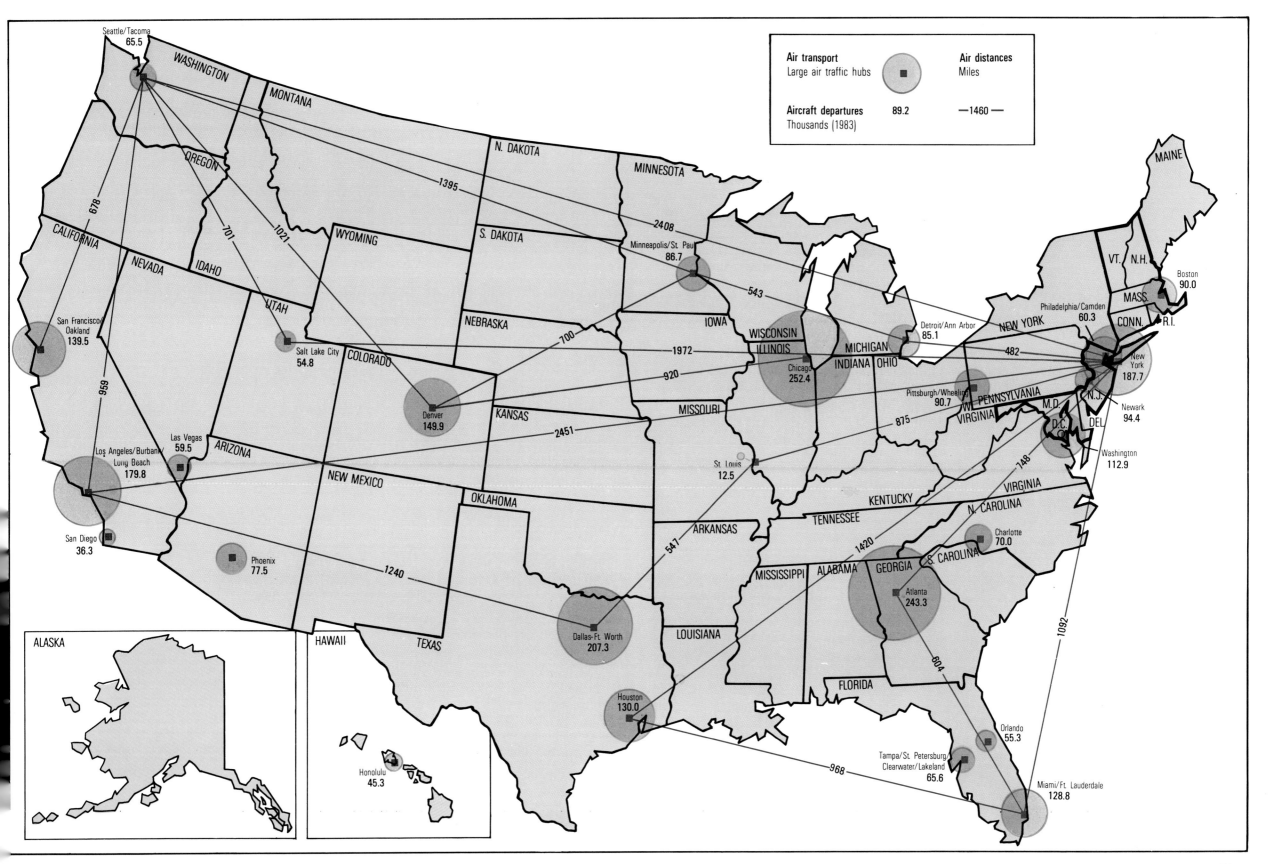

Air transport
Large air traffic hubs

Aircraft departures
Thousands (1983)   89.2

Air distances
Miles

—1460—

ALASKA

HAWAII

Seattle/Tacoma
65.5

WASHINGTON

MONTANA

N. DAKOTA

MINNESOTA

OREGON

IDAHO

WYOMING

S. DAKOTA

Minneapolis/St. Paul
86.7

CALIFORNIA

NEVADA

UTAH

COLORADO

NEBRASKA

IOWA

WISCONSIN

ILLINOIS

MICHIGAN

Detroit/Ann Arbor
85.1

NEW YORK

MAINE

VT.   N.H.

MASS.

Boston
90.0

CONN.   R.I.

Philadelphia/Camden
60.3

San Francisco/
Oakland
139.5

Salt Lake City
54.8

Denver
149.9

KANSAS

MISSOURI

INDIANA   OHIO

Chicago
252.4

Pittsburgh/Wheeling
90.7

W. PENNSYLVANIA

VIRGINIA

M.D.

N.J.

New York
187.7

Newark
94.4

Las Vegas
59.5

Los Angeles/Burbank/
Long Beach
179.8

ARIZONA

NEW MEXICO

OKLAHOMA

St. Louis
12.5

D.C.

DEL

Washington
112.9

VIRGINIA

San Diego
36.3

Phoenix
77.5

ARKANSAS

TENNESSEE

KENTUCKY

N. CAROLINA

Charlotte
70.0

MISSISSIPPI   ALABAMA   GEORGIA   S. CAROLINA

Atlanta
243.3

Dallas-Ft. Worth
207.3

TEXAS

LOUISIANA

FLORIDA

Houston
130.0

Honolulu
45.3

Orlando
55.3

Tampa/St. Petersburg/
Clearwater/Lakeland
65.6

Miami/Ft. Lauderdale
128.8

678
701
1021
1395
2408
543
959
700
1972
920
875
482
2451
547
1240
1420
748
604
1092
968

COMMUNICATIONS

One of the most striking features of social development in the twentieth century has been the expansion of the communications media, and in this change the United States has led the world. Nearly every U.S. home today has at least one TV set and radio. Over 1,700 daily newspapers circulate over 62.5 million copies in total. Billions of pieces of mail are delivered each year.

The map shows how the states compare in two respects. The color of each state indicates the circulation of daily newspapers per 1,000 people, and the symbols show the number of telephones per 100 people. The District of Columbia is once again far ahead of others: 2.44 daily papers are bought there per capita, and there are more telephones than households. Mississippi is at the other end of the scale, with 161 daily newspapers for every 1,000 people, and 49 telephones for every 100 inhabitants.

In 1960 there were 74 million telephones in use in the United States, making 182 million calls each day. In 1981 this had risen to 158 million telephones, and 800 million calls per day. In 1960 312 morning daily newspapers circulated over 24 million copies. In 1982 the number of morning daily newspapers had increased to

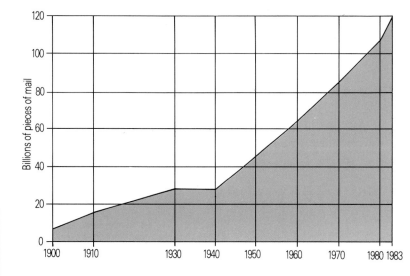

Diagram C: Number of pieces of mail, in billions, handled each year by the U.S. Postal Service, 1900-1983

434 and circulation to over 33 million copies. The number of evening papers, however, decreased over the same period from 1,459 to 1,284 and circulation from 34.9 million to 28.8 million.

Television is now the most influential form of mass communication. The average American watches about 7 hours of TV each day. Whereas in 1961 56 TV stations broadcast a total of 2,186 hours each week, in 1982 there were 291 stations broadcasting 30,337 hours weekly.

Diagram A shows how commercial TV has grown since 1960 in terms of gross broadcast revenues. While the figure for radio expanded from $665 million to $3.58 billion in the period 1960-1980, the equivalent amounts for television are $1.5 billion and $10.5 billion.

Diagram B shows the main source of these massive funds — TV network advertising expenditures. Food, tobacco, and automotive products account for a large part of the total. TV advertising expenditures are now on the way to overtaking the total amount spent on local and national newspaper advertising.

Diagram C graphs the expansion of the U.S. Postal Service. At the turn of the century it handled 7.1 billion pieces of mail in a year. By 1983 this figure had risen to 120 billion. Over the same period, Postal Service revenues increased from $108 million to over $25 billion. This amounts to a rise from $1.34 per capita in 1900, to over $24 per capita in 1983.

Source: U.S. Federal Communications Commission

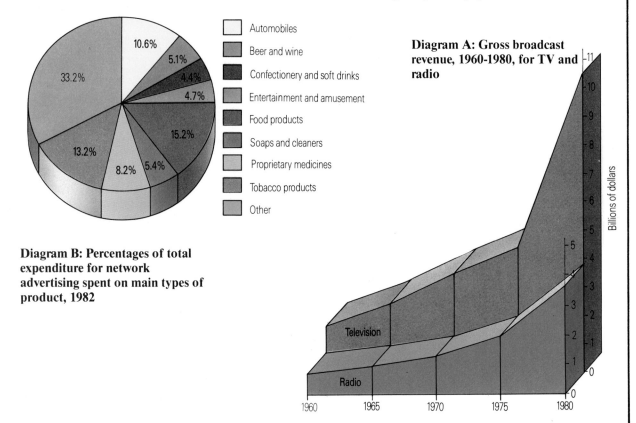

Automobiles
Beer and wine
Confectionery and soft drinks
Entertainment and amusement
Food products
Soaps and cleaners
Proprietary medicines
Tobacco products
Other

10.6%
5.1%
4.4%
4.7%
33.2%
15.2%
13.2%
8.2%
5.4%

Diagram A: Gross broadcast revenue, 1960-1980, for TV and radio

Billions of dollars

Television

Radio

1960   1965   1970   1975   1980

Diagram B: Percentages of total expenditure for network advertising spent on main types of product, 1982

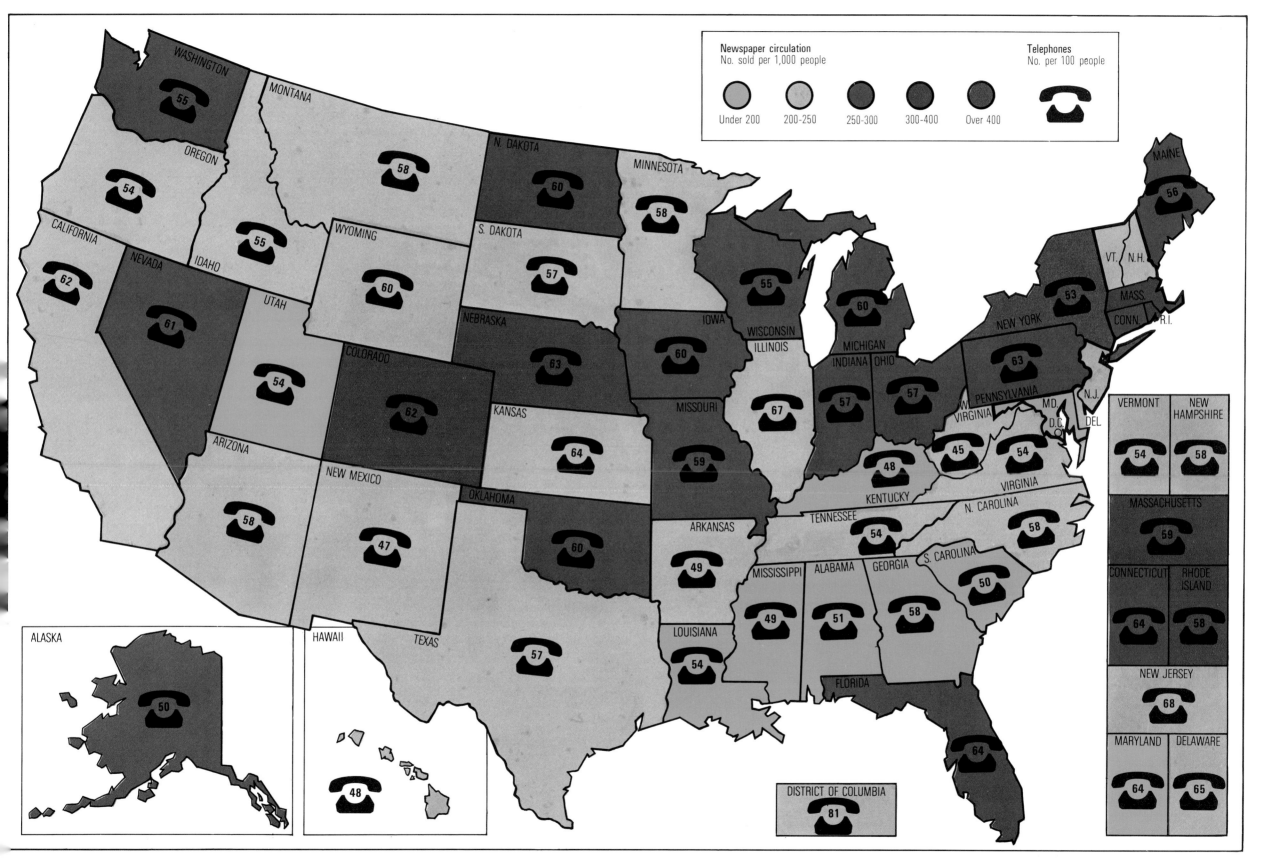

Newspaper circulation
No. sold per 1,000 people

Under 200 | 200-250 | 250-300 | 300-400 | Over 400

Telephones
No. per 100 people

WASHINGTON 55
MONTANA 58
N. DAKOTA 60
MINNESOTA 58
MAINE 56
OREGON 54
IDAHO 55
WYOMING 60
S. DAKOTA 57
WISCONSIN 55
NEW YORK 53
CALIFORNIA 62
NEVADA 61
UTAH 54
NEBRASKA 63
IOWA 60
MICHIGAN 60
ILLINOIS 67
INDIANA 57
OHIO 57
PENNSYLVANIA 63
COLORADO 62
KANSAS 64
MISSOURI 59
W. VIRGINIA 48
VIRGINIA 54
KENTUCKY 45
ARIZONA 58
NEW MEXICO 47
OKLAHOMA 60
ARKANSAS 49
TENNESSEE 54
N. CAROLINA 58
S. CAROLINA 50
MISSISSIPPI 49
ALABAMA 51
GEORGIA 58
LOUISIANA 54
TEXAS 57

ALASKA 50
HAWAII 48

DISTRICT OF COLUMBIA 81

VERMONT 54
NEW HAMPSHIRE 58
MASSACHUSETTS 59
CONNECTICUT 64
RHODE ISLAND 58
NEW JERSEY 68
MARYLAND 64
DELAWARE 65

FLORIDA 64

REVENUE AND EXPENDITURE

The map deals with state and local revenue and expenditure. The states are colored according to the per capita revenue raised, while the numbers in the symbols give the·corresponding per capita expenditure. Alaska and the District of Columbia are by far the highest, because of their unique nature. Of the other states Wyoming is the highest, both for revenue and expenditure, while Arkansas is the lowest.

The pie chart on each state is divided according to the distribution of expenditure by function. On average, about 36 percent of state and local expenditure is spent on education. Utah, spending 48 percent on education, comes first in this respect, followed by Indiana and South Carolina with 44 percent each.

Diagram A: Distribution of federal and state and local government expenditure, by main functions, 1970 and 1982

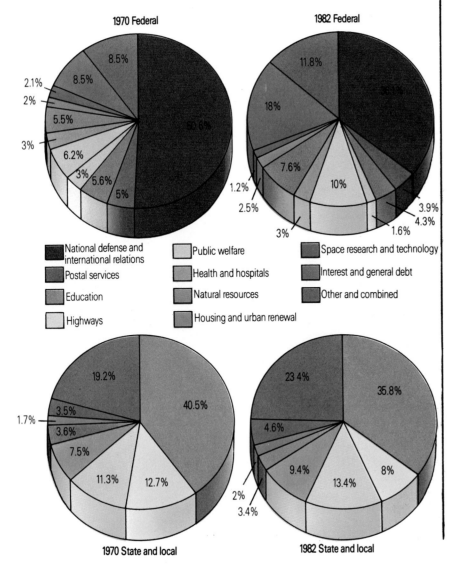

1970 Federal

1982 Federal

- National defense and international relations
- Postal services
- Education
- Highways
- Public welfare
- Health and hospitals
- Natural resources
- Housing and urban renewal
- Space research and technology
- Interest and general debt
- Other and combined

1970 State and local

1982 State and local

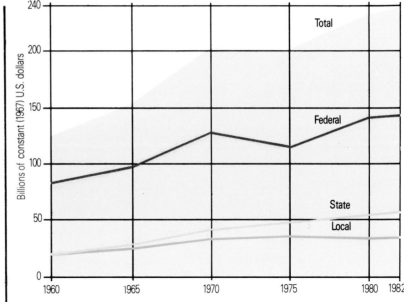

Diagram B: Tax revenue, 1960-1982, for all governments and for federal, state, and local governments

The four pie charts of Diagram A show the proportions of total national expenditure devoted to various purposes, both by federal, and state and local authorities, in 1970 and in 1982.

Diagram B depicts the steady rise in tax revenue since 1960, graphing federal, state and local, and total taxes, allowing for inflation. State and local taxes represent a rising proportion of the total.

In 1960, total tax revenue of all governments amounted to $113 billion. Of this, 68 percent went to the federal government, 16 percent to state governments, and 16 percent to local governments. In 1982, when the total tax revenue amounted to $671 billion, 60 percent went to federal government, 24 percent to state government and 16 percent to local governments.

A major factor in economic life is the indebtedness of the government. In 1983 the total public debt amounted to $1,377.2 billion, or $5,870 per capita. In 1970, the total was $370.1 billion, or $1,814 per capita. Interest payments on this debt made up 9.9 percent of total federal outlays in 1970. In 1983, it was 16.2 percent.

The debts of some of our large cities are now also substantial. In 1982 New York City owed $1,472 per capita. But this was far behind some others, notably Atlanta, Georgia ($2,354), Washington, D.C. ($2,783), Wichita, Kansas ($2,860), and Austin, Texas ($2,899). In the years since then, the debt of some cities has increased while the debt of others has decreased.

Source: U.S. Bureau of the Census

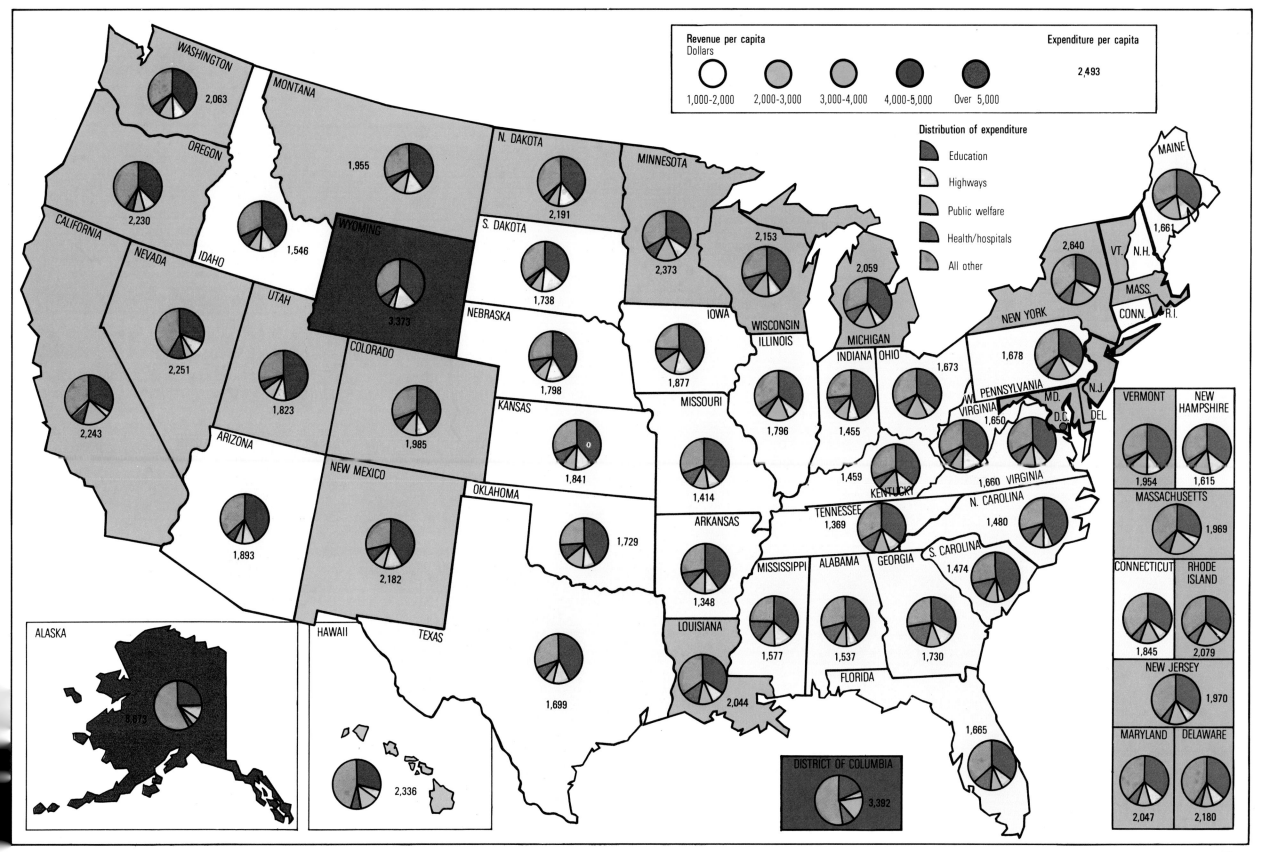

Revenue per capita
Dollars

○ 1,000-2,000   ○ 2,000-3,000   ○ 3,000-4,000   ● 4,000-5,000   ● Over 5,000

Expenditure per capita

2,493

Distribution of expenditure

Education
Highways
Public welfare
Health/hospitals
All other

WASHINGTON 2,063
MONTANA 1,955
OREGON 2,230
IDAHO 1,546
CALIFORNIA 2,243
NEVADA 2,251
UTAH 1,823
WYOMING 3,373
N. DAKOTA 2,191
S. DAKOTA 1,738
MINNESOTA 2,373
COLORADO 1,985
NEBRASKA 1,798
KANSAS 1,841
ARIZONA 1,893
NEW MEXICO 2,182
OKLAHOMA 1,729
TEXAS 1,699
WISCONSIN 2,153
IOWA 1,877
ILLINOIS 1,796
MISSOURI 1,414
ARKANSAS 1,348
LOUISIANA 2,044
MICHIGAN 2,059
INDIANA 1,455
OHIO 1,673
KENTUCKY 1,459
TENNESSEE 1,369
MISSISSIPPI 1,577
ALABAMA 1,537
GEORGIA 1,730
PENNSYLVANIA 1,678
W. VIRGINIA 1,650
VIRGINIA 1,660
N. CAROLINA 1,480
S. CAROLINA 1,474
FLORIDA 1,665
NEW YORK 2,640
MAINE 1,661

VERMONT 1,954
NEW HAMPSHIRE 1,615
MASSACHUSETTS 1,969
CONNECTICUT 1,845
RHODE ISLAND 2,079
NEW JERSEY 1,970
MARYLAND 2,047
DELAWARE 2,180

ALASKA 5,873
HAWAII 2,336
DISTRICT OF COLUMBIA 3,392

PERSONAL WEALTH

This map deals with the distribution of personal wealth. States are colored according to the average personal income per capita of residents in 1983. Also shown are the number of wealthholders, those whose gross estate is $60,000 or more. "Gross estate" is the total value of all assets, including life insurance. Numbers of wealthholders are estimates derived by the Internal Revenue Service from a sample of federal estate tax returns for deceased people.

On average, the residents of the United States had an income of $11,675 per capita in 1983. (This rose to $12,707 in 1984.) The average for individual states in 1983 varied from $8,072 in Mississippi and $8,937 in Arkansas, to $14,826 in Connecticut and $16,820 in Alaska. The District of Columbia's average was $16,409. The map shows the per capita income for each of the states and its relation to other states.

Overall, the people with $60,000 or more gross estate make up 3.7 percent of the population. In Alaska this percentage is 6, in Connecticut 5.7, in Mississippi 2.8, and in Arkansas 1.8, correlating with the per capita income levels. (These figures relate to 1976.)

In 1965, per capita personal income in the United States was $2,782, and in 1975 $5,857. In terms of constant (1972) dollars, the per capita incomes were:

1965	$3,171
1975	$4,051
1983	$4,670

In 1983, the median family income — the level at which 50 percent of all U.S. families received this amount or less — was estimated at $24,580. Diagram A shows the distribution of the aggregate income received by families in 1983. The percentage of the total aggregate income for the entire country is plotted against the percentage of families receiving the corresponding income or less.

At the bottom end of the scale, 20 percent of all families received 4.7 percent of the total income, and 40 percent received 15.8 percent of the total. At the other end of the scale, the top 5 percent of families received 15.8 percent of the total income.

Diagram B graphs the growth in the median family income since 1950 in constant (1983) dollars. It also shows black and white families separately. The rise in income levels in all cases is striking, until 1973, when the steady increase came to an end. Although the percentage difference between white and black families is plain, it has slowly been decreasing.

Diagram A: Percentage of aggregate personal income received by various percentages of all families, 1983

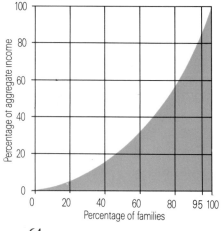

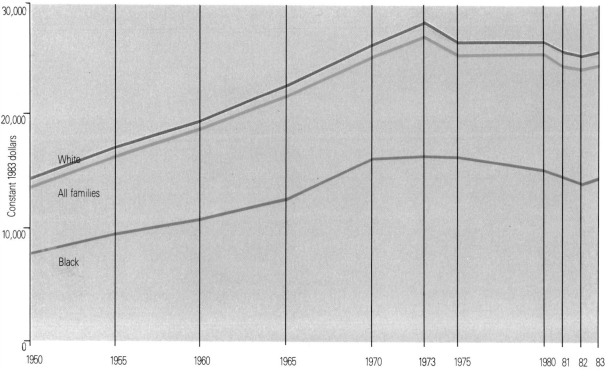

In 1983, 10.3 percent of households had an income of $50,000 or more. The percentage for white households was 11.1, for black households 3.1, and for households of Spanish origin 4.5. At the other end of the scale, 9.2 percent of households received a money income of $5,000 or less, 7.7 percent for whites, 21.1 percent for blacks, and 12.5 percent for households of Spanish origin.

Families are classified as being above or below the poverty level using the poverty index originated in 1964. This is based on income and reflects the different food consumption requirements of families according to their size. The poverty thresholds are updated every year to reflect changes in the Consumer Price Index. In 1983 the threshold for a family of four stood at $10,178, and 35.5 million people were classified as being below the poverty level. They accounted for 12.1 percent of the white population, 35.7 percent of the black population, and 28.4 percent of people of Spanish origin.

Turning to the distribution of personal wealth, data are less plentiful and less up-to-date. (Most of the data come from the U.S. Internal Revenue Service.) In 1976, it is estimated, 1 percent of the population held 19.2 percent of the nation's total personal wealth, and just 0.5 percent owned 14.3 percent.

Diagram B: Median income of families, in constant (1983) dollars, all families, black and white

Sources: U.S. Bureau of Economic Analysis, *Survey of Current Business;*
U.S. Bureau of the Census, *Current Population Reports;*
U.S. Internal Inland Revenue Service, *Statistics of Income*

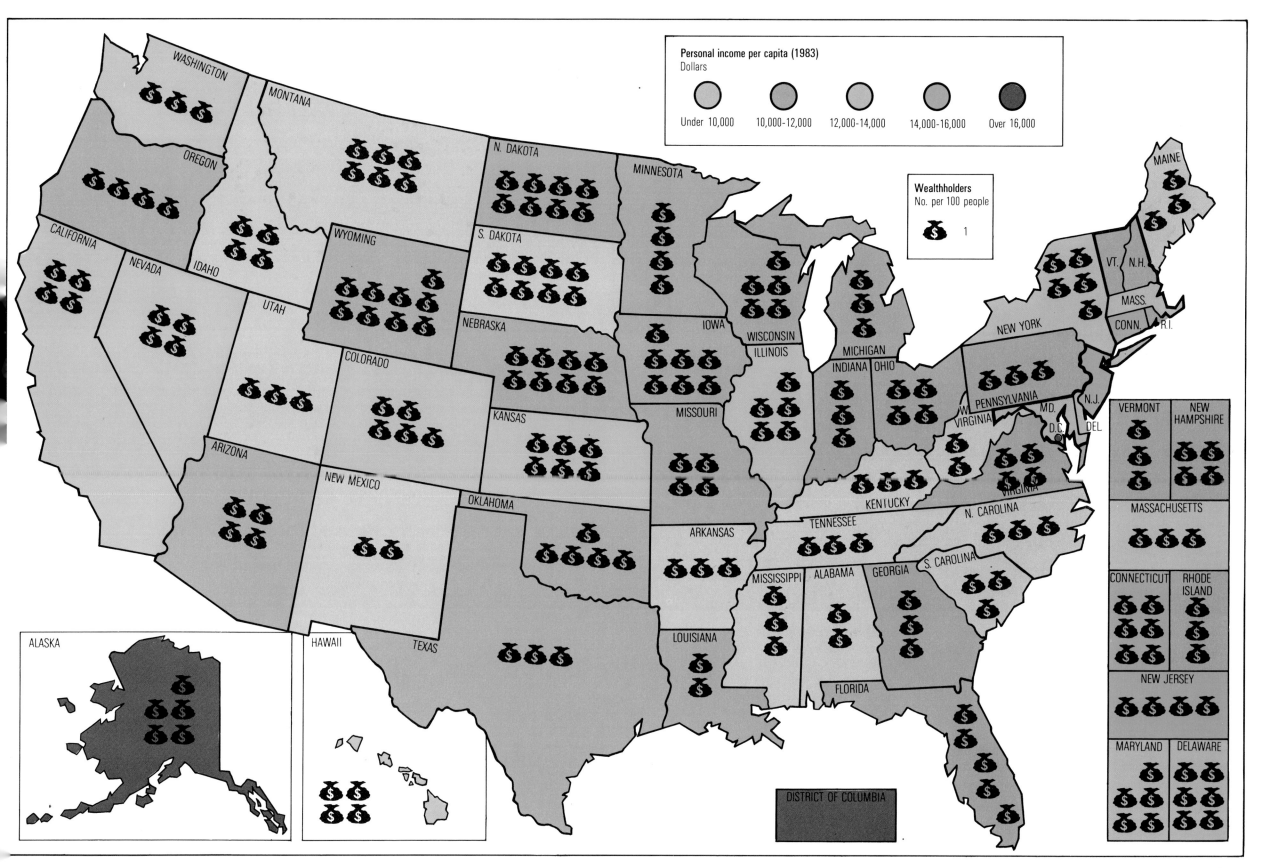

Personal income per capita (1983)
Dollars

Under 10,000   10,000-12,000   12,000-14,000   14,000-16,000   Over 16,000

Wealthholders
No. per 100 people
$ = 1

WASHINGTON
MONTANA
OREGON
N. DAKOTA
MINNESOTA
MAINE
CALIFORNIA
NEVADA
IDAHO
WYOMING
S. DAKOTA
VT. N.H.
MASS.
UTAH
NEBRASKA
IOWA
WISCONSIN
MICHIGAN
NEW YORK
CONN. R.I.
COLORADO
ILLINOIS
INDIANA OHIO
PENNSYLVANIA
N.J.
ARIZONA
KANSAS
MISSOURI
W. VIRGINIA
MD. DEL
D.C.
NEW MEXICO
OKLAHOMA
KENTUCKY
VIRGINIA
N. CAROLINA
TENNESSEE
ARKANSAS
MISSISSIPPI
ALABAMA
GEORGIA
S. CAROLINA
LOUISIANA
TEXAS
ALASKA
HAWAII
FLORIDA
DISTRICT OF COLUMBIA

VERMONT
NEW HAMPSHIRE
MASSACHUSETTS
CONNECTICUT
RHODE ISLAND
NEW JERSEY
MARYLAND
DELAWARE

65

THE FAMILY

This map deals with statistics about the family. States are colored according to the number of marriages per 1,000 people in 1982. The average marriage rate for the whole country was 10.8.

It must be pointed out, that the rate for a state refers to the number of marriages *performed* there, related to the population *residing* in that state. This explains the anomalous figure for Nevada in particular, which recorded 123.9 marriages for every thousand residents in 1982. Apart from this state, marriage rates per thousand in 1982 ranged from 8.1 in New Jersey to 16.7 in South Carolina.

It should also be borne in mind that the marriage rate measured in this way is strongly affected by the age structure, that is, by the proportion of the population in the age groups most likely to be marrying. This is important when considering trends in the marriage rate, since the percentage of the population in the 25 to 44 year age group declined up to 1970, and then rose again.

The map also contains two symbols for each state. One indicates the number of married couples with children, as a percentage of all families. (The Bureau of the Census defines a family to be "a group of two or more persons related by birth, marriage, or adoption and residing together in a household.") The other symbol shows the birth rate per 1,000 people for 1981.

The variations between states are in all cases affected by their age distribution. So it is not surprising that the lowest figure for married couples with children per 100 families is 22 for the District of Columbia, followed by 33 for Florida.

Similarly, the fact that Alaska shows the second highest birth rate — 24.3 per 1,000 — is clearly related to the age distribution. Utah comes first with 27.3, while Connecticut has the lowest figure, 12.7 per 1,000 people.

Diagram A shows that, in 1983, 63.9 percent of the population aged 18 and over were married, a decline from the 1970 figure of 71.7 percent. Conversely 6.9 percent of people aged 18 and over in 1983 were divorced, compared with the 1970 figure of 3.2 percent. In 1970, there were 47 divorced people for every 1,000 married people, while in 1983 the figure had risen to 114.

The rate of divorce per 1,000 of total population rose rapidly during the 1960s and early 1970s, from 2.2 in 1960, to 3.5 in 1970, reaching 4.8 in 1975. However, the rate of increase then slowed down. In 1981 the figure had reached 5.3; it then began to fall again, in 1982 to 5.1 and in 1983 to 5.0.

Diagram B graphs the marriage rate, per 1,000 unmarried women aged 15 and over, and the divorce rate, also expressed per 1,000 married women, aged 15 and over, from 1960 to 1981. The marriage rate reached its peak in 1969; and declined quite rapidly from 1973 to 1978. It then showed signs of rising again. The divorce rate expressed per 1,000 married women reached a peak of 22.8 in 1979.

Many states now report a "median duration of marriage" figure, and an estimate can be made for the country as a whole. In 1981 it was 7.0 years.

The median age at first marriage is also estimated by the Bureau of the Census. In 1981 it was 23.9 years for men and 22.0 for women. Both figures had shown a tendency to rise over the past two decades. In 1960, the median age for men was 22.8, that for women, 20.3.

The median age at remarriage, on the other hand, also estimated by the Bureau, has fallen. In 1965 it was 39.6 years for men, and 35.5 for women. In 1981 it was 35.3 for men, and 32.1 for women.

Diagram C shows the characteristics of family households in 1983, separating black and white. Almost 85 percent of white households included a married couple, compared to 53.4 percent of black households. In 12.2 percent of white households, the householder was a woman, with no spouse present. For black households, the percentage was 41.9. In the remaining 3.1 percent of white and 4.7 percent of black households, the householder was male, with no spouse present.

Sources: U.S. National Center for Health Statistics; U.S. Bureau of the Census

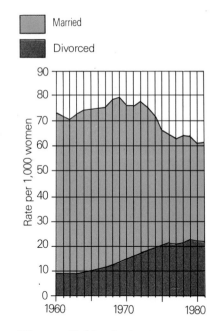

Diagram B: Marriage rate, per 1,000 unmarried women, and divorce rate, per 1,000 married women, 1960-1981

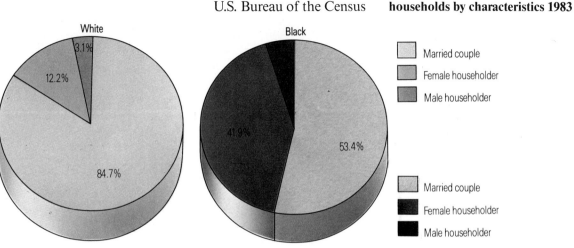

Diagram C: Distribution of family households by characteristics 1983

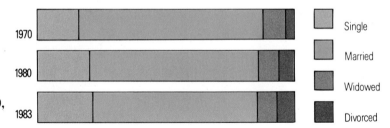

Diagram A: Marital status, 1970, 1980, and 1983

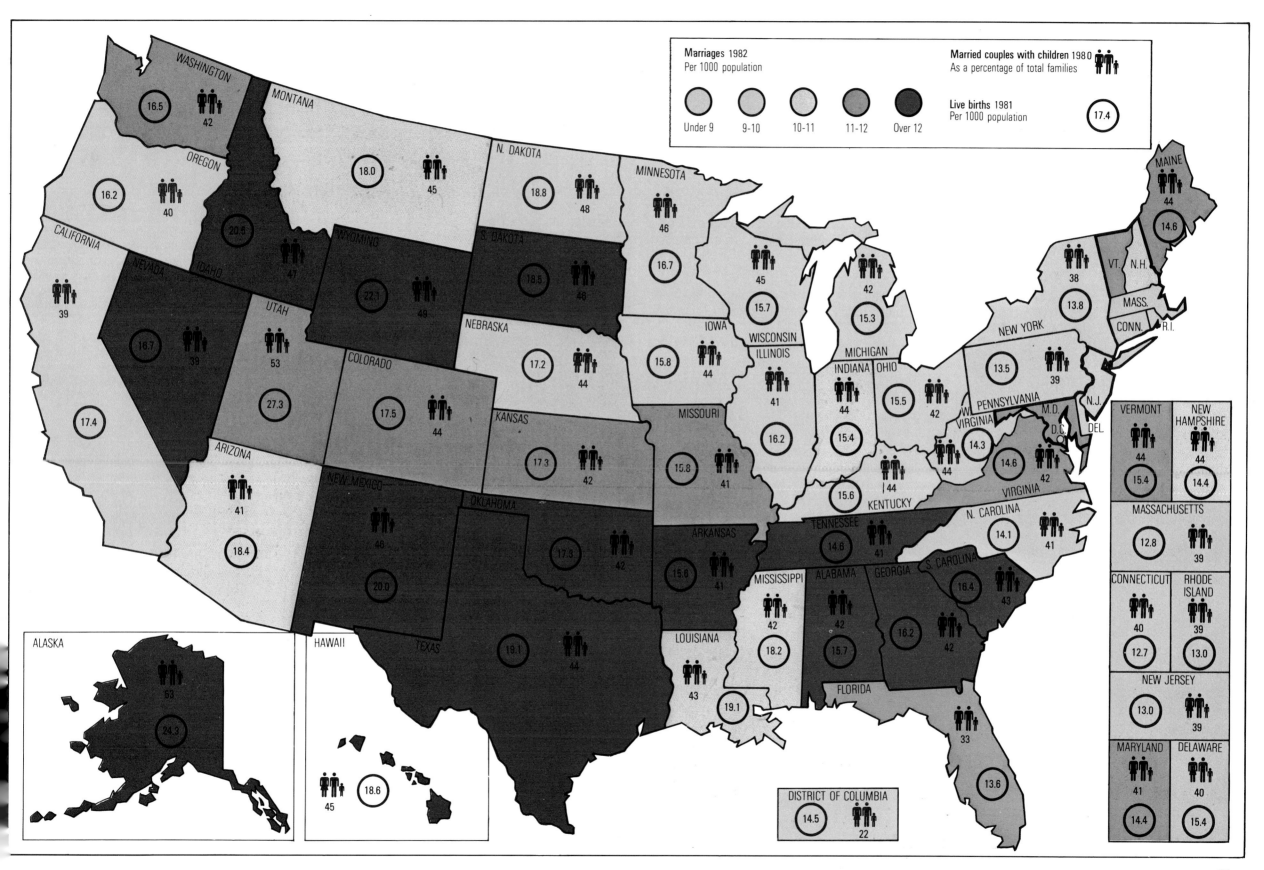

Marriages 1982
Per 1000 population

Married couples with children 1980
As a percentage of total families

Live births 1981
Per 1000 population

Under 9 · 9-10 · 10-11 · 11-12 · Over 12

17.4

WASHINGTON 16.5 · 42
OREGON 16.2 · 40
MONTANA 18.0 · 45
N. DAKOTA 18.8 · 48
MINNESOTA 16.7 · 46
MAINE 14.6 · 44
IDAHO 20.6 · 47
WYOMING 22.1 · 49
S. DAKOTA 18.5 · 48
WISCONSIN 15.7 · 45
VT. N.H.
MASS. 13.8
NEVADA 16.7 · 39
CALIFORNIA 17.4
UTAH 27.3 · 53
COLORADO 17.5 · 44
NEBRASKA 17.2 · 44
IOWA 15.8 · 44
ILLINOIS 15.3 · 42
MICHIGAN 16.2 · 41
NEW YORK 13.5 · 39
CONN. R.I.
ARIZONA 18.4 · 41
NEW MEXICO 20.0 · 46
KANSAS 17.3 · 42
MISSOURI 15.8 · 41
INDIANA 15.4 · 44
OHIO 15.5 · 42
PENNSYLVANIA 14.3 · 44
N.J.
M.D. D.C. DEL
OKLAHOMA 17.3 · 42
ARKANSAS 15.6 · 41
KENTUCKY 15.6 · 44
W. VIRGINIA 14.6 · 42
VIRGINIA
N. CAROLINA 14.1 · 41
TENNESSEE 14.6 · 41
S. CAROLINA 16.4 · 43
TEXAS 19.1 · 44
LOUISIANA 19.1 · 43
MISSISSIPPI 18.2 · 42
ALABAMA 15.7 · 42
GEORGIA 16.2 · 42
FLORIDA 13.6 · 33

ALASKA 24.3 · 63
HAWAII 18.6 · 45

VERMONT 15.4 · 44
NEW HAMPSHIRE 14.4 · 44
MASSACHUSETTS 12.8 · 39
CONNECTICUT 12.7 · 40
RHODE ISLAND 13.0 · 39
NEW JERSEY 13.0 · 39
MARYLAND 14.4 · 41
DELAWARE 15.4 · 40

DISTRICT OF COLUMBIA 14.5 · 22

EDUCATION ENROLLMENT

On this map, the states are colored according to the percentage of adults — 25 years and over — in 1980, who had completed at least 4 years of high school education. Nationwide, this percentage was 66.5, but there is a considerable variation between the states.

In Kentucky 53.1 percent of adults had completed 4 years of high school, and in Mississippi 54.8 percent, while 80 percent of Utah adults had reached this level of education, exceeded only by Alaska's 82.5 percent.

The map also shows two other percentages for each state: the enrollment rate in public elementary and secondary schools, and the percentage of adults who had completed 4 years or more of college. The enrollment rate expresses the number of schoolchildren in the fall of 1982 as a percentage of the number of children aged between 5 and 17 years. Rhode Island shows the lowest enrollment rate, at 80.3 percent, followed by Pennsylvania, with 80.5 percent. At the other end of the scale, Utah again stands out with 97.4, followed by Wyoming, with 96.2. The average for the whole country was 87.3.

The percentage of people with 4 years' college education, which was 16.2 percent nationwide in 1980, was highest in the District of Columbia, where 27.5 percent of adults had attained this educational level. Next came Colorado, with 23 percent. Lowest were Arkansas, with 10.8, and Kentucky, with 11.1 percent.

Diagram A traces the history of school enrollment for the years 1960 to 1983, showing the total numbers of pupils, and the numbers in elementary and high schools, and in colleges. The numbers reflect changes in the age structure over the post-war period, as well as changes in educational standards.

Diagram A: School enrollment, by level of instruction, 1960-1983

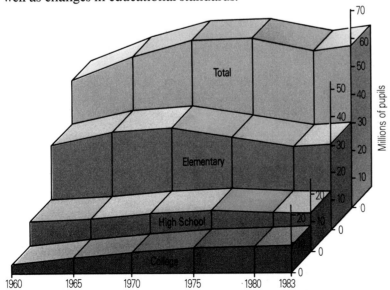

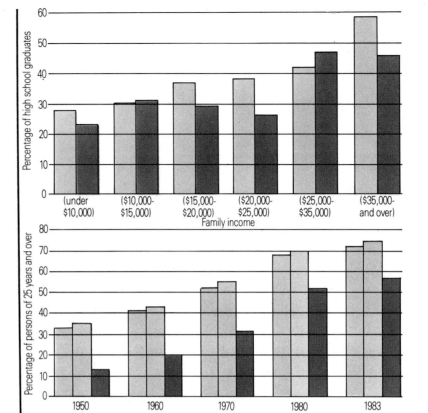

All races

Black

White

Diagram B: Percentage of high school graduates enrolling in college, by family income, 1983. Figures are for dependent family members, 18-24 years old

Diagram C: Percentage of adults — 25 years or over — who have completed 4 years or more of high school education, 1950-1983

In 1980, 42 percent of the population aged between 16 and 24 were enrolled in school. In 1950, this percentage was only 27. Most striking was the rise in the number of girls who continued their education. In 1950, 103,000 women were awarded bachelor's degrees, and 329,000 men, but in 1982 the women obtaining bachelor's degrees outnumbered men, by 480,000 to 473,000.

Enrollment rates are strongly affected by family income and by race. Diagram B shows the percentage of high school graduates aged 18 to 24, broken down into black people and white people, and into family income groups. While 27.9 percent of high school graduates from families with an annual income of under $10,000 were in college, the percentage rose to 58.2 percent for the "$35,000 and over" group.

The overall percentage for black people is lower than that for white people, but this difference is not found in every income group. Diagram C also bears on the difference in educational levels achieved by black people and white people in the period 1950-1983. While, at the start of this period, the percentage of black people aged 25 or over who had completed 4 years or more of high school was far smaller than the percentage of white people, the gap has decreased steadily as the overall percentage has increased.

Sources: U.S. Bureau of the Census;
U.S. National Center for Education Statistics

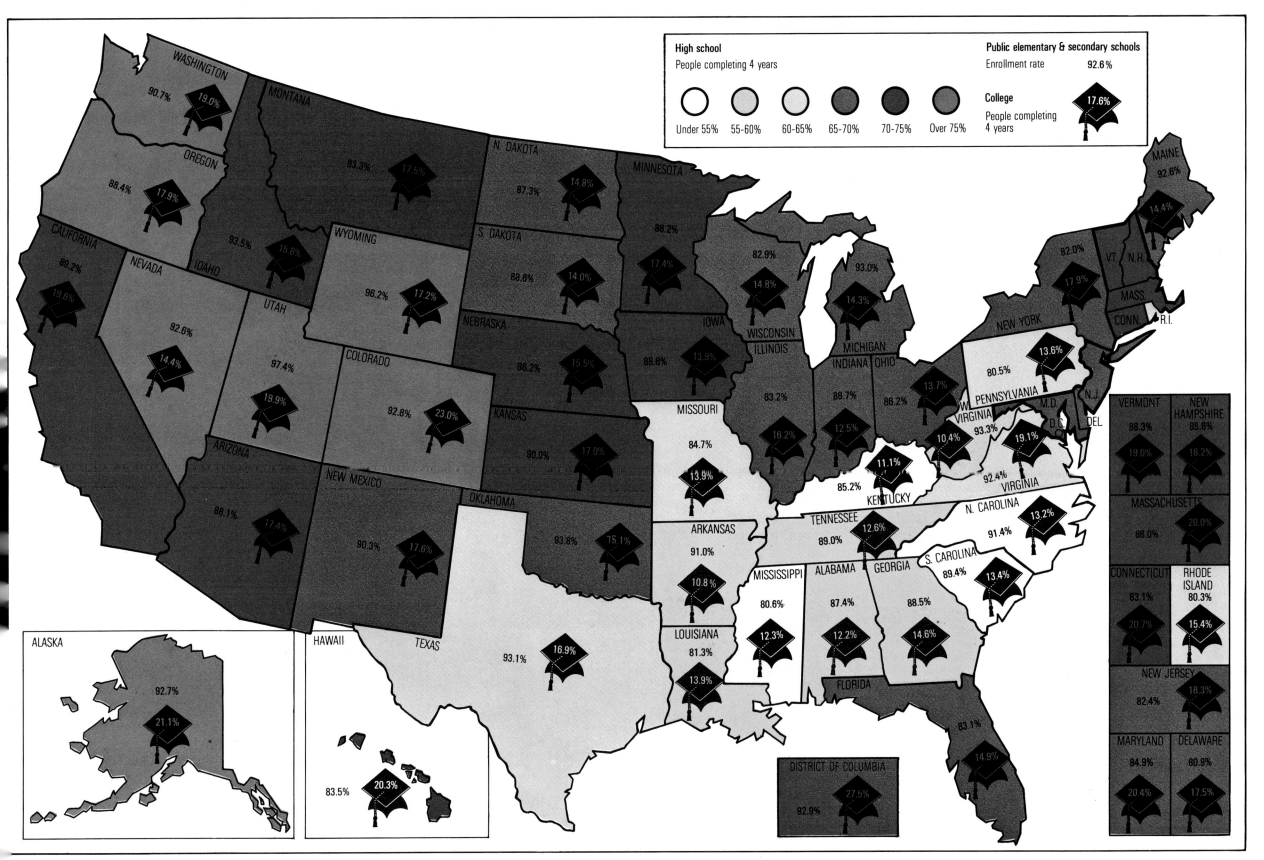

High school
People completing 4 years

Under 55% · 55-60% · 60-65% · 65-70% · 70-75% · Over 75%

Public elementary & secondary schools
Enrollment rate 92.6%

College
People completing 4 years 17.6%

WASHINGTON 90.7% 19.0%

MONTANA 93.3% 17.5%

N. DAKOTA 87.3% 14.8%

MINNESOTA 88.2%

MAINE 92.6% 14.4%

OREGON 88.4% 17.9%

IDAHO 93.5% 15.8%

WYOMING 96.2% 17.2%

S. DAKOTA 88.8% 14.0%

WISCONSIN 82.9% 14.8%

MICHIGAN 93.0%

NEW YORK 82.0%

VT. N.H.

MASS.

CONN. R.I.

CALIFORNIA 89.2% 19.6%

NEVADA 92.6% 14.4%

UTAH 97.4% 19.9%

COLORADO 92.8% 23.0%

NEBRASKA

IOWA 88.6% 13.9%

ILLINOIS 83.2% 16.2%

INDIANA 88.7% 12.5%

OHIO 86.2% 13.7%

PENNSYLVANIA 80.5% 13.6%

17.9%

ARIZONA 88.1% 17.4%

NEW MEXICO 90.3% 17.6%

KANSAS 90.0% 17.0%

MISSOURI 84.7% 13.9%

KENTUCKY 85.2% 11.1%

W. VIRGINIA 93.3% 10.4%

VIRGINIA 92.4% 19.1%

M.D.

N.J.

D.C. DEL

OKLAHOMA 93.8% 75.1%

ARKANSAS 91.0% 10.8%

TENNESSEE 89.0% 12.6%

N. CAROLINA 91.4% 13.2%

S. CAROLINA 89.4% 13.4%

MISSISSIPPI 80.6% 12.3%

ALABAMA 87.4% 12.2%

GEORGIA 88.5% 14.6%

LOUISIANA 81.3% 13.9%

TEXAS 93.1% 16.9%

FLORIDA 83.1% 14.9%

ALASKA 92.7% 21.1%

HAWAII 83.5% 20.3%

DISTRICT OF COLUMBIA 92.9% 27.5%

VERMONT 88.3% 19.0%

NEW HAMPSHIRE 85.8% 18.2%

MASSACHUSETTS 88.0% 20.0%

CONNECTICUT 83.1% 20.7%

RHODE ISLAND 80.3% 15.4%

NEW JERSEY 82.4% 18.3%

MARYLAND 84.9% 20.4%

DELAWARE 80.9% 17.5%

EDUCATION RESOURCES

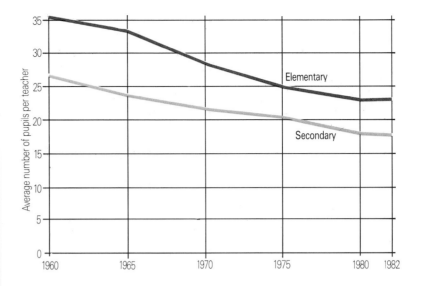

Diagram B: Average number of pupils per teacher in public elementary and secondary schools, 1960-1982

This map shows information about the resources devoted to education. States are colored to represent the 1984 expenditure per pupil, according to the average daily attendance at public elementary and secondary schools.

Alaska had the highest expenditure per pupil, $7,026. This is far above the second highest, New Jersey, which spent $4,943 per pupil. At the other end of the scale, Mississippi spent $1,962 per pupil in 1984. The average for the entire country was $3,173.

Diagram A presents expenditure per capita in 1982 for each state, in descending order. Wyoming comes first on this list, spending $724 per pupil. Some way behind is New York State, with $564. At the bottom are Kentucky, with $328 per pupil, and Mississippi with $317.

Also shown on the map for each state are average teachers' salaries for the year ending in June 1984. This figure covers all teachers in public elementary and secondary schools. The national average was $22,000, but there is a remarkable variation in teachers' salaries between different parts of the country. In

Alaska, the average salary was $36,564. The District of Columbia came next with $27,659, followed by New York State at $27,330. In South Dakota, on the other hand, teachers averaged $16,480 per year, and in Arkansas, $16,929.

Diagram B graphs the number of children per teacher. This "pupil-teacher ratio" has fallen fairly steadily over the period, and further falls are projected in the next decade.

The map also gives the number of institutions of higher education in 1982 for each state. This covers universities, colleges, professional schools, and junior and teachers' colleges. There was a total of 3,280 such institutions in the United States in 1982, with a total enrollment of 8.58 million. Of these, 296 were in New York State, and 273 in California.

Source: U.S. National Center for Education Statistics

Diagram A: Per capita expenditure on education, 1982, by state

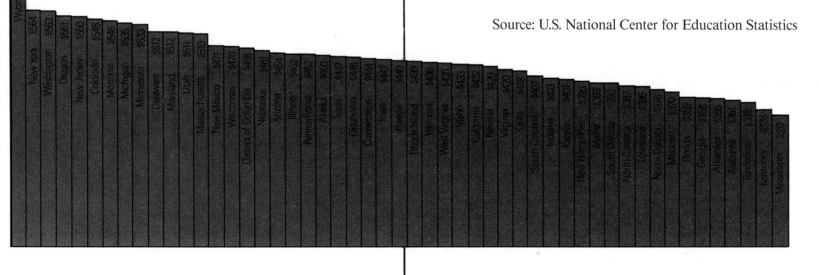

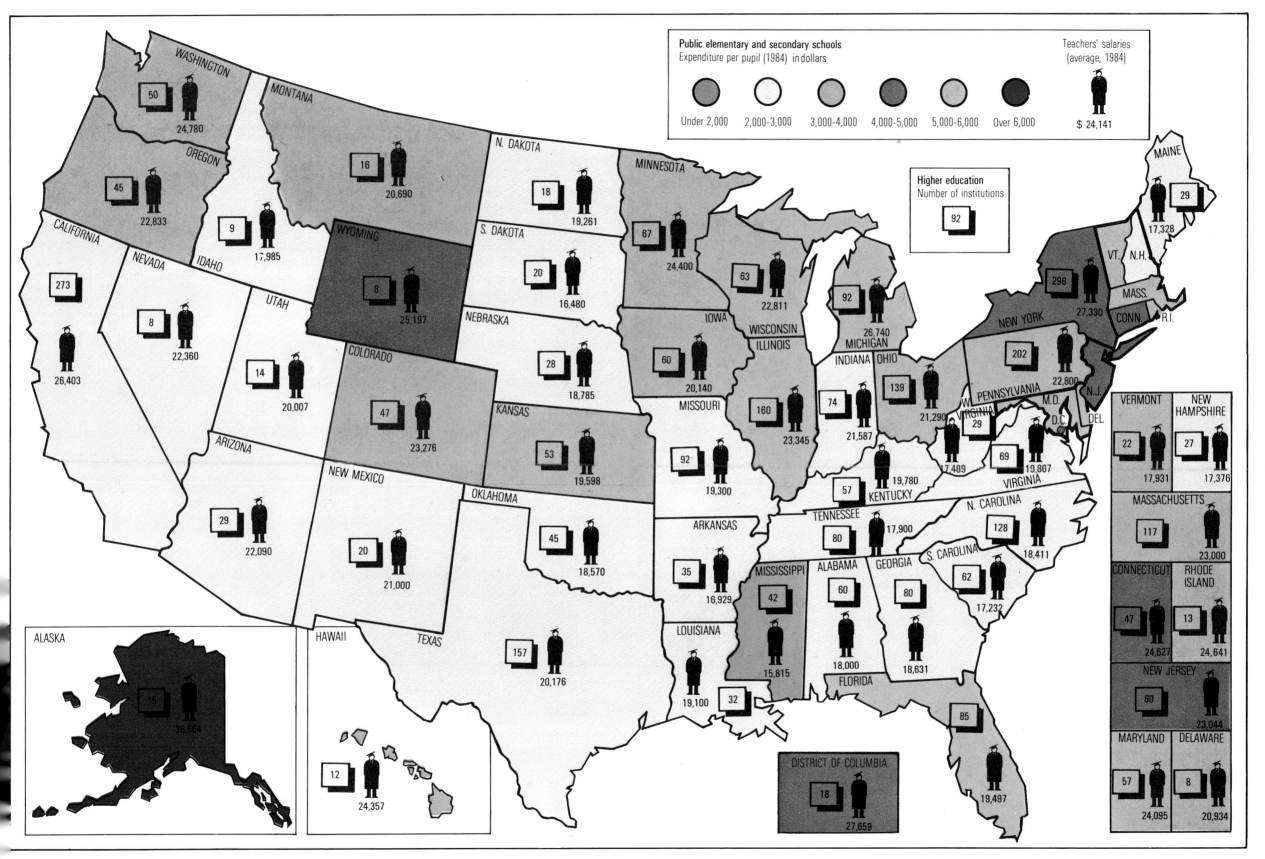

Public elementary and secondary schools
Expenditure per pupil (1984) in dollars

Under 2,000 | 2,000-3,000 | 3,000-4,000 | 4,000-5,000 | 5,000-6,000 | Over 6,000

Teachers' salaries (average, 1984)
$ 24,141

Higher education
Number of institutions
92

WASHINGTON 50 — 24,780
OREGON 45 — 22,833
CALIFORNIA 273 — 26,403
NEVADA 8 — 22,360
IDAHO 9 — 17,985
MONTANA 16 — 20,690
WYOMING 8 — 25,197
UTAH 14 — 20,007
COLORADO 47 — 23,276
ARIZONA 29 — 22,090
NEW MEXICO 20 — 21,000
N. DAKOTA 18 — 19,261
S. DAKOTA 20 — 16,480
NEBRASKA 28 — 18,785
KANSAS 53 — 19,598
OKLAHOMA 45 — 18,570
TEXAS 157 — 20,176
MINNESOTA 67 — 24,400
IOWA 63 — 22,811
WISCONSIN 92 — 26,740
MISSOURI 92 — 19,300
ARKANSAS 35 — 16,929
LOUISIANA 19,100
MISSISSIPPI 42 — 15,815
ALABAMA 60 — 18,000
ILLINOIS 160 — 23,345
MICHIGAN 92 — 26,740
INDIANA 74 — 21,587
OHIO 139 — 21,290
KENTUCKY 57 — 17,900
TENNESSEE 80 — 17,900
GEORGIA 80 — 18,631
S. CAROLINA 62 — 17,232
N. CAROLINA 128 — 18,411
FLORIDA 85 — 19,497
W. VIRGINIA 29 — 17,489
VIRGINIA 69 — 19,867
PENNSYLVANIA 202 — 22,800
NEW YORK 296 — 27,330
MAINE 29 — 17,328

ALASKA 15 — 36,564
HAWAII 12 — 24,357
DISTRICT OF COLUMBIA 18 — 27,659

VERMONT 22 — 17,931
NEW HAMPSHIRE 27 — 17,376
MASSACHUSETTS 117 — 23,000
CONNECTICUT 47 — 24,627
RHODE ISLAND 13 — 24,641
NEW JERSEY 60 — 23,044
MARYLAND 57 — 24,095
DELAWARE 8 — 20,934

PUBLIC HEALTH

In 1983 the total expenditure on the nation's health amounted to over $355 billion, or $1,459 per capita (and 11 percent of the GNP). In 1960 the expenditure per capita was exactly one-tenth of that (and 5 percent of the GNP). Allowing for inflation, the cost of health services and supplies rose during the 1960s and 1970s and, according to informed forecasts, is likely to go on rising.

The map provides three general indicators of health and health services: the ratio of physicians to total population, the availability of hospital beds, and infant mortality rates.

The ratio of physicians to total population is generally high, and highest of all in the Northeast and California, traditionally prosperous regions with high urban population. The true figures are probably slightly higher than the map suggests since certain small categories, such as physicians in federal employment or doctors of osteopathy, are excluded.

In general, there are fewer differences between the states in health care now than there were one or two generations ago. Thus, the availability of hospital beds is reasonably consistent nationwide (the national average is 6 beds per 1,000 people), and the comparatively low figure in Alaska, for example, may be largely explained by the low proportion of elderly Alaskans. The term "hospital" here encompasses all institutions registered by the American Hospital Association (approximately 7,000 in all), including psychiatric and other specialized hospitals.

Infant mortality rates are used all over the world as an indication of health care. They represent babies that were born alive but died before their first birthday. These figures are encouraging inasmuch as they show an improvement of 40 percent in the decade ending in 1981. Moreover, the gap between white and black people has tended to close, although the mortality rate is still markedly higher among black babies.

It is largely this fact that explains the very high figure for infant mortality in the District of Columbia (notwithstanding its high proportion of hospital beds) and contributes to the relatively high figures in the South. Every southern state has a rate higher than the national average, with Mississippi the highest at 15 per thousand live births.

Diagram A shows the life expectancy at birth for white and black people. Although the life expectancy at birth of a black male is still six years less than that of a white male, it has improved. The figures overall are inspiring: general life expectancy has increased from 54 to 74 years in half a century.

Diagram B lays out, in broad categories, expenditure on health services and supplies in 1983. This category includes personal expenses, hospital care, physicians', dentists', and other professional services, drugs, eyeglasses, home nursing and other services, but not medical research or building works, etc. The gap between private and public (federal, state, local) expenditure has narrowed considerably in recent years. In 1960, before the introduction of Medicare, public expenditure amounted to less than 21 percent of the total; by 1980 this percentage had almost doubled.

A notable feature of private expenditure is the rising cost of medical insurance. In 1960 insurance premiums accounted for less than 45 percent of total expenditure in the private sector. In 1983 they accounted for over 55 percent.

Source: U.S. National Center for Health Statistics

Diagram A: Life expectancy at birth, 1920-1980

- White male
- White female
- Black male
- Black female

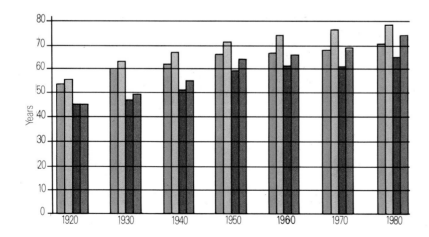

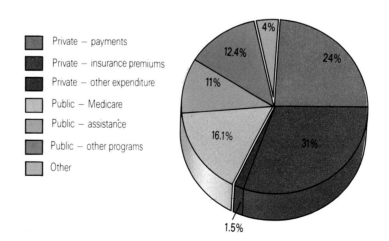

- Private — payments
- Private — insurance premiums
- Private — other expenditure
- Public — Medicare
- Public — assistance
- Public — other programs
- Other

Diagram B: National health expenditure, 1983

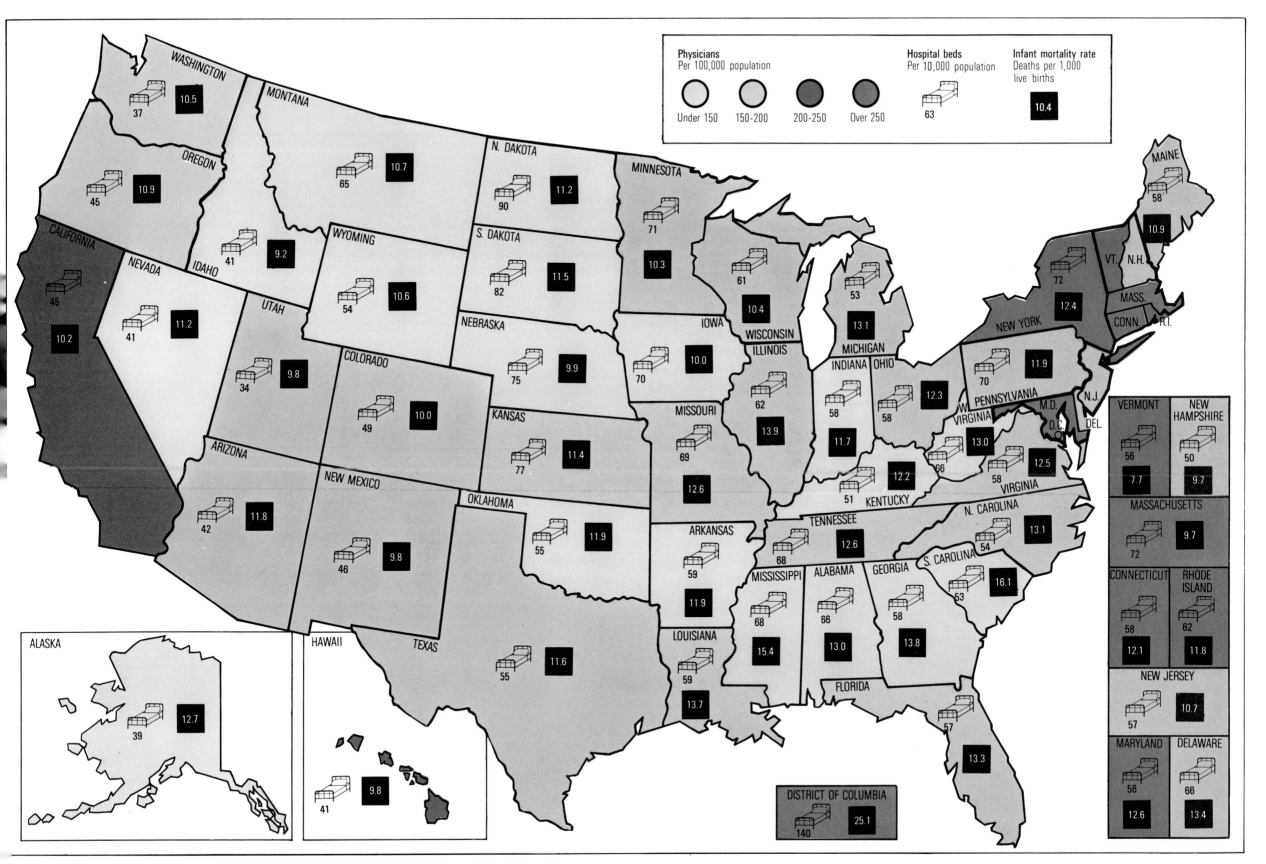

Physicians
Per 100,000 population

Under 150 | 150-200 | 200-250 | Over 250

Hospital beds
Per 10,000 population

63

Infant mortality rate
Deaths per 1,000 live births

10.4

WASHINGTON 10.5 — 37

OREGON 10.9 — 45

CALIFORNIA 10.2 — 45

NEVADA 11.2 — 41

IDAHO 9.2 — 41

UTAH 9.8 — 34

ARIZONA 11.8 — 42

MONTANA 10.7 — 65

WYOMING 10.6 — 54

COLORADO 10.0 — 49

NEW MEXICO 9.8 — 46

N. DAKOTA 11.2 — 90

S. DAKOTA 11.5 — 82

NEBRASKA 9.9 — 75

KANSAS 11.4 — 77

OKLAHOMA 11.9 — 55

TEXAS 11.6 — 55

MINNESOTA 10.3 — 71

IOWA 10.4 — 61

MISSOURI 12.6 — 69

ARKANSAS 11.9 — 59

LOUISIANA 13.7 — 59

WISCONSIN 10.0 — 70

ILLINOIS 13.9 — 62

MICHIGAN 13.1 — 53

INDIANA 11.7 — 58

OHIO 12.3 — 58

KENTUCKY 12.2 — 51

TENNESSEE 12.6 — 68

MISSISSIPPI 15.4 — 68

ALABAMA 13.0 — 66

GEORGIA 13.8 — 58

FLORIDA 13.3 — 57

W. VIRGINIA 13.0 — 66

VIRGINIA 12.5 — 58

N. CAROLINA 13.1 — 54

S. CAROLINA 16.1 — 53

PENNSYLVANIA 11.9 — 70

NEW YORK 12.4 — 72

MAINE 10.9 — 58

ALASKA 12.7 — 39

HAWAII 9.8 — 41

DISTRICT OF COLUMBIA 25.1 — 140

VERMONT 7.7 — 56

NEW HAMPSHIRE 9.7 — 50

MASSACHUSETTS 9.7 — 72

CONNECTICUT 12.1 — 58

RHODE ISLAND 11.8 — 62

NEW JERSEY 10.7 — 57

MARYLAND 12.6 — 58

DELAWARE 13.4 — 66

CRIME

This map deals with crime and law enforcement. States are colored according to the number of criminal offenses known to the police, per 100,000 population in 1983. The average for the entire country was 5,159.

The crime rate for individual states varies from 2,419 for West Virginia, to 6,251 for California. Variations in the crime rate closely match the varying degrees of urbanization. The rate of crime in metropolitan areas in 1983 averaged 5,852, while the rate in rural areas was 1,881 offences per 100,000 population.

Diagram A graphs the rate of all criminal offenses, including non-violent crimes in the period 1974-1983. The rate has decreased since 1980 for every category of crime. On the map, the percentage fall in the crime rate is shown for each state.

Diagram B is a pie chart showing the distribution of serious criminal offenses between various categories of crime according to arrests. Larceny (theft of property without use of force or fraud) forms the largest category, making up 56 percent of the total. Burglary comes next, at 19 percent. Violent crimes (comprising murder, forcible rape, robbery and aggravated assault) make up 21 percent of all serious criminal offenses.

The contrast between metropolitan and rural areas is more striking in the incidence of violent crime than for crime in general. In metropolitan areas in 1983, there were 627 violent crimes per 100,000 population, compared with 161 in rural areas. In cities with populations of 250,000 or more, the rate for violent crime was 1,294, and for "property crime" 7,345 offenses per 100,000 people.

Detroit, Michigan, had the highest rate of violent crime in 1983: 2,169 per 100,000 residents. It was followed by Baltimore, Maryland, at 2,003, and Washington, D.C. at 1,915.

There were a total of 10.3 million arrests for serious crimes in 1983: 74 percent of these were of people in the 18-44 year age group, and 83 percent were males. The proportion of persons arrested who were under 18 has been declining steadily since the mid-1970s, while the proportion in the 18-44 year age group has been rising.

In 1982, 608,000 persons were in locally operated jails or in state or federal prisons — 38 for every 10,000 adult residents. There were 1,287,300 people under the supervisory authority of a probation agency. In 1983, 11,896 persons were released from their first term of imprisonment in a federal institution. On average they had served 15.9 months of an average sentence of 35.4 months.

Diagram C graphs the number of prisoners in federal and state prisons, per 100,000 population, from 1950 to 1983. This rate fell during the 1960s, but thereafter rose rapidly. In 1983, there were well over twice as many prisoners as in 1970.

In 1981, Juvenile Courts disposed of 1.35 million delinquency cases, 44 for every 1,000 people in the 10-17 years age group. This was an improvement on the 1980 figure, when the rate was 46.4. However, in 1960, the rate was 20.1. At that time 19.3 percent of these cases concerned girls, but in 1981 the percentage had risen to 24.0.

Sources: U.S. Federal Bureau of Investigation;
U.S. Bureau of Justice Statistics

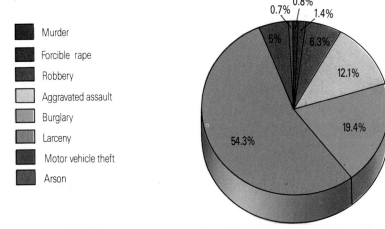

Murder
Forcible rape
Robbery
Aggravated assault
Burglary
Larceny
Motor vehicle theft
Arson

Diagram B: Distribution of criminal offenses by type of crime, 1983

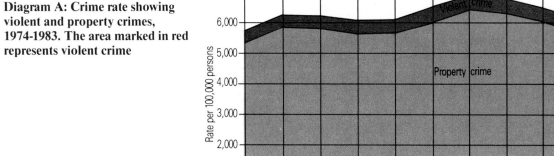

Diagram A: Crime rate showing violent and property crimes, 1974-1983. The area marked in red represents violent crime

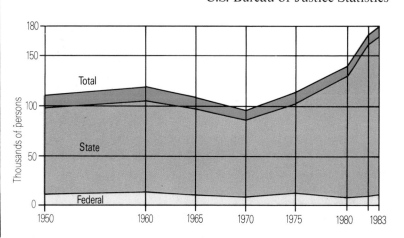

Diagram C: Federal and state prisoners, 1950-1983

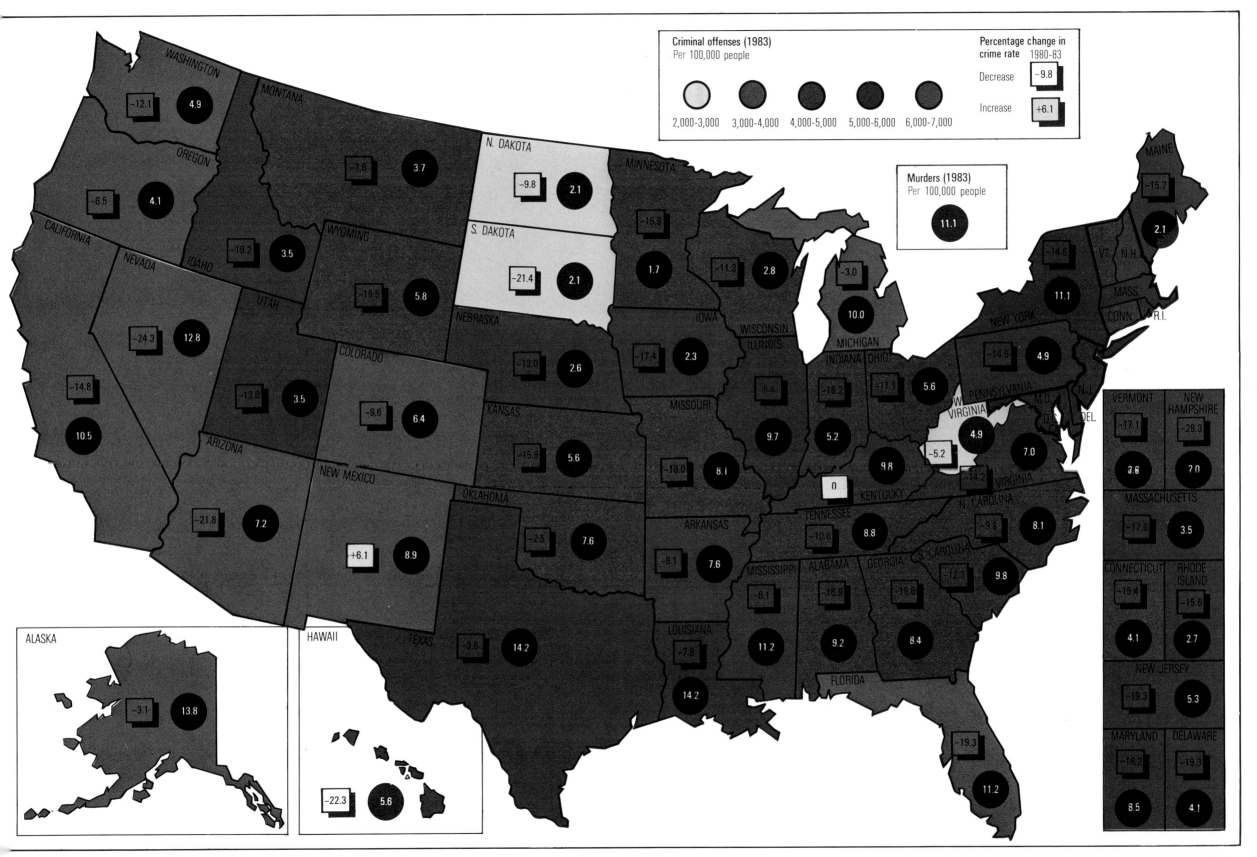

Criminal offenses (1983)
Per 100,000 people

Percentage change in crime rate 1980-83

Decrease -9.8

Increase +6.1

2,000-3,000   3,000-4,000   4,000-5,000   5,000-6,000   6,000-7,000

Murders (1983)
Per 100,000 people

11.1

WASHINGTON -12.1 4.9

MONTANA -7.6 3.7

N. DAKOTA -9.8 2.1

MINNESOTA -15.9 1.7

MAINE -15.7 2.1

OREGON -6.5 4.1

S. DAKOTA -21.4 2.1

WISCONSIN -11.3 2.8

-14.6 11.1

VT. N.H.

CALIFORNIA

NEVADA

IDAHO -19.2 3.5

WYOMING -19.5 5.8

NEBRASKA

IOWA 1.7

MICHIGAN -3.0 10.0

NEW YORK -14.5 4.9

MASS.

CONN. R.I.

-24.3 12.8

UTAH -13.0 3.5

COLORADO -9.6 6.4

ILLINOIS -12.0 2.6

INDIANA n.d.

OHIO -16.2 5.6

PENNSYLVANIA -17.1

N.J.

-14.8

10.5

KANSAS -15.8 5.6

MISSOURI -10.0 8.1

9.7

5.2

W. VIRGINIA 4.9

-5.2

VIRGINIA -14.2 7.0

M.D.

DEL.

VERMONT -17.1 3.6

NEW HAMPSHIRE -28.3 2.0

ARIZONA -21.8 7.2

NEW MEXICO +6.1 8.9

OKLAHOMA -2.5 7.6

ARKANSAS -8.1 7.6

9.8

KENTUCKY 0

TENNESSEE -10.8 8.8

N. CAROLINA -9.8 8.1

MASSACHUSETTS -17.6 3.5

CONNECTICUT -15.4 4.1

RHODE ISLAND -15.6 2.7

ALASKA -3.1 13.8

HAWAII -22.3 5.6

TEXAS -9.8 14.2

LOUISIANA -7.8 11.2

MISSISSIPPI -6.1

ALABAMA -16.9 9.2

GEORGIA -19.6 8.4

S. CAROLINA -12.3 9.8

NEW JERSEY -19.3 5.3

MARYLAND -18.2 8.5

DELAWARE -19.3 4.1

FLORIDA -19.3 11.2

14.2

75

ELECTIONS

The presidential elections of 1984 were won by the Republican candidate, the incumbent President Reagan. As the map shows, he won every state except Minnesota, the home state of his Democratic opponent, and the District of Columbia.

In terms of the total popular vote, however, President Reagan's victory was less overwhelming. He obtained 58.8 percent of the votes cast, against 40.5 percent for the Democratic candidate (Mondale). That is certainly a substantial majority, but it was exceeded by Johnson's victory over Goldwater in 1964 and by Nixon's over McGovern in 1972.

When people vote in a presidential election, they are voting for a group of electors who make up the electoral college (equal in number to the members of Congress for each state), which decides by a simple majority the winning candidate in each state. It was only in 1961, after the adoption of the Twenty-Third Amendment to the Constitution, that the people living in the District of Columbia were able to vote for president. They still do not have a representative or senator in Congress.

The map also shows the state of the two parties in Congress after the 1984 elections. In spite of the "coattail" effect (the tendency for the head of the ticket to pull along the other candidates with him), the Democrats held a comfortable majority in the House of Representatives, which is elected as a whole every two years. In the Senate, where one-third of the members are elected every two years (two senators for each state regardless of population), the Republicans held a small majority.

Citizens of other democratic countries are often surprised by the low proportion of persons voting in federal elections. Less than three-quarters of eligible citizens are registered to vote, and of those who are registered, approximately one-quarter fail to do so. Votes cast in the 1984 presidential election numbered 92.6 million, about 53 percent of possible (including nonregistered) voters. The percentage figure was almost identical in the 1932 election. In spite of efforts to persuade more eligible people (especially blacks in the South) to register, little progress had been made toward making elections more fully democratic.

Of the 16 presidential elections between 1924 and 1984, 8 were won by candidates of each party. This equilibrium surprises middle-aged Democrats in particular, who tend to think of the Republicans as essentially a minority party (between 1932 and 1968 there was only one successful Republican presidential candidate, Eisenhower).

Diagram A shows that Democratic candidates in general took a higher share of the popular vote between 1932 and 1984, which is confirmed by the results of Congressional elections and by the Democratic predominance among state governors (Table A). President Reagan's victory over Carter by a large majority in 1980, the first defeat of an elected incumbent president since 1932, appears all the more remarkable.

An interesting feature revealed in Diagram A is the high proportion of presidential elections that have been won by either a very narrow or a very substantial majority.

The two-party system has remained deeply entrenched since the early years of the twentieth century and shows no signs of changing. Nevertheless, on two occasions in particular a third candidate has made a considerable impact. In 1968 Governor Wallace of Alabama attracted nearly 10 million votes; in 1980 John Anderson secured nearly 6 million. In the 1984 election, however, a number of fringe candidates managed only 0.7 percent of the popular vote between them.

Sources: U.S. Bureau of the Census;
U.S. Information Service

TABLE A
PARTY AFFILIATION OF STATE GOVERNORS, 1960-1984

	Dem.	Rep.
1960	34	16
1964	34	16
1968	24	26
1972	30	20
1976*	36	13
1980	31	19
1984	35	15

* Excludes 1 independent state governor

Diagram A: Voting in presidential elections, 1932-1984

Democrat

Republican

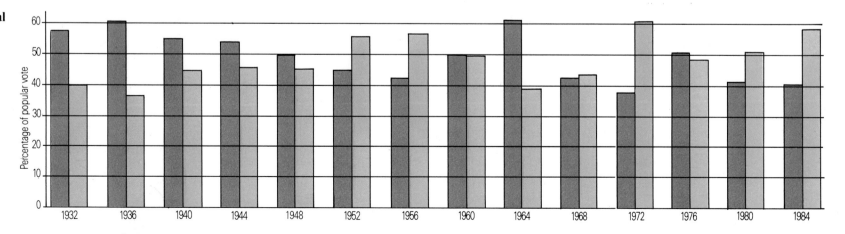

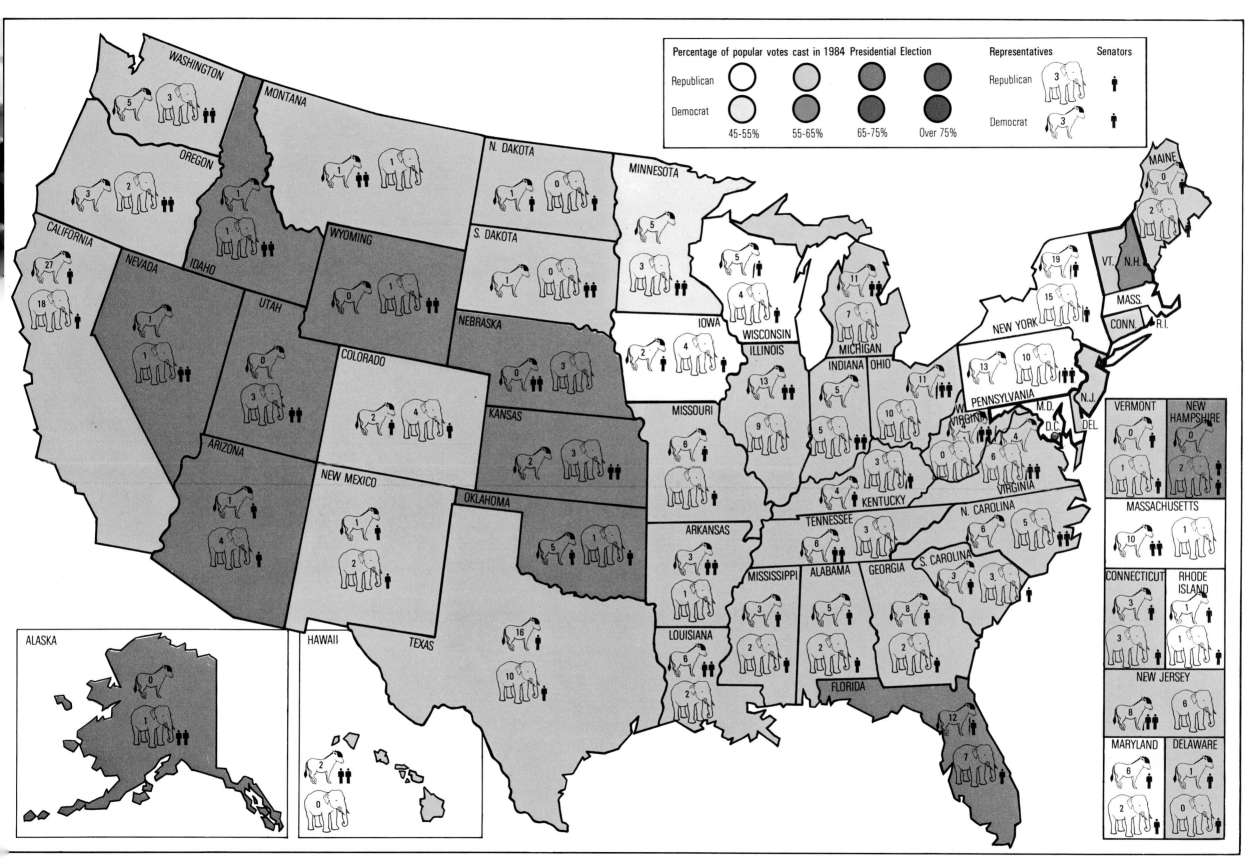

NATIONS OF THE WORLD

On January 10, 1946, 51 countries attended the first meeting of the General Assembly of the United Nations. Subsequently, the number of member states rose steadily as former possessions of European colonial powers gained independence. In 1985, 159 countries were members of the UN General Assembly.

The map shows most countries (some independent islands are too small to be depicted) and certain territories. The following table lists these countries in alphabetical order, together with their population (1984 estimates) and area. Familiar or abbreviated names of countries have been used in preference to the sometimes lengthy official ones, for example North Korea (listed as Korea, North) rather than "Democratic People's Republic of Korea."

Sources: World Bank; U.S. Bureau of the Census

Country	Population (millions)	Area (thousands of square miles)	Country	Population (millions)	Area (thousands of square miles)	Country	Population (millions)	Area (thousands of square miles)	Country	Population (millions)	Area (thousands of square miles)
Afghanistan	14.4	250	El Salvador	4.9	8	Laos	3.7	91	Saudi Arabia	10.8	830
Albania	2.9	11	Equatorial Guinea	0.3	11	Lebanon	2.6	4	Senegal	6.5	76
Algeria	21.4	920	Ethiopia	32.0	472	Lesotho	1.5	12	Sierra Leone	3.8	28
Angola	7.7	481	Fiji	0.7	7	Liberia	2.2	43	South Africa	31.7	471
Argentina	30.2	1,068	Finland	4.9	130	Libya	3.7	679	Soviet Union	275.1	8,649
Australia	15.5	2,968	France	54.9	211	Luxembourg	0.4	1	Spain	38.4	195
Austria	7.5	32	Gabon	1.0	103	Madagascar	9.7	227	Sri Lanka	15.9	25
Bangladesh	99.6	56	Gambia	0.7	4	Malawi	6.8	46	Sudan	21.2	967
Belgium	9.9	12	Germany, East	16.7	42	Malaysia	15.3	127	Surinam	0.4	63
Belize	0.2	9	Germany, West	61.4	96	Mali	7.6	479	Swaziland	0.7	7
Benin	3.9	43	Ghana	13.8	92	Mauritania	1.6	398	Sweden	8.3	174
Bhutan	1.4	18	Greece	10.0	51	Mexico	77.7	762	Switzerland	6.5	16
Bolivia	6.0	424	Greenland[1]	0.1	840	Mongolia	1.9	604	Syria	10.2	71
Botswana	1.0	232	Guatemala	8.0	42	Morocco	23.6	172	Taiwan	19.1	12
Brazil	134.4	3,286	Guinea	5.6	95	Mozambique	13.4	309	Tanzania	21.0	365
Brunei	0.2	2	Guinea-Bissau	0.8	14	Namibia	1.1	318	Thailand	51.7	198
Bulgaria	9.0	43	Guyana	0.8	83	Nepal	16.6	54	Togo	2.9	22
Burkina Faso	6.7	106	Haiti	5.7	11	Netherlands	14.4	16	Tunisia	7.2	63
Burma	36.2	262	Honduras	4.2	43	New Caledonia[2]	0.2	9	Turkey	50.2	301
Burundi	4.7	11	Hungary	10.7	36	New Zealand	3.3	104	Uganda	14.3	91
Cameroon	9.5	184	Iceland	0.2	40	Nicaragua	2.9	50	United Arab Emirates	1.3	32
Canada	25.1	3,852	India	746.4	1,267	Niger	6.3	489	United Kingdom	56.0	94
Central African Republic	2.9	241	Indonesia	169.4	735	Nigeria	88.1	357	United States	236.7	3,615
Chad	5.1	496	Iran	43.8	636	Norway	4.1	125	Uruguay	2.9	68
Chile	11.7	292	Iraq	15.0	168	Oman	1.2	82	Venezuela	17.3	352
China	1,031.6	3,705	Ireland	3.6	27	Pakistan	96.6	310	Vietnam	59.0	128
Colombia	28.9	440	Israel	4.0	8	Panama	2.0	29	Yemen, South	2.1	129
Congo	1.7	132	Italy	57.0	116	Papua New Guinea	3.2	178	Yemen	5.9	75
Costa Rica	2.6	20	Ivory Coast	9.7	125	Paraguay	3.6	157	Yugoslavia	23.0	99
Cuba	10.0	44	Jamaica	2.4	4	Peru	19.0	496	Zaire	32.0	906
Cyprus	0.7	4	Japan	120.0	144	Philippines	55.5	116	Zambia	6.6	291
Czechoslovakia	15.5	49	Jordan	2.7	38	Poland	36.9	121	Zimbabwe	8.4	151
Denmark	5.1	17	Kampuchea	6.1	70	Portugal	10.0	36			
Djibouti	0.3	8	Kenya	19.4	225	Puerto Rico[3]	3.3	3			
Dominican Republic	6.4	19	Korea, North	19.6	47	Qatar	0.3	4			
Ecuador	8.6	109	Korea, South	42.0	38	Romania	22.7	92			
Egypt	47.0	387	Kuwait	1.8	7	Rwanda	6.0	10			

[1] Greenland is an overseas territory of Denmark.
[2] New Caledonia is an overseas territory of France.
[3] Puerto Rico is an outlying U.S. area.

GREENLAND

UNION OF SOVIET SOCIALIST REPUBLICS

ALASKA

CANADA

MONGOLIA

ICELAND

NORWAY
SWEDEN
FINLAND

UNITED KINGDOM
DENMARK
POLAND

AFGHAN

CHINA

N. KOREA

JAPAN

UNITED STATES OF AMERICA

FRANCE
ITALY
YUGO
ROMANIA

SPAIN

PORTUGAL

GREECE
TURKEY
IRAN

PAKISTAN

NEPAL
BHUTAN

TAIWAN

HONG KONG

MOROCCO

TUNISIA

LIBYA

IRAQ

SAUDI ARABIA

INDIA

BANG

BURMA

LAOS

VIETNAM

PHILIPPINES

MEXICO

CUBA

HAITI
DOMINICAN REPUBLIC
PUERTO RICO

EGYPT

OMAN

MALI

NIGER

SUDAN

S. YEMEN

SRI LANKA

THAILAND

KAM

BRUNEI

MALAYSIA
SING

HAWAII

BELIZE
GUATEMALA
HONDURAS
EL SALVADOR
NICARAGUA

JAMAICA

MAURITANIA

SENEGAL
GAMBIA
GUINEA-BISSAU

B.F.

NIGERIA

CHAD

C.A.R.

ETHIOPIA

SOMALIA

INDONESIA

PAPUA
NEW GUINEA

COSTA RICA

PANAMA

VENEZUELA

COLOMBIA

GUYANA

SURINAM
FRENCH GUIANA

SIERRA LEONE
LIBERIA
IVORY
COAST

GHANA

TOGO
BENIN
CAMEROON
EQUATORIAL GUINEA

GABON

CONGO

ZAIRE

UG

KENYA

TANZANIA

FIJI

ECUADOR

NEW CALEDONIA

PERU

BRAZIL

BOLIVIA

ANGOLA

ZAMBIA

MALAWI

MOZAMBIQUE

MADAGASCAR

AUSTRALIA

CHILE

PARAGUAY

NAMIBIA

ZIMB-
ABWE

BOTSWANA

SWAZILAND

NEW ZEALAND

ARGENTINA

URUGUAY

SOUTH
AFRICA

LESOTHO

Key to map abbreviations	Key to map abbreviations
A (Austria)	HUNG (Hungary)
ALB (Albania)	J (Jordan)
B (Burundi)	KAM (Kampuchea)
Bang (Bangladesh)	L (Luxembourg)
Bel (Belgium)	NL (Netherlands)
B.F. (Burkino Faso)	R (Rwanda)
BULG (Bulgaria)	S (Switzerland)
C.A.R. (Central African Republic)	SING (Singapore)
CY (Cyprus)	SY (Syria)
CZ (Czechoslovakia)	UG (Uganda)
	YUGO (Yugoslavia)

79

WORLD POPULATION DENSITY

This map colors different countries according to the number of people per square mile of land area. Many countries have too small an area to be shown on the map, but Table A lists the population densities of almost all countries, in ascending order.

Clearly, there is a huge variation between the population densities of different countries, ranging from Macao's 63,000 people per square mile, to Greenland's sparseness, with less than 1 person for each 100 square miles.

But presenting a single figure for each country greatly understates the variation in density. People do not spread themselves out evenly over large areas, but tend to cluster together in cities. Urbanization is indeed the main factor in determining population density. In the modern metropolis, densities of several thousand people per square mile are common.

Since the 1960s two opposing tendencies have emerged in the developed and the developing countries.

In many areas of Asia, Africa, and Latin America the largest metropolitan areas have shown rapid rises in population. This is due not only to migration from the outlying areas, but also to the higher rate of natural increase in the city because of relatively higher living standards. On the other hand, in countries like the United States, the traditional movement from the country to the town has slowed markedly since the 1960s.

Table B shows the populations of the 10 largest urban clusters in the world, for 1950 and for 1975, and population projections for the year 1990, on the basis of present trends. In 1950 only Buenos Aires, Calcutta, and Shanghai appeared on the list as representatives of developing countries. By 1975, Sao Paulo and Mexico City were among the top ten, pushing Chicago and Moscow off the list. By the late 1970s the population of Mexico City had already outstripped that of New York City. By 1990, if present rates of increase are maintained, New York City and Los Angeles will be the only other representatives of North America. All the other cities among the 10 most populous will be in Asia and South America, while Europe will no longer figure here at all. It even looks as if Jakarta will replace Los Angeles on the list by the year 2000.

This means that the world picture of population density will have completely changed by the end of this century.

Source: U.S. Bureau of the Census

POPULATION DENSITY (people per square mile)

Country	Density	Country	Density
Greenland	0.06	Fiji	97
French Guiana	2	Swaziland	97
Mongolia	3	Honduras	98
Namibia	3	Mexico	102
Botswana	4	Tunisia	114
Mauritania	4	Malaysia	120
Australia	5	Egypt	122
Surinam	6	Lesotho	126
Libya	6	Costa Rica	132
Iceland	6	Ireland	132
Canada	7	Togo	135
Gabon	9	Morocco	137
Guyana	10	Sierra Leone	137
Chad	10	Burma	138
Central African Republic	11	Syria	142
Nigeria	13	Malawi	149
Saudi Arabia	13	Ghana	150
Bolivia	14	Uganda	157
Oman	14	Gambia	166
Mali	16	Turkey	167
Angola	16	Cyprus	185
South Yemen	17	Guatemala	192
New Caledonia	18	Greece	196
Belize	18	Spain	197
Papua, New Guinea	18	Bulgaria	209
Sudan	22	Cuba	226
Algeria	23	Indonesia	230
Paraguay	23	Austria	233
Zambia	23	Yugoslavia	233
Equatorial Guinea	25	Nigeria	247
Somalia	26	Romania	247
Argentina	28	Kuwait	256
New Zealand	31	France	260
U.S.S.R.	32	Thailand	261
Norway	33	Albania	282
Djibouti	34	Portugal	283
Zaire	35	Hungary	297
Finland	37	Nepal	305
Peru	38	Poland	306
United Arab Emirates	39	Denmark	307
Chile	40	Pakistan	311
Brazil	41	Czechoslovakia	313
Laos	41	Dominican Republic	341
Bahamas	42	Luxembourg	367
Madagascar	43	East Germany	400
Mozambique	43	Switzerland	406
Uruguay	43	North Korea	422
Sweden	48	Burundi	434
Venezuela	49	Vietnam	460
Liberia	50	Philippines	479
Cameroon	52	Italy	490
Zimbabwe	56	Israel	512
Afghanistan	58	Haiti	528
Tanzania	58	Congo	544
Nicaragua	58	Guam	550
Guinea	59	Jamaica	564
Burkina Faso	64	India	589
United States	65	Trinidad	589
Colombia	66	Rwanda	592
South Africa	67	Britain	595
Ethiopia	68	El Salvador	597
Iran	69	Sri Lanka	629
Panama	69	West Germany	640
Qatar	69	Lebanon	648
Jordan	71	Japan	835
Bhutan	76	Belgium	838
Ivory Coast	78	Grenada	850
North Yemen	78	Netherlands	915
Ecuador	79	Puerto Rico	971
Kenya	86	South Korea	1,105
Senegal	86	Taiwan	1,530
Kampuchea	88	Bangladesh	1,791
Iraq	89	Singapore	11,304
Benin	90	Hong Kong	13,404
Brunei	96	Macao	63,344

Table A: Population densities

Table B: Populations of the 10 largest urban clusters in 1950, 1975, and 1990 (projected)

LEADING URBAN CLUSTERS
1950-1990 (projected)
(in millions of people)

1950

New York/Northeast New Jersey	12.3
London	10.4
Rhine/Ruhr	6.9
Tokyo/Yokohama	6.9
Shanghai	5.8
Paris	5.5
Greater Buenos Aires	5.3
Chicago/Northwest Indiana	4.9
Moscow	4.8
Calcutta	4.4

1975

New York/Northeast New Jersey	19.8
Tokyo/Yokohama	17.7
Mexico City	11.9
Shanghai	11.6
Los Angeles/Long Beach	10.8
São Paulo	10.7
London	10.4
Rhine/Ruhr	9.3
Greater Buenos Aires	9.3
Paris	9.2

1990

Tokyo/Yokohama	23.4
Mexico City	22.9
New York/Northeast New Jersey	21.8
São Paulo	19.9
Shanghai	17.7
Peking	15.3
Rio de Janeiro	14.7
Los Angeles/Long Beach	13.3
Greater Bombay	12.0
Calcutta	11.9

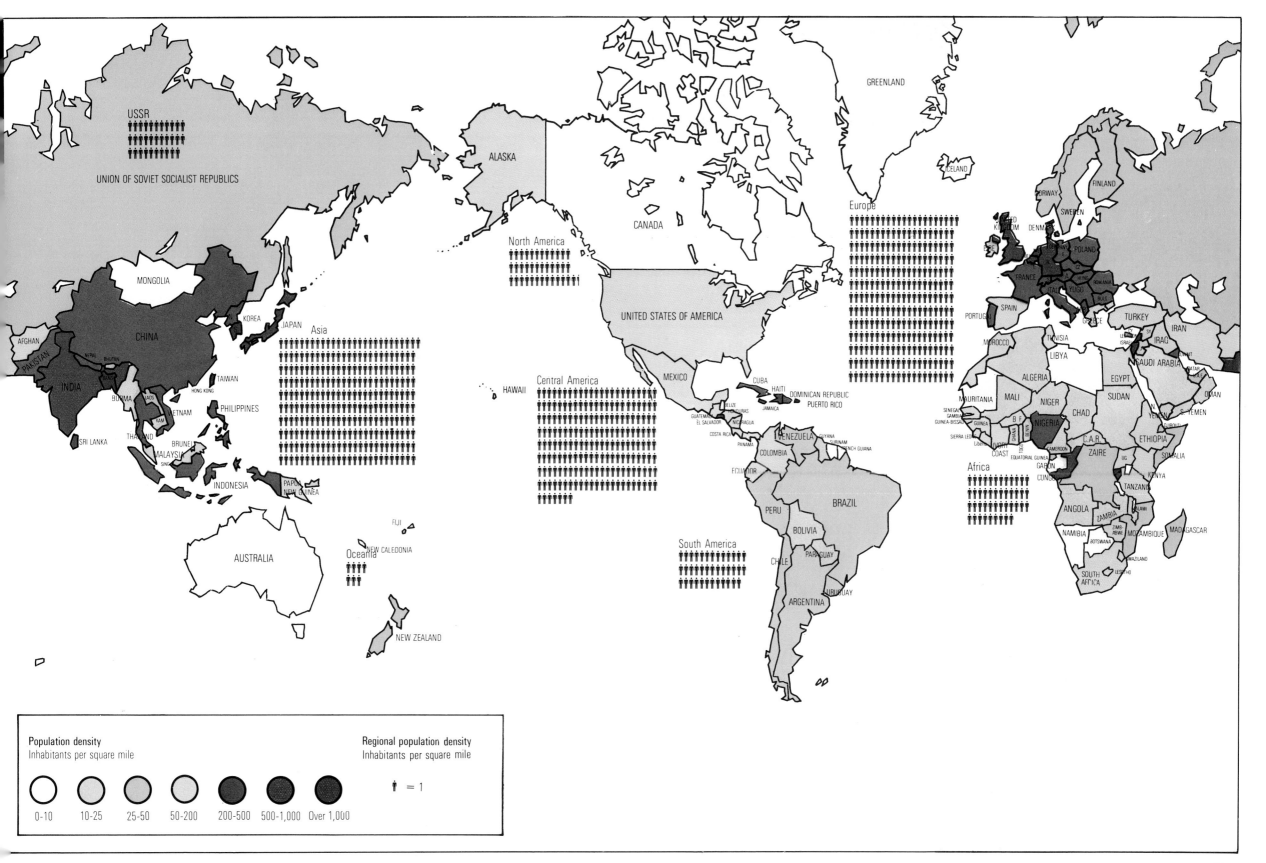

USSR
UNION OF SOVIET SOCIALIST REPUBLICS

GREENLAND

ALASKA

ICELAND

CANADA

North America

Europe

NORWAY   FINLAND

UNITED KINGDOM   SWEDEN

DENMARK

Asia

UNITED STATES OF AMERICA

SPAIN

FRANCE   POLAND

ITALY   YUGO   ROMANIA

BULG

GREECE   TURKEY   IRAN

PORTUGAL

MONGOLIA

KOREA

JAPAN

AFGHAN

CHINA

PAKISTAN   NEPAL   BHUTAN

INDIA   BURMA

SRI LANKA   THAILAND

LAOS

VIETNAM

TAIWAN

HONG KONG

PHILIPPINES

MALAYSIA

BRUNEI

SINGA

INDONESIA

PAPUA
NEW GUINEA

MEXICO

CUBA

HAITI

DOMINICAN REPUBLIC
PUERTO RICO

JAMAICA

BELIZE

GUATEMALA   HONDURAS

EL SALVADOR   NICARAGUA

COSTA RICA

PANAMA

Central America

HAWAII

MOROCCO   TUNISIA

ALGERIA   LIBYA

MAURITANIA   MALI   NIGER

SENEGAL

GAMBIA

GUINEA-BISSAU   GUINEA

SIERRA LEONE

IVORY
COAST

NIGERIA

CHAD   SUDAN

EGYPT

SAUDI ARABIA

N
YEMEN   OMAN

S-YEMEN

QATAR

KUWAIT

IRAQ

ISRAEL

VENEZUELA   GUYANA

SURINAM

FRENCH GUIANA

COLOMBIA

ECUADOR

PERU   BRAZIL

BOLIVIA

Africa

C.A.R.

CAMEROON

ZAIRE

GABON   CONGO

ETHIOPIA

SOMALIA

KENYA

UG

TANZANIA

FIJI

NEW CALEDONIA

Oceania

AUSTRALIA

South America

PARAGUAY

CHILE

URUGUAY

ARGENTINA

ANGOLA   ZAMBIA

NAMIBIA

ZIMB-
ABWE

BOTSWANA

MOZAMBIQUE   MADAGASCAR

MALAWI

SWAZILAND

SOUTH
AFRICA   LESOTHO

NEW ZEALAND

Population density
Inhabitants per square mile

⬤ 0-10   ⬤ 10-25   ⬤ 25-50   ⬤ 50-200   ⬤ 200-500   ⬤ 500-1,000   ⬤ Over 1,000

Regional population density
Inhabitants per square mile

👤 = 1

WORLD POPULATION GROWTH

The map shows the wide differences between the rates of change of population in different countries. Each country is colored according to the percentage natural increase per year. Natural increase expresses the total annual change of population of a country — births plus immigration minus deaths plus emigration — as a percentage of population. This map also shows life expectancy at birth for males and females.

Nearly everywhere the tendency is for people to live longer. Better living standards and improved medical knowledge and provision make this likely, an important part of this effect being the increase in the number of babies surviving to adulthood.

The other side of the picture is that higher standards of living lead eventually to a fall in the number of babies born. But the problem is that these two changes, longer life and fewer babies, do not coincide. Between them lies what has been called the "demo-

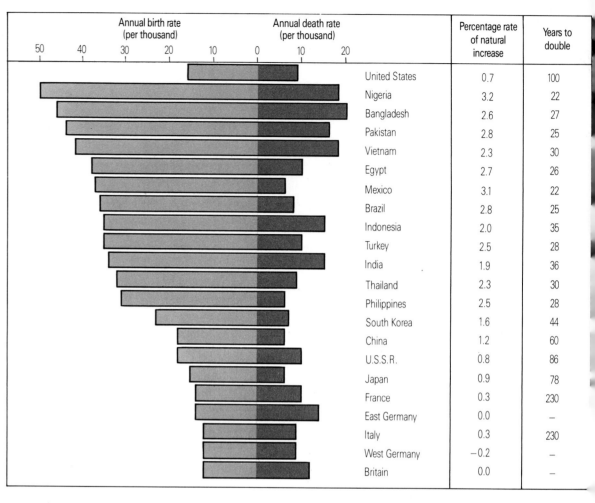

graphic transition": about the same number of people are born, and they tend to live longer. The result is a period of rapid rise in population.

Diagram A illustrates the growth of the population in various parts of the world, 1970-1982. Asia has well over half of the total world population, but its rate of increase is less than that of Africa and Latin America.

Diagram B shows the crude birth rate (the number of babies born in one year for each thousand in the population) and the crude death rate (the number of deaths per year per thousand people) for some of the most populous countries. We can easily see how the industrialized nations — the U.S.A., U.S.S.R., Japan, and Western Europe — have completed the transition to a pattern of low birth rate and low death rate. China seems to be approaching this situation. In these countries, the size of the population has about stabilized. The other countries shown face the problems associated with the "population explosion", combining lower death rates than in former times with a still high birth rate.

Source: *World Bank Atlas, 1985*

Diagram A: Population growth by region, 1970-1982. Figures above each group show the percentage increase over the 12-year period

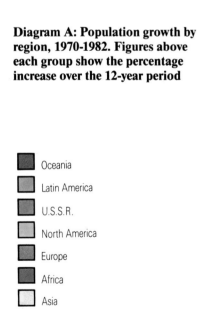

- Oceania
- Latin America
- U.S.S.R.
- North America
- Europe
- Africa
- Asia

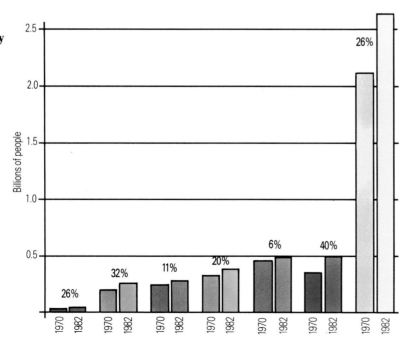

Diagram B: Population growth rate for selected countries, 1982

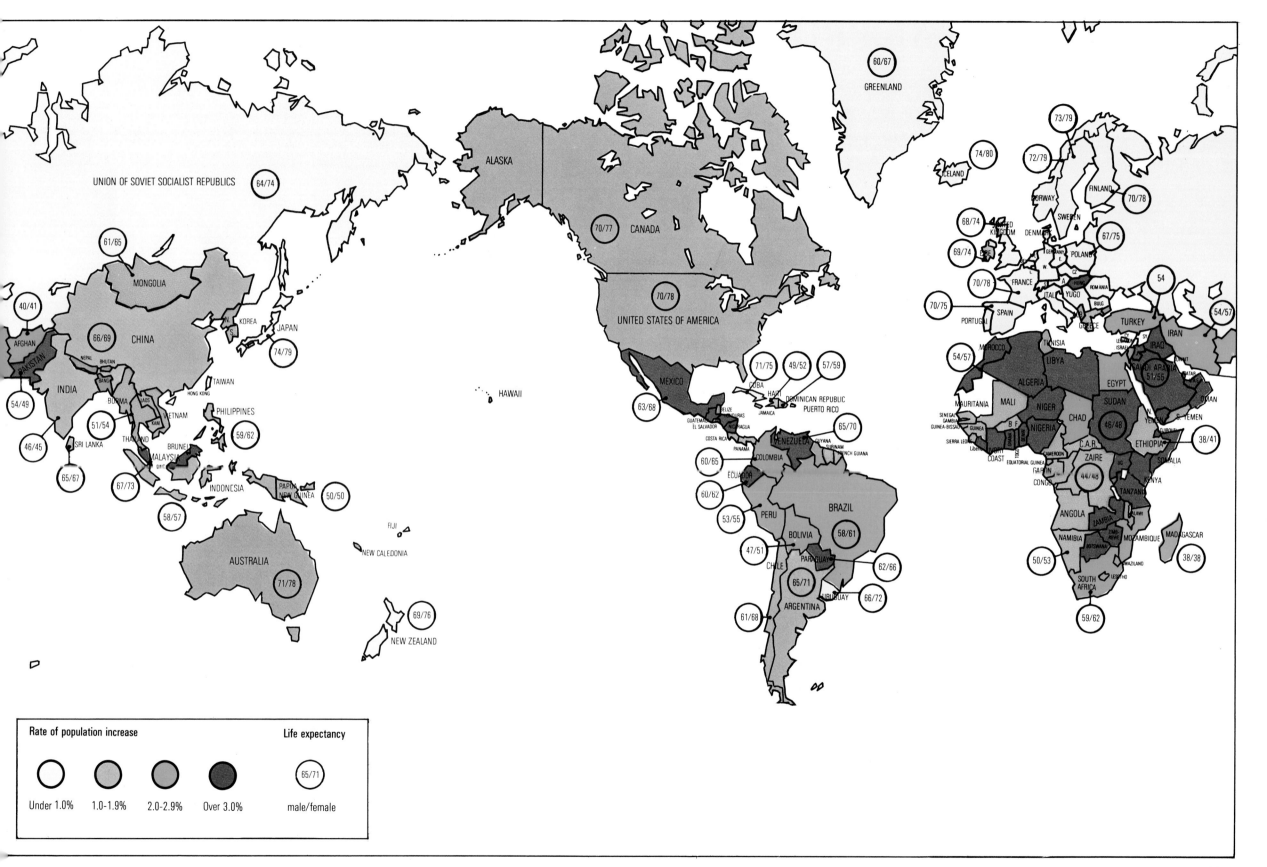

Rate of population increase

Life expectancy

Under 1.0%	1.0-1.9%	2.0-2.9%	Over 3.0%	65/71
○	⬤	⬤	⬤	male/female

UNION OF SOVIET SOCIALIST REPUBLICS   64/74

MONGOLIA   61/65

CHINA   66/69

JAPAN   74/79

N. KOREA

TAIWAN

HONG KONG

AFGHAN   40/41

PAKISTAN

INDIA   54/49

NEPAL   BHUTAN   BANGL

BURMA   LAOS   VIETNAM   51/54

SRI LANKA   46/45

THAILAND   65/67

PHILIPPINES   59/62

MALAYSIA   67/73

BRUNEI

INDONESIA   58/57

PAPUA NEW GUINEA   50/50

FIJI

NEW CALEDONIA

AUSTRALIA   71/78

NEW ZEALAND   69/76

ALASKA

CANADA   70/77

UNITED STATES OF AMERICA   70/78

MEXICO   63/68

HAWAII

CUBA   71/75

HAITI   49/52

DOMINICAN REPUBLIC   57/59

PUERTO RICO

JAMAICA

GUATEMALA   BELIZE   HONDURAS

EL SALVADOR   NICARAGUA

COSTA RICA   PANAMA

VENEZUELA   65/70

COLOMBIA   60/65

GUYANA   SURINAM   FRENCH GUIANA

ECUADOR   60/62

PERU   53/55

BRAZIL   58/61

BOLIVIA   47/51

CHILE   61/68

PARAGUAY   62/66

ARGENTINA   65/71

URUGUAY   66/72

GREENLAND   60/67

ICELAND   74/80

NORWAY   73/79

SWEDEN   72/79

FINLAND   70/78

UNITED KINGDOM   68/74

DENMARK

IRELAND   69/74

FRANCE   70/78

PORTUGAL   70/75

SPAIN

GERMANY E   GERMANY W

POLAND   67/75

CZ

A   H

ITALY

YUGO

ROMANIA

BULG

GREECE

54

TURKEY

SY   LEBANON   ISRAEL

IRAQ

IRAN   54/57

MOROCCO   54/57

ALGERIA

TUNISIA

LIBYA

EGYPT

SAUDI ARABIA   51/55

KUWAIT   QATAR

OMAN

YEMEN   S. YEMEN   38/41

DJIBOUTI

MAURITANIA

MALI

NIGER

CHAD   46/48

SUDAN

ETHIOPIA

SOMALIA

SENEGAL   GAMBIA

GUINEA-BISSAU   GUINEA

SIERRA LEONE   Liberia

IVORY COAST   B   F   NIGERIA   BENIN   TOGO   GHANA

CAMEROON

EQUATORIAL GUINEA   GABON   CONGO

C.A.R.

ZAIRE   44/48

UG   KENYA

TANZANIA

ANGOLA

ZAMBIA

MALAWI

NAMIBIA   50/53

BOTSWANA   ZIMBABWE

MOZAMBIQUE

MADAGASCAR   38/38

SWAZILAND

SOUTH AFRICA   59/62

LESOTHO

83

GROSS NATIONAL PRODUCT

TOP TEN: COUNTRIES WITH HIGHEST GNP PER CAPITA
(1983, in U.S. dollars)

United Arab Emirates	21,340
Qatar	21,170
Brunei	21,140
Kuwait	18,180
Switzerland	16,390
U.S.A.	14,090
Norway	13,820
Bermuda	13,320
Sweden	12,400
Luxembourg	12,190

Diagram A: Countries of more than 20 million inhabitants, ranked in order of 1983 GNP per capita. The width of each block is proportional to population. Some countries have been omitted due to unavailability of comparable data. There are also a number of countries with a population of less than 20 million that have a high GNP per capita, some of which rank among the top ten countries (see table)

Diagram B: Proportions of world population living in countries having different levels of per capita GNP

The map provides one way of comparing the economic development of different countries. It is colored according to the 1983 average annual Gross National Product (GNP) per capita for each country, measured in current U.S. dollars. (For the meaning of GNP, see note opposite.) As can be seen, only a few countries share with the United States, Canada, and northwestern Europe the position of having over $5,000 per person, and hardly any are close to the U.S. figure of $14,090. Apart from some underdeveloped countries, the countries for which no comparable data are available are the U.S.S.R. and Eastern Europe.

Diagram A brings out the comparison in another way. Each block represents a country, and the countries are ranked in order of their GNP per capita, which is measured by the *height* of the block. The *width* of each block is proportional to that country's population, so that the *area* is a measure of the total GNP.

The diagram thus illustrates the distribution of the total world GNP between various countries. It must be stressed that this is *not* the distribution of wealth between individual people. Apart from its other limitations as a measure of general well-being, GNP tells us nothing at all about the spread of income *within* a country. In both the map, and in diagram A, each country is taken as a unit, represented by its average GNP per capita.

Diagram B gives another summary of this information. It is a pie chart showing the percentages of the population of the world in 1983 that lived in countries whose per capita GNP fell into the different bands.

In 1983, just under 50 percent of the world's population lived in countries with an average GNP per capita of $400 a year or less. At the other end of the scale, 16 percent of the people of the world lived in countries with an average of $5,000 or more.

The United States, with about 5 percent of the world's population, accounted for 33 percent of the total GNP, the countries of the European Economic Community, with some 8 percent of the population, for 20 percent, and Japan, with 3 percent of the population for 12 percent. The remainder, 84 percent of the world's people, were responsible for only 35 percent of the world total GNP.

Source: *World Bank Atlas, 1985*

> Note. GNP is an estimate of the total value of goods and services produced in a country per year. It is the national income less depreciation. Gross Domestic Product (GDP) is equivalent to GNP less net income from abroad.

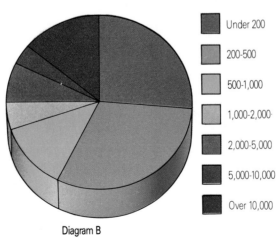

■	Under 200
■	200-500
■	500-1,000
■	1,000-2,000
■	2,000-5,000
■	5,000-10,000
■	Over 10,000

Diagram A

Diagram B

United States – 14,090
Canada – 12,000
West Germany – 11,420
France – 10,390
Japan – 10,100
Britain – 9,050
Italy – 6,350
Spain – 4,800
Yugoslavia – 2,570
South Africa – 2,450
Algeria – 2,400
Mexico – 2,240
Argentina – 2,030
S. Korea – 2,010
Brazil – 1,890
Colombia – 1,410
Thailand – 810
Nigeria – 760
Philippines – 760
Morocco – 750
Egypt – 700
Indonesia – 560
Sudan – 400
Pakistan – 390
China – 290
India – 180
Burma – 180
Zaire – 160
Ethiopia – 140
Bangladesh – 140

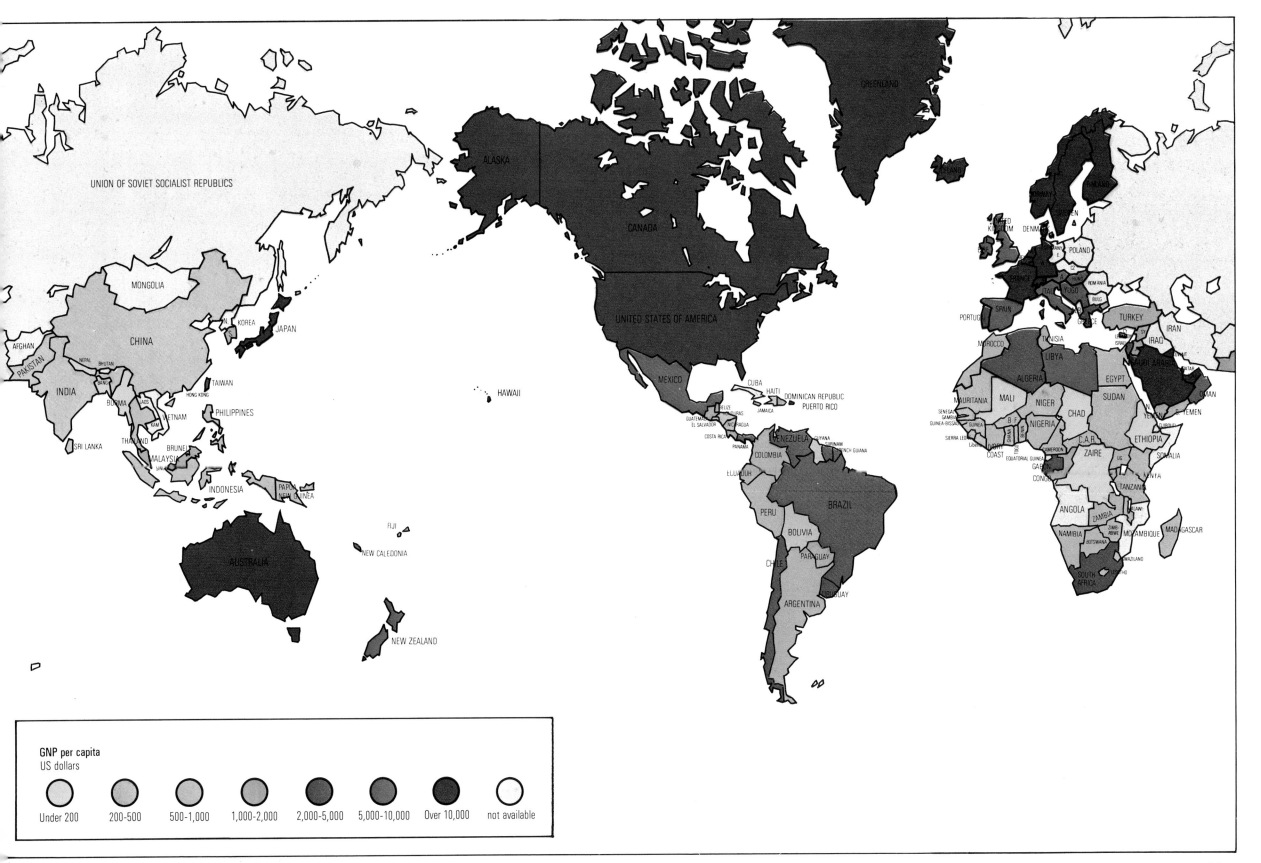

GNP per capita
US dollars

Under 200	200-500	500-1,000	1,000-2,000	2,000-5,000	5,000-10,000	Over 10,000	not available

GNP GROWTH RATE

On this map, the countries are colored according to the annual average percentage rate of growth of GNP per capita, over the ten-year period, 1973-1982. GNP is an estimate of the total output of goods and services of a country. The GNP given on the map is an average figure, so temporary fluctuations are ironed out. But this also means that it cannot reflect the sometimes quite considerable effects of recent world economic changes.

There are clearly wide differences between countries. The more developed economies show only moderate growth rates, approximately 1 or 2 percent. The United States averaged 1.5 percent in this decade, the United Kingdom 1.0, France 2.2 and West Germany 2.3, while Japan's GNP grew at an average of 3.3 percent. But among the less developed countries there was a remarkably high degree of variation, several of them registering falls in per capita GNP.

Diagram A: Percentage rates of growth in per capita GNP, averaged over 1973-1982

Two different factors affect per capita GNP: on the one hand, the development of production, on the other, the increase in population. In fact, the rate of growth in a per capita figure is approximately equal to the rate of growth of the total amount, less the rate of natural increase in population.

In many countries — Uganda or Ghana, for example — the population is increasing much faster than the production of wealth. On the other hand, countries like Egypt and Saudi Arabia show much higher rates of growth of production than of population.

Diagram A compares the rates of growth in per capita GNP for the most populous countries. Each block represents a country, with height proportional to GNP growth rate, and width according to population. The countries are arranged in order of increasing per capita GNP, as in the diagram on page 84, with the poorest on the left.

There is no obvious pattern relating per capita GNP to per capita GNP growth rate, but there is a general tendency for some of the countries with the lowest GNP figures to be falling still farther behind countries with high GNP figures.

Sources: International Bank for Reconstruction and Development, *World Development Report, 1975 to 1985*; *World Bank Atlas, 1985*

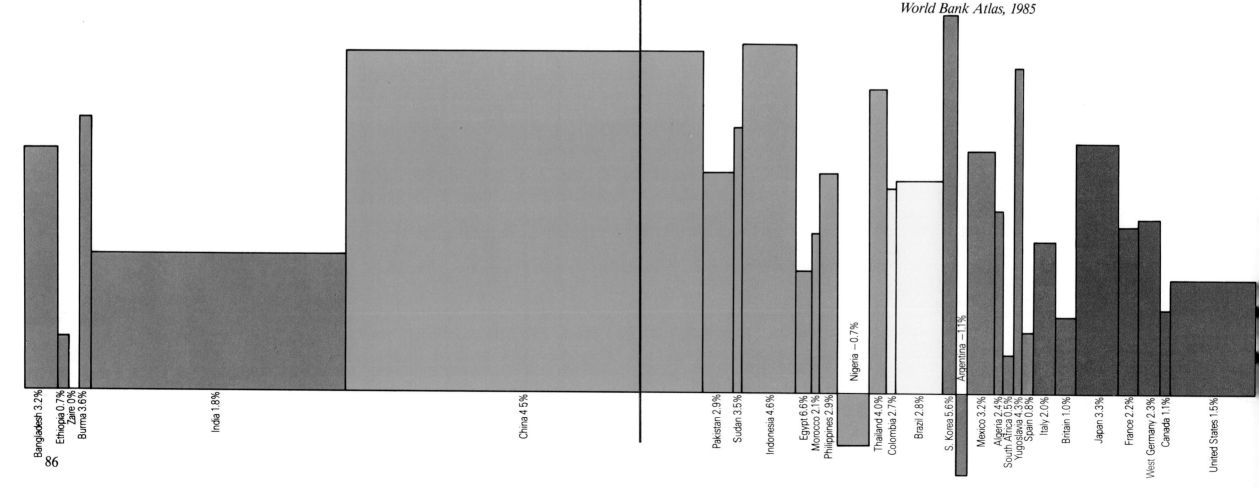

Bangladesh 3.2% · Ethiopia 0.7% · Zaire 0% · Burma 3.6% · India 1.8% · China 4 5% · Pakistan 2.9% · Sudan 3.5% · Indonesia 4.6% · Egypt 6.6% · Morocco 2.1% · Philippines 2.9% · Nigeria −0.7% · Thailand 4.0% · Colombia 2.7% · Brazil 2.8% · S. Korea 5.6% · Argentina −1.1% · Mexico 3.2% · Algeria 2.4% · South Africa 0.5% · Yugoslavia 4.3% · Spain 0.8% · Italy 2.0% · Britain 1.0% · Japan 3.3% · France 2.2% · West Germany 2.3% · Canada 1.1% · United States 1.5%

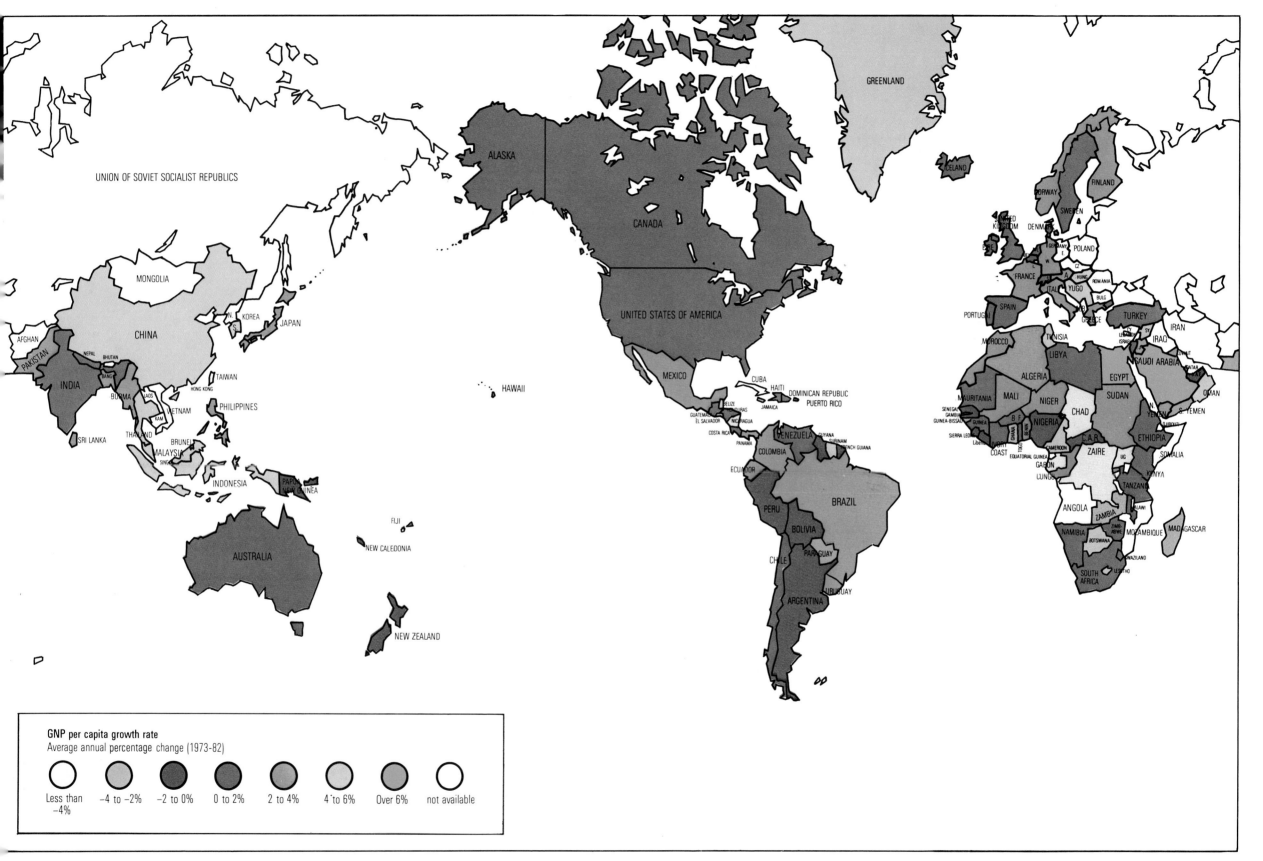

GNP per capita growth rate
Average annual percentage change (1973-82)

Less than −4% | −4 to −2% | −2 to 0% | 0 to 2% | 2 to 4% | 4 to 6% | Over 6% | not available

WORLD FOOD PRODUCTION

Cereals form the most important food supplies on a world-wide basis. This map shows total world production of cereals by countries in millions of metric tons for 1982. The squares, colored for wheat, rice, corn, and other cereals, show how a country's total production is made up of these main categories. The arrows show net exports and imports and the main direction of such flows.

There are a number of countries that cannot feed themselves. Rapid increases in population mean that more countries are likely to be added to this food deficit list.

Five countries are major net exporters of grain after meeting all their own needs. These are the United States, which exports 100 million metric tons of grain, Canada (26 million), Australia (15 million), Argentina (15 million), and Thailand (7 million). The United States is by far the world's largest grain exporter, its 100 million tons being more than the total of 63 million exported by the other principal grain surplus countries.

The net importers of grain are the key to the world grain trade. These are the U.S.S.R. (38 million metric tons), the EEC (6 million), Eastern Europe (7 million), China (20 million), Japan (24 million), Egypt (7 million), South Korea (5.5 million), and Saudi Arabia (5.5 million).

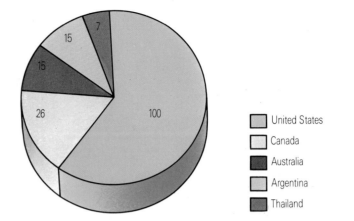

Diagram B: The principal grain exporters' share of the world market, in millions of metric tons

These figures vary enormously from year to year, depending upon weather conditions and whether, for example, the U.S.S.R. has had a good or bad harvest. In recent years satellites have been used to show in advance the probable yield of the coming Soviet harvest, a matter of great interest to the entire world.

The world's four leading grain producers are: the United States (339 million metric tons), China (306 million), the U.S.S.R. (173 million), and India (134 million). These figures, however, must be related to the populations of the four countries. The United States with 236 million people to feed produces almost twice as much grain as does the U.S.S.R., which has to feed 271 million people. China must feed 1 billion people, India 700 million.

A similar pattern can be seen in meat production, where China, the United States and the U.S.S.R. account between them for almost 50 percent of the total world production. The notable exception here is India, where religious practices result in low meat production figures.

Fish represents a significant component of food supplies in certain countries. The list shows that Japan and the U.S.S.R. are far and away the leading nations by catch. The Japanese fish catch is more than five times the size of the country's meat production by weight.

Source: Food and Agriculture Organization of the United Nations

TOP TEN: FISHING NATIONS BY CATCH, 1982
(thousands of metric tons)

Japan	10,775.1
U.S.S.R.	9,956.7
China	4,926.7
United States	3,988.3
Chile	3,673.0
Peru	3,452.0
Norway	2,499.9
India	2,335.2
South Korea	2,281.3
Indonesia	2,020.0

TOP TEN: MEAT PRODUCING NATIONS, 1982
(thousands of metric tons)

China	20,570
United States	17,057
U.S.S.R.	12,562
Germany, West	4,647
France	3,815
Brazil	3,322
Argentina	2,927
Poland	2,397
Italy	2,311
Australia	2,307

Diagram A: The top ten grain producers, in millions of metric tons

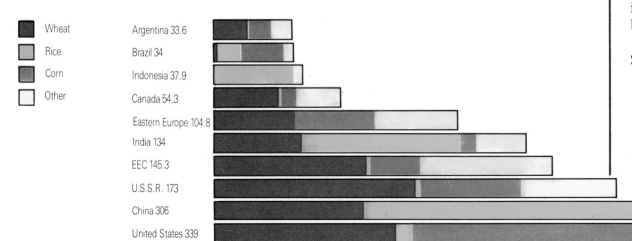

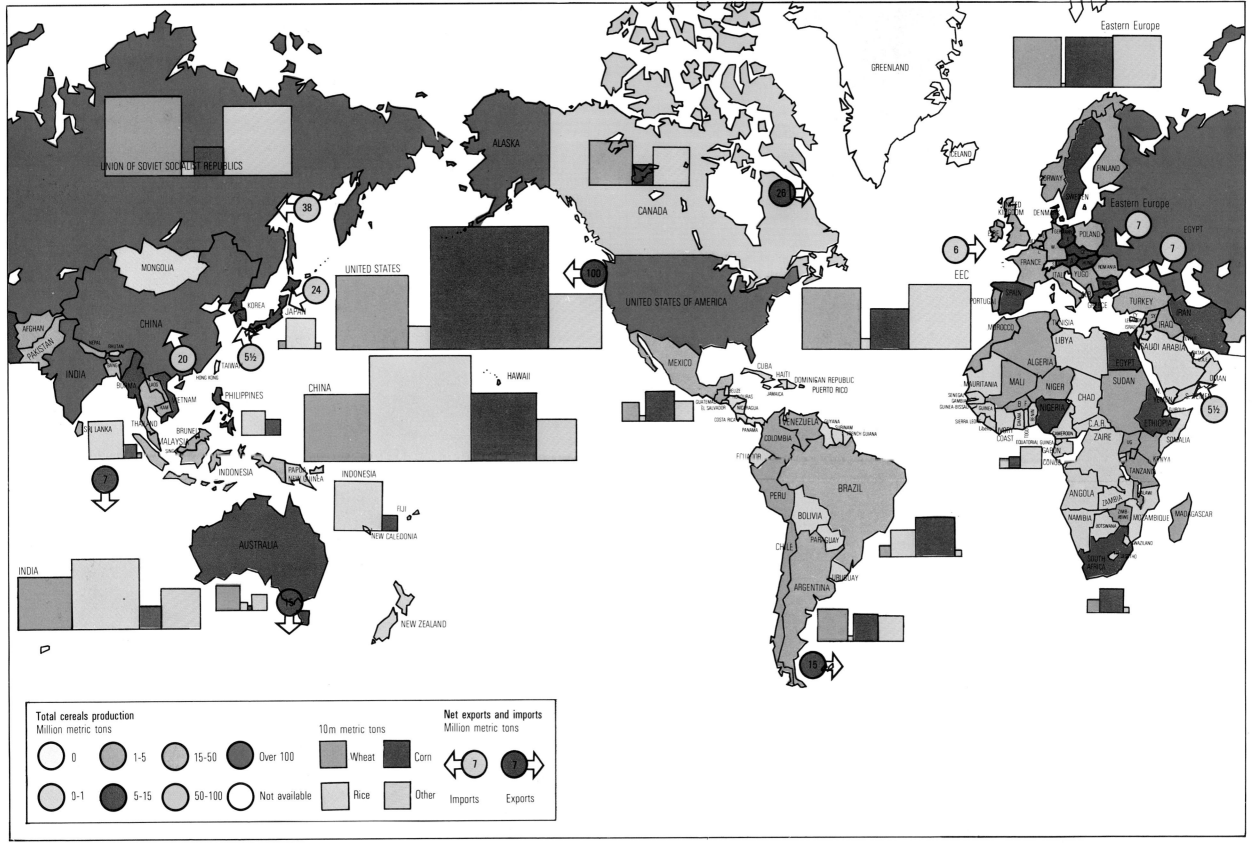

Eastern Europe

GREENLAND

ICELAND

ALASKA

UNION OF SOVIET SOCIALIST REPUBLICS

38

CANADA

26

100

UNITED STATES OF AMERICA

UNITED STATES

24

MONGOLIA

KOREA

JAPAN

5½

CHINA

AFGHAN

PAKISTAN

NEPAL BHUTAN

INDIA

BANG

BURMA

LAOS

VIETNAM

KAM

THAILAND

SRI LANKA

MALAYSIA

BRUNEI

SINGA

HONG KONG

TAIWAN

20

CHINA

HAWAII

PHILIPPINES

INDONESIA

PAPUA NEW GUINEA

INDONESIA

FIJI

NEW CALEDONIA

7

INDIA

AUSTRALIA

NEW ZEALAND

5½

7

6

EEC

Eastern Europe

7

EGYPT

NORWAY

SWEDEN

FINLAND

UNITED KINGDOM

DENMARK

IRE

GER

POLAND

FRANCE

YUGO

ROMANIA

ITALY

SPAIN

PORTUGAL

GREECE

TURKEY

IRAN

IRAQ

MOROCCO

TUNISIA

LIBYA

SAUDI ARABIA

QATAR

OMAN

EGYPT

MAURITANIA

MALI

NIGER

CHAD

SUDAN

YEMEN

5½

ALGERIA

SENEGAL

GAMBIA

GUINEA-BISSAU

GUINEA

B F

NIGERIA

C.A.R.

ETHIOPIA

SIERRA LEONE

IVORY COAST

GHANA

BENIN

TOGO

CAMEROON

ZAIRE

UG

KENYA

SOMALIA

EQUATORIAL GUINEA

GABON

CONGO

TANZANIA

ANGOLA

ZAMBIA

MALAWI

MOZAMBIQUE

MADAGASCAR

NAMIBIA

ZIMBABWE

BOTSWANA

SWAZILAND

SOUTH AFRICA

LESOTHO

MEXICO

CUBA

HAITI

DOMINICAN REPUBLIC

PUERTO RICO

JAMAICA

BELIZE

GUATEMALA

HONDURAS

EL SALVADOR

NICARAGUA

COSTA RICA

PANAMA

VENEZUELA

GUYANA

SURINAM

FRENCH GUIANA

COLOMBIA

ECUADOR

PERU

BRAZIL

BOLIVIA

CHILE

PARAGUAY

ARGENTINA

URUGUAY

15

Total cereals production					Net exports and imports		
Million metric tons				10m metric tons	Million metric tons		

Total cereals production
Million metric tons

0   1-5   15-50   Over 100

0-1   5-15   50-100   Not available

10m metric tons

Wheat   Corn

Rice   Other

Net exports and imports
Million metric tons

7   7

Imports   Exports

89

WORLD FOOD CONSUMPTION

The level of food consumption per capita is one of the most obvious indicators of national well-being. This map shows the dietary energy supplies of countries, ranging from those that are 15 percent below requirements to those that are more than 30 percent above requirements, such as the United States. Dietary requirements are the minimum amount of animal and vegetable foods deemed necessary to maintain health. This varies according to age and climate, for example more is required in a cold than a hot climate.

Twenty-three countries have dietary energy supplies more than 30 percent above their requirements. At the other end of the scale there are seven countries — Afghanistan, Chad, Ethiopia, Guinea, Mali, Mozambique, and Zimbabwe — where dietary energy supplies are more than 15 percent below requirements.

The total number of countries with less than their food requirements (those which fall under the first four categories of shading on the map) come to 43.

The countries possessing far more food than requirements broadly coincide with the nations of North America, Europe (both west and east), the U.S.S.R., Japan, Australasia, and one or two others which are also the most developed countries in other respects.

Diagram A: Shipments of food aid in cereals (1,000 tons grain equivalent) by donor

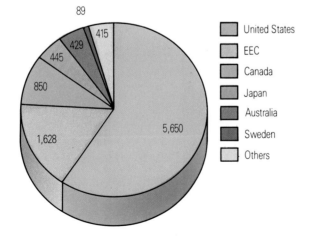

- United States
- EEC
- Canada
- Japan
- Australia
- Sweden
- Others

The bars relating to each country show how available proteins are divided between sources — animal or vegetable — in percentage terms on a daily basis.

North America, Australasia and Europe average a higher proportion of animal to vegetable protein. The U.S.S.R. and Japan have approximately equal amounts of vegetable and animal protein. China has a far higher proportion — five to one — of vegetable to animal protein.

Those countries with adequate or above average requirements of food supplies per capita are likely to also be the most productive and efficient economies. On the other hand, countries with less than the required level of food are likely to be less productive since their people lack the energy required to sustain maximum output.

Many countries which at present face food shortages have the land and the people to produce more. What they lack are the modern agricultural inputs — machinery, fertilizers, and techniques — and it will be many years before all developing countries have reached anything near their maximum potential output.

Some developing countries may have the capacity to produce all their food requirements but poor infrastructure — lack of roads and railways — make it extremely costly to move supplies from areas which produce a surplus to those in need.

Some developing countries in Africa, while receiving food aid, also export food. This is because their development has been deliberately geared to producing cash crops such as cocoa, sugar, tea, and coffee for export to earn hard currency, and in consequence they have neglected the production of staple foods such as maize for home consumption.

China, with the world's largest population (1 billion), can as a rule feed all its people because over many centuries it has developed techniques of intensive farming. Yet in a year of bad weather or floods it may have to import huge quantities of grain, as it has done from both the United States and Canada.

Emergencies and abnormal food shortages have become increasingly frequent in the 1970s and 1980s. In response to these needs, the FAO has created a Global Information and Early Warning System designed to cope with such emergencies. This, however, must depend upon reserve stocks of grains. These in turn have to come from the principal food surplus countries led by the United States.

Source: Food and Agriculture Organization of the United Nations

AFRICAN COUNTRIES AFFECTED BY ABNORMAL FOOD SHORTAGES IN 1984

Angola	Morocco
Botswana	Mozambique
Burkina Faso	Niger
Burundi	Rwanda
Cape Verde	Senegal
Chad	Somalia
Ethiopia	Sudan
Kenya	Tanzania
Lesotho	Zambia
Mali	Zimbabwe
Mauritania	

Dietary energy supplies per capita
Percentage above or below requirements

● Worse than 15% below
○ 15-10% below
○ 10-5% below
○ Up to 5% below
○ 0-5% over
○ 5-15% over
● 15-30% over
● More than 30% over
○ Not available

Proteins per capita
Grams per day

50
10

Vegetable
Animal

GREENLAND

UNION OF SOVIET SOCIALIST REPUBLICS

MONGOLIA

CHINA

AFGHAN

PAKISTAN

NEPAL BHUTAN

INDIA

BURMA

SRI LANKA

THAILAND

MALAYSIA

BRUNEI

INDONESIA

VIETNAM

KAM

PHILIPPINES

TAIWAN

HONG KONG

JAPAN

KOREA

PAPUA
NEW GUINEA

AUSTRALIA

NEW CALEDONIA

FIJI

NEW ZEALAND

ALASKA

CANADA

UNITED STATES OF AMERICA

MEXICO

HAWAII

CUBA

HAITI

JAMAICA

DOMINICAN REPUBLIC

PUERTO RICO

BELIZE

GUATEMALA

HONDURAS

EL SALVADOR NICARAGUA

COSTA RICA

PANAMA

VENEZUELA

GUYANA

SURINAM

FRENCH GUIANA

COLOMBIA

ECUADOR

PERU

BRAZIL

BOLIVIA

CHILE

PARAGUAY

ARGENTINA

URUGUAY

ICELAND

NORWAY

SWEDEN

FINLAND

UNITED
KINGDOM

DENMARK

GERMANY

POLAND

FRANCE

SPAIN

PORTUGAL

ITALY

YUGO

ROMANIA

BULG

GREECE

TURKEY

IRAN

IRAQ

SYRIA

MOROCCO

TUNISIA

LIBYA

EGYPT

SAUDI ARABIA

QATAR

OMAN

N. YEMEN

S. YEMEN

ALGERIA

MAURITANIA

MALI

NIGER

CHAD

SUDAN

SENEGAL

GAMBIA

GUINEA-BISSAU

GUINEA

SIERRA LEONE

LIBERIA

IVORY
COAST

B F

NIGERIA

BENIN

TOGO

CAMEROON

EQUATORIAL GUINEA

GABON

CONGO

C.A.R.

ZAIRE

ETHIOPIA

SOMALIA

KENYA

TANZANIA

ANGOLA

ZAMBIA

MALAWI

ZIMBABWE

MOZAMBIQUE

MADAGASCAR

NAMIBIA

BOTSWANA

SWAZILAND

SOUTH
AFRICA

LESOTHO

91

FOREIGN AID

This map illustrates the distribution of U.S. government aid to foreign countries in 1983, in the form of grants and credits. Well over half of the total went to the countries of the Near East. Israel received the largest single amount, $2.3 billion, and Egypt received $1.8 billion. Of the $457 million aid going to the Far East, $448 million went to South Korea. Of the $576 million aid going to South East Asia, $251 million went to Indonesia and $215 million to the Philippines. These figures cover both military and economic aid programs.

Foreign assistance is divided into three groups. Grants are transfers for which no payment is expected. These include military supplies and services. Credits are loans with specific obligations for repayment. Finally, there is the transfer of U.S. farm products in exchange for foreign currencies.

Military aid to friendly countries is given under the Mutual Defense Assistance Program, set up in 1949. Between World War II and 1983, the United States gave a total of $100.5 billion in such aid, $74.6 billion of this as grants. In 1983, military aid totaled $5.6 billion, $4.2 billion of this going to the Near East and South Asia.

Total economic aid in 1983 was $8.6 billion, just over one-third of this being given to Near Eastern and South Asian countries. $1.1 billion went to the African continent, $2 million of this to Ethiopia.

Diagram A: U.S. foreign aid compared with other leading countries, 1983

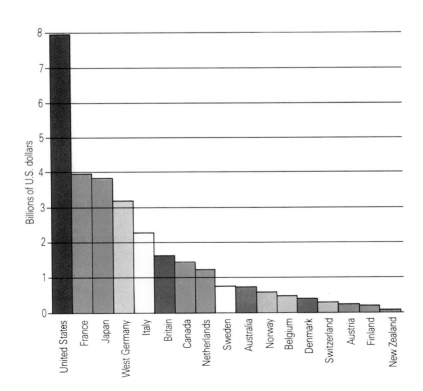

Diagram B: Per capita public aid to developing countries, 1983 (excluding military aid)

The distribution of U.S. government aid to foreign countries has changed considerably since the years immediately following World War II. From 1945 to 1954, aid to Western Europe accounted for the vast majority of the total U.S. foreign aid. After 1954, the Near East, South Asia, and the Far East represent the largest categories, the Far East playing a less important part since the mid-1970s.

Diagrams A and B show international aid to developing countries in 1983, excluding military aid. Diagram A gives the total amounts of such aid from different countries. The U.S. figure of $8 billion is by far the highest. Only France ($3.9 billion), Japan ($3.8 billion) and West Germany ($3.2 billion) come anywhere near it. Diagram B, however, expresses the same figures as amounts per capita: the United States appears farther down on this list.

Sources: U.S. Agency for International Development;
U.S. Bureau of Economic Analysis

GREENLAND

UNION OF SOVIET SOCIALIST REPUBLICS

ALASKA

CANADA

ICELAND

NORWAY   FINLAND
          SWEDEN
UNITED
KINGDOM   DENMARK
                    POLAND
MONGOLIA   38   FRANCE   ITALY YUGO.   ROMANIA
                                                                     BULG.
                    457   137
                                     545   PORTUGAL SPAIN   GREECE   TURKEY   IRAN
N. KOREA   IRAQ
CHINA   JAPAN   2322   MOROCCO   TUNISIA
AFGHAN.   LIBYA   SAUDI ARABIA   QATAR
                    691   2861   EGYPT
PAKISTAN   MAURITANIA   MALI   NIGER   SUDAN   OMAN
         TAIWAN   764   258   SENEGAL   N. YEMEN
INDIA   MEXICO   CUBA HAITI   GAMBIA   S. YEMEN
BURMA   HONG KONG   HAWAII DOMINICAN REPUBLIC   GUINEA-BISSAU   ALGERIA CHAD
         VIETNAM   576   JAMAICA PUERTO RICO   SIERRA LEO. NIGERIA   ETHIOPIA
SRI LANKA LAOS   IVORY   C.A.R.
         THAILAND   BELIZE HONDURAS   LIBERIA COAST CAMEROON   SOMALIA
MALAYSIA BRUNEI   GUATEMALA NICARAGUA   VENEZUELA GUYANA   EQUATORIAL GUINEA ZAIRE
         SINGAPORE EL SALVADOR   SURINAM   GABON CONGO   KENYA
INDONESIA PAPUA   COSTA RICA PANAMA   FRENCH GUIANA   TANZANIA
         NEW GUINEA   COLOMBIA
                   205   ECUADOR   ANGOLA ZAMBIA ZIM-   MADAGASCAR
         FIJI   BABWE MOZAMBIQUE
         NEW CALEDONIA   PERU   BRAZIL   BOTSWANA MALAWI
                             BOLIVIA   NAMIBIA   SWAZILAND
AUSTRALIA   PARAGUAY   SOUTH   LESOTHO
                             CHILE   AFRICA
                                     URUGUAY
NEW ZEALAND   ARGENTINA

Direction of US foreign aid
Millions of dollars excluding international and regional organizations

- Western Europe
- Eastern Europe
- Near and Middle East
- Indian sub-continent
- South East Asia
- Far East
- Australia and Pacific Islands
- Canada
- Central America and the Caribbean
- South America
- Israel
- Africa

WORLD IRON AND STEEL MINERALS

This map is designed to show the main producers of steel related minerals: both iron ore, which remains the basis of industrial production, and the much rarer steel alloy metals — six are listed here. Countries are shaded in different colors according to their iron ore supplies, while pie charts representing the six steel alloy metals show the major producing countries for each metal.

Iron ore is the world's most common mineral ore and is widely distributed throughout the earth's crust. Estimates suggest that at present rates of extraction known resources will satisfy the needs of industry for 300 years. Diagram A shows that although many countries produce at least some iron ore, only two — Brazil and the U.S.S.R. — produce more than 10 percent of the world's output, with the U.S.S.R. accounting for one-third of the world total.

The next group of countries — those producing between 5 and 10 percent of total world output — has only three members: Australia, China, and the United States.

A third group of countries produces between 1 and 5 percent of world output each. These include Canada, France, North Korea, Liberia, Mauritania, Mexico, South Africa, Spain, Sweden, and Venezuela. But many other countries produce at least enough ore for their own needs, and in some cases enough for export as well. World resources of this metal are enormous.

The picture for the rarer steel alloy metals is far more erratic. For example, virtually none of these are produced in Europe except for chromium ores in Albania and Turkey. Similarly, out of fifty countries in Africa only South Africa, Zimbabwe, and Gabon are shown as producing any of these rare metals, while in Latin America only Brazil, Bolivia, Chile, Cuba, and Mexico do so.

The United States is a producer of vanadium and molybdenum but not of the other four listed minerals. The U.S.S.R., on the other hand, is a source of all six steel alloy minerals, and in substantial quantities as well. China produces three of these rare minerals, as do Australia and South Africa.

Source: *U.N. Monthly Bulletin of Statistics*

Diagram A: Leading iron ore producers, 1983, in millions of metric tons

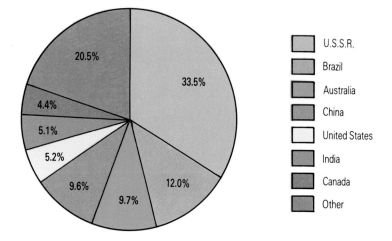

- U.S.S.R.
- Brazil
- Australia
- China
- United States
- India
- Canada
- Other

MAJOR PRODUCERS, 1983	

Nickel (thousand metric tons)		Vanadium (thousand metric tons)	
U.S.S.R.	172.0	U.S.S.R.	9.5
Canada	128.1	South Africa	8.1
Australia	76.6	China	4.5
New Caledonia	54.3	Finland	3.4
Cuba	39.3		
Indonesia	38.4	World total	27.4
World total	668.0		

Molybdenum (thousand metric tons)		Tungsten (thousand metric tons)	
		China	12.5
		U.S.S.R.	9.1
Chile	14.5	Korea, South	2.5
United States	13.6	Bolivia	2.4
U.S.S.R.	11.3	Australia	2.1
Canada	10.5		
Mexico	5.9	World total	40.0
World total	64.0		

Manganese (million metric tons)		Chromium ores and concentrates (million metric tons)	
		U.S.S.R.	2.5
U.S.S.R.	9.9	South Africa	2.2
South Africa	2.6	Albania	1.5
Brazil	2.1	Zimbabwe	0.4
Gabon	1.9		
China	1.0	World total	7.7
World total	22.0		

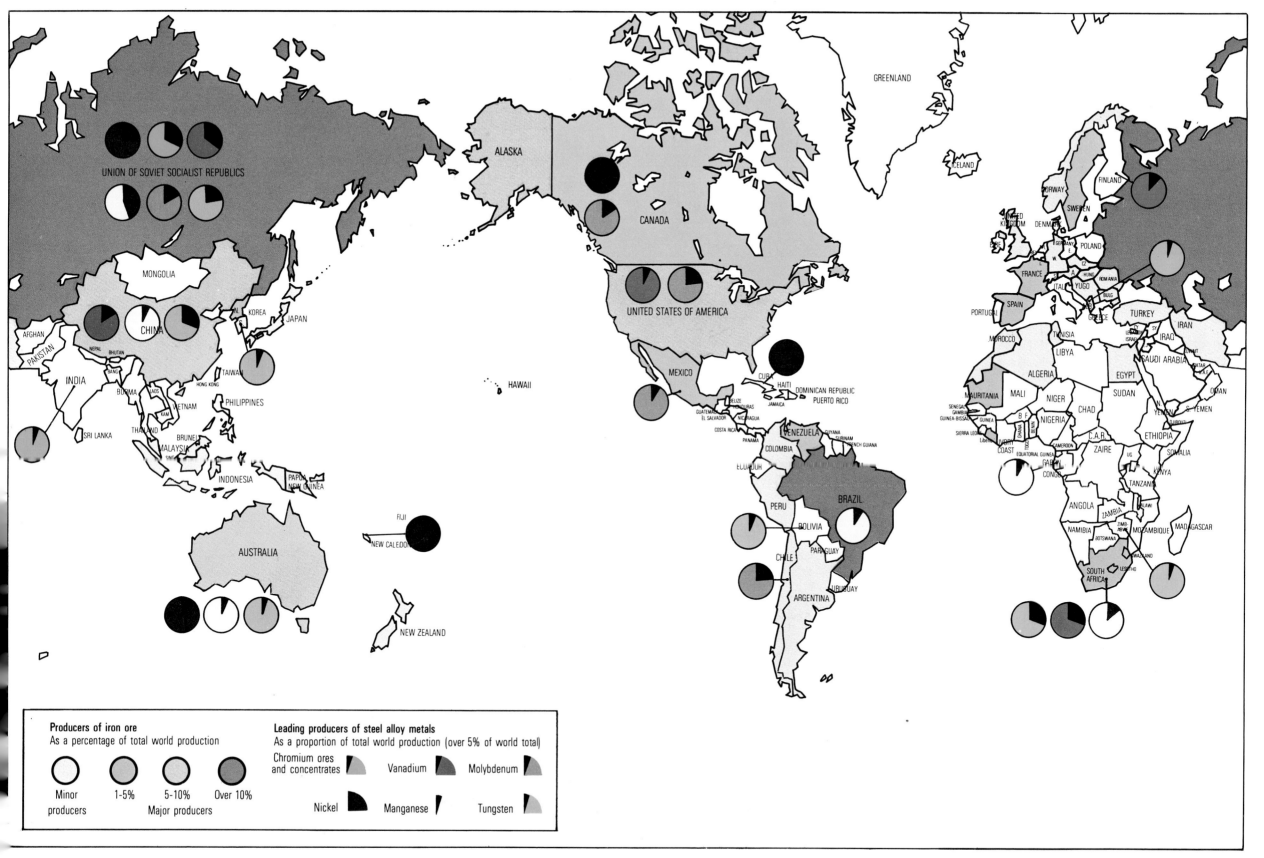

GREENLAND
ALASKA
CANADA
UNION OF SOVIET SOCIALIST REPUBLICS
MONGOLIA
UNITED STATES OF AMERICA
N. KOREA
JAPAN
CHINA
AFGHAN
PAKISTAN
INDIA
NEPAL
BHUTAN
BANG
BURMA
LAOS
VIETNAM
THAILAND
SRI LANKA
TAIWAN
HONG KONG
PHILIPPINES
BRUNEI
MALAYSIA
SINGAPORE
INDONESIA
PAPUA
NEW GUINEA
AUSTRALIA
FIJI
NEW CALEDONIA
NEW ZEALAND
HAWAII
MEXICO
CUBA
HAITI
DOMINICAN REPUBLIC
PUERTO RICO
JAMAICA
BELIZE
GUATEMALA
HONDURAS
EL SALVADOR
NICARAGUA
COSTA RICA
PANAMA
VENEZUELA
GUYANA
SURINAM
FRENCH GUIANA
COLOMBIA
ECUADOR
PERU
BRAZIL
BOLIVIA
PARAGUAY
CHILE
ARGENTINA
URUGUAY
ICELAND
NORWAY
SWEDEN
FINLAND
UNITED KINGDOM
DENMARK
GERMANY
POLAND
FRANCE
ROMANIA
YUGO
BULG
PORTUGAL
SPAIN
ITALY
GREECE
TURKEY
IRAN
IRAQ
SAUDI ARABIA
QATAR
KUWAIT
MOROCCO
TUNISIA
LIBYA
EGYPT
ALGERIA
MAURITANIA
MALI
NIGER
CHAD
SUDAN
YEMEN
S-YEMEN
OMAN
SENEGAL
GAMBIA
GUINEA-BISSAU
GUINEA
SIERRA LEONE
LIBERIA
IVORY COAST
GHANA
TOGO
BENIN
NIGERIA
CAMEROON
C.A.R.
ETHIOPIA
EQUATORIAL GUINEA
GABON
CONGO
ZAIRE
UG
KENYA
SOMALIA
TANZANIA
ANGOLA
ZAMBIA
MALAWI
MOZAMBIQUE
MADAGASCAR
NAMIBIA
ZIMB
BOTSWANA
SWAZILAND
SOUTH AFRICA
LESOTHO

Producers of iron ore
As a percentage of total world production

○ Minor producers
◔ 1-5%
◔ 5-10%
● Over 10%

Major producers

Leading producers of steel alloy metals
As a proportion of total world production (over 5% of world total)

Chromium ores and concentrates ◤
Vanadium ◣
Molybdenum ◥

Nickel ◣
Manganese ◣
Tungsten ◥

95

MINERAL WEALTH

This map shows countries possessing one or more of seven of the world's most important minerals in quantities exceeding 2 percent of total world production of the mineral. The seven selected minerals are: aluminum (bauxite), zinc, titanium, lead, silver, copper, and gold. All quantities are given as percentages of world production, in 1983.

Four countries — Australia, Canada, the U.S.S.R., and the United States have six or seven of these minerals each and produce at least 2 percent of each one. Three countries — China, Mexico, and South Africa — produce four each.

To form an idea of the world distribution of two of these minerals — aluminum and copper — production details of leading countries are given below.

Twelve countries produce substantial quantities of aluminum (bauxite): Australia (31.6 percent of total world production), Brazil (5.5 percent), China (2.5 percent), France (2 percent), Greece (3 percent), Guinea (16.7 percent), Hungary (3.8 percent), India (2.4 percent), Jamaica (10 percent), Surinam (3.6 percent), the U.S.S.R. (8 percent), and Yugoslavia (4.5 percent).

The world's main copper producers are: Australia (3 percent), Canada (7 percent), Chile (15 percent), China (2 percent), Mexico (2.5 percent), Papua New Guinea (2.1 percent), Peru (4 percent), Poland (5 percent), South Africa (2.5 percent), Zaire (6 percent), Zambia (7 percent), U.S.S.R. (14 percent), United States (13 percent), with the rest of the world accounting for 16.9 percent.

Out of all the nations of the world only 33 countries produce 2 percent or more of these seven minerals; many other countries, however, produce relatively small, but significant, quantities. And several countries, such as Afghanistan and Iran, are known to possess large resources, for example of copper, which have not as yet been exploited.

Seven countries between them account for 86 percent of the world's gold production. South Africa, the leading producer, accounts for 48 percent of total world output.

Source: *U.N. Monthly Bulletin of Statistics*

MAJOR PRODUCERS, 1983

Lead (thousand metric tons)		Zinc (thousand metric tons)	
U.S.S.R.	580.0	Canada	1,069.7
Australia	480.6	U.S.S.R.	1,025.0
United States	449.0	Australia	696.1
Canada	251.5	Peru	553.1
Peru	205.1	United States	275.3
Mexico	167.4	Mexico	257.4
China	160.0	Japan	255.7
World total	3,400.0	World total	6,500.0

Silver (metric tons)		Gold (kilograms)	
Mexico	1,910	South Africa	677,870
Peru	1,792	U.S.S.R.	268,000
U.S.S.R.	1,600	Canada	70,746
United States	1,350	United States	60,883
Canada	1,203	Brazil	53,684
Australia	1,052	Australia	30,597
World total	12,441	Philippines	24,900
		World total	1,400,000

Diagram A: Comparison of mineral production between the United States, U.S.S.R., Australia and Canada, 1983

- Aluminum
- Zinc
- Titanium
- Lead
- Silver
- Copper
- Gold

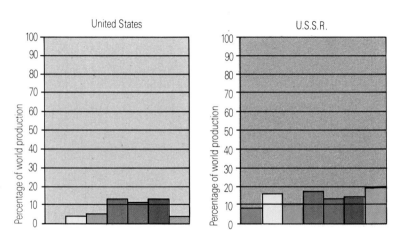

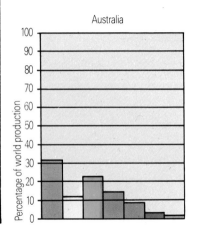

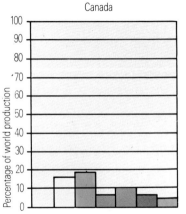

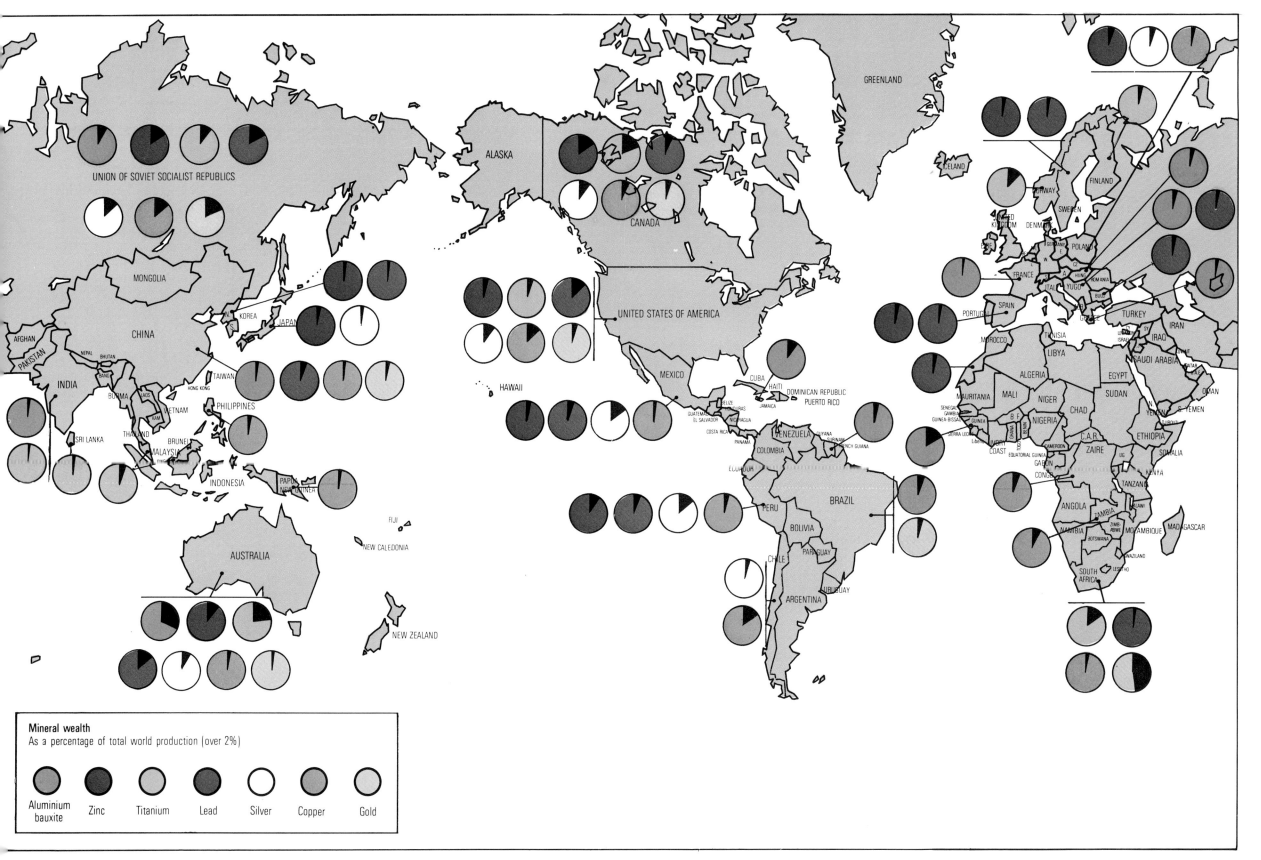

GREENLAND

ALASKA

CANADA

UNITED STATES OF AMERICA

UNION OF SOVIET SOCIALIST REPUBLICS

MONGOLIA

CHINA

KOREA

JAPAN

TAIWAN

HONG KONG

AFGHAN

PAKISTAN

NEPAL BHUTAN

INDIA

BANG

BURMA

LAOS

VIETNAM

SRI LANKA

THAILAND

PHILIPPINES

BRUNEI

MALAYSIA

KAM

INDONESIA

PAPUA
NEW GUINEA

FIJI

NEW CALEDONIA

AUSTRALIA

NEW ZEALAND

HAWAII

MEXICO

CUBA

HAITI

JAMAICA

DOMINICAN REPUBLIC

PUERTO RICO

BELIZE

GUATEMALA

HONDURAS

EL SALVADOR

NICARAGUA

COSTA RICA

PANAMA

VENEZUELA

COLOMBIA

GUYANA

SURINAM

FRENCH GUIANA

ECUADOR

PERU

BRAZIL

BOLIVIA

PARAGUAY

CHILE

URUGUAY

ARGENTINA

ICELAND

NORWAY

SWEDEN

FINLAND

UNITED
KINGDOM

DENMARK

GERMANY

POLAND

W.

CZ

FRANCE

A

HUNG

ROMANIA

ITALY

YUGO

BULG

GREECE

PORTUGAL

SPAIN

TURKEY

TUNISIA

LEB

SY

IRAN

MOROCCO

ISRAEL

IRAQ

LIBYA

EGYPT

SAUDI ARABIA

KUWT

QATAR

ALGERIA

NIGER

CHAD

SUDAN

YEMEN

S-YEMEN

OMAN

MAURITANIA

MALI

SENEGAL

GAMBIA

GUINEA-BISSAU

GUINEA

SIERRA LEONE

Liberia

IVORY
COAST

GHANA

TOGO

BENIN

NIGERIA

CAMEROON

EQUATORIAL GUINEA

GABON

CONGO

C.A.R.

ZAIRE

ETHIOPIA

SOMALIA

UG

KENYA

TANZANIA

ANGOLA

ZAMBIA

MALAWI

ZIMB-
ABWE

MOZAMBIQUE

MADAGASCAR

NAMIBIA

BOTSWANA

SWAZILAND

SOUTH
AFRICA

LESOTHO

Mineral wealth
As a percentage of total world production (over 2%)

Aluminium
bauxite

Zinc

Titanium

Lead

Silver

Copper

Gold

WORLD ENERGY PRODUCTION

This map is designed to show the extent of energy production in 1982 from all sources given in millions of metric tons coal equivalent (mtce). Only two countries, the United States and the U.S.S.R., produced in excess of 1 billion mtce, with the United States at 1,996 million mtce and the U.S.S.R. at 2,013 million mtce. The United States is a substantial exporter of coal but a major importer of oil to fuel its great industrial sector. The U.S.S.R. is an exporter of oil, principally to the COMECON countries, and also an exporter of natural gas.

At the bottom of the scale come those countries, mainly in Africa, that produced less than 1 million or between 1-10 million mtce a year.

The pie charts show the proportions of total fuel production of the four main fuel resources: coal, petroleum, gas, and electricity (from either hydro or nuclear power). Here it is possible to see how much a country is dependent upon a particular fuel. The United States, for example, gets its energy in roughly equal proportions from oil, gas and coal. Britain, which in recent years has become a net oil exporter as a result of the North Sea finds, now obtains 50 percent of its energy from oil. It is easy to spot the oil exporting countries, since the greater part of their pie charts is white, for oil.

The third largest producer of energy in the world in 1982, after the United States and the U.S.S.R. was China with 637 million mtce. In China's case the energy comes from coal, 75 percent, and oil, 20 percent, with only very small amounts coming from other resources.

When making comparisons, it is important to remember the great differences in population. The United States with an annual production of 1,996 million mtce had a population of 232 million in 1982 whereas China with less than a third that level of production had a population over 4 times as large at 1 billion. This means that the real level of fuel available per capita of the population is approximately 15 times as much for an American as it is for a Chinese.

Some countries could produce far more energy than they do. Saudi Arabia is an example. Its production (1982) at 490 million mtce is much lower than its production at the height of the oil boom. Production of energy is related to home needs plus developed export markets.

Diagram A shows the world's top 10 energy producers. The two superpowers are major exporters and produce all the main fuels. China, with its huge population, comes third on the list and Saudi Arabia fourth, with a vast surplus of oil to its needs. Britain joined the top rank of energy producers following the discovery of North Sea oil. The next important producers after the leading 10, in order are: Iran, Australia, India, Indonesia, United Arab Emirates, South Africa, Nigeria.

Diagram B is a pie chart showing global regional coal production. The world has vast resources of coal, especially across the northern hemisphere but also in southern Africa and Australia.

Source: *U.N. World Energy Statistics Yearbook*

WORLD'S LEADING NATURAL GAS PRODUCERS, 1983
(in billions of cubic meters)

U.S.S.R.	502
United States	450
Netherlands	73
Canada	71
Romania	40
Britain	40
Algeria	36

PERCENTAGE SHARES OF OIL PRODUCTION, 1983

U.S.S.R.	22.4
United States	15.6
Saudi Arabia	9.4
Britain	4.2
China	3.8
Rest of world	44.6

OPEC, apart from Saudi Arabia, accounts for a further 23.1 percent of the 44.6 percent figure for the rest of the world.

Diagram A: Energy production by the top 10 energy producers of the world, 1982

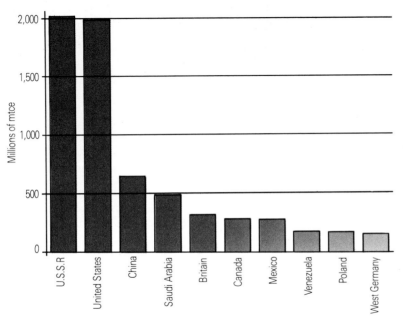

Diagram B: Regional percentage shares of coal production, 1982

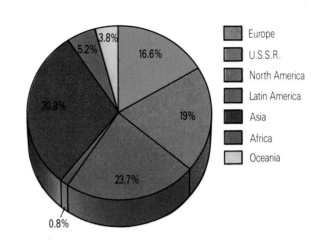

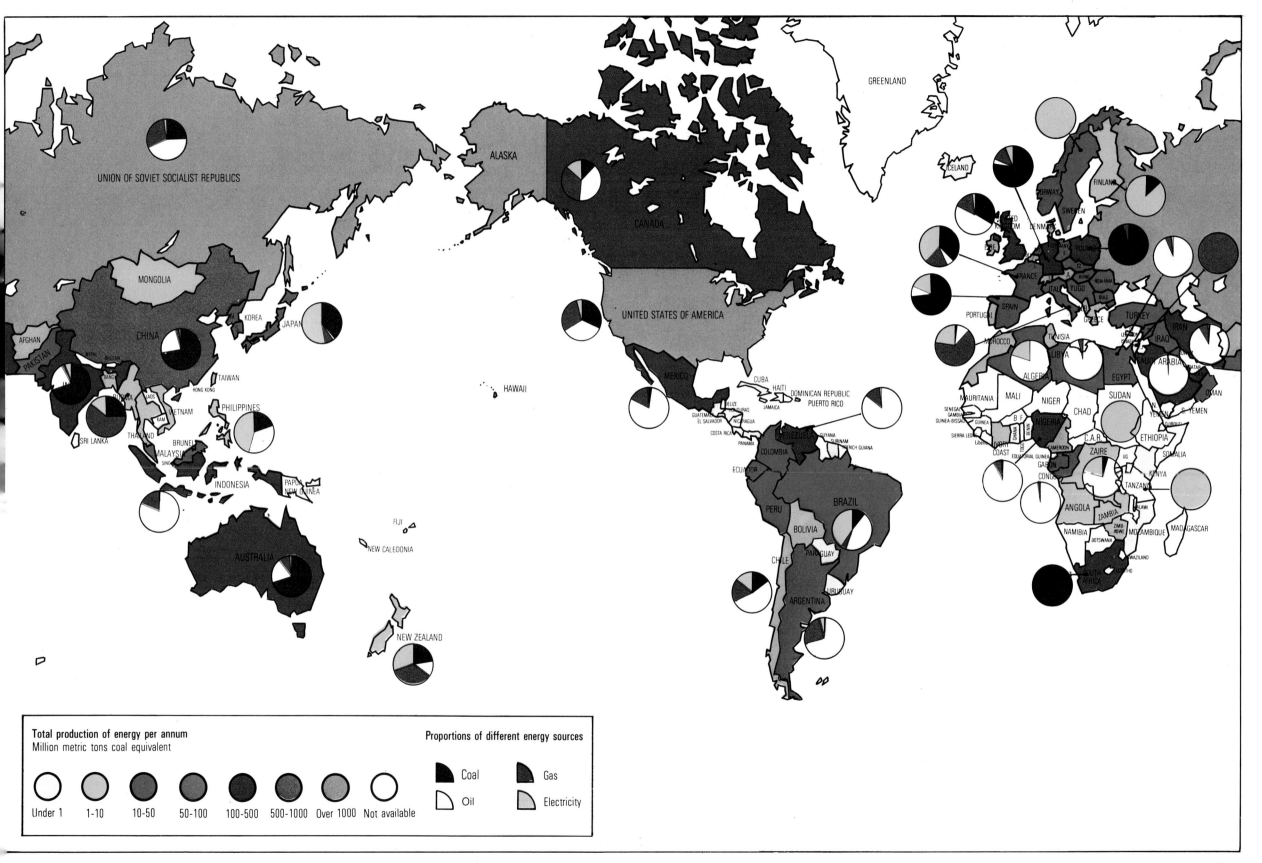

Total production of energy per annum
Million metric tons coal equivalent

Proportions of different energy sources

Coal
Oil
Gas
Electricity

Under 1   1-10   10-50   50-100   100-500   500-1000   Over 1000   Not available

WORLD ENERGY CONSUMPTION

The amount of energy a nation uses is a key to its industrial power and to the level of its development. Energy is derived from many sources — oil, coal, natural gas, hydropower, nuclear power — but for convenience the calorific value of a country's combined energy consumption from all sources has been converted to a coal equivalent (see Note 1).

The map is designed to show world levels of energy consumption in 1982 at both the national level (in metric tons coal equivalent — mtce) and at the per capita level (in kilogram coal equivalent). (See Note 2.)

The square boxes containing figures show the particular country's total consumption in millions of metric tons coal equivalent. The United States, the world's greatest industrial power, consumes 2.2 billion mtce. The U.S.S.R., the second industrial power, follows with a figure of 1.6 billion mtce, more than 600 million tons less than the United States. This difference is equivalent to the entire energy consumption of China with its population of 1 billion people.

On an individual (per capita) basis the amount of fuel consumed is a reasonable guide to the standard of living a country enjoys. (It is, however, a very rough guide, and many other factors have to be taken into account as well.)

The countries are colored according to the amount of energy they consume. This ranges from less than 100 kg coal equivalent per capita to more than 10,000 kg coal equivalent per capita. Most of the poorest countries are found in Africa, the world's least developed region. A few countries, such as Bahrain and Brunei, have a consumption above 10,000 kg coal equivalent, but these figures are based upon huge oil production in relation to tiny populations rather than actual consumption.

Per capita consumption in the United States stands at 9,431 kg coal equivalent, while that for the U.S.S.R. stands at 5,768 kg coal equivalent. The difference between the two is greater at this individual level than when comparing the national consumption of the two powers. The reason can be found partly in the difference in size of populations: in 1982 the United States had a population of 232 million, the U.S.S.R. of 270 million. The average real income per capita can be roughly calculated in proportion to the energy available per person.

Industrial power can be gauged according to energy consumption. Diagram A shows ten selected countries represented as blocks, the height of each block corresponding to the country's level of energy consumption.

Diagram B shows electrical power production (from all sources — hydro, nuclear, and thermal) for ten selected countries in 1982. This is another excellent indicator of a country's level of development.

Source: *U.N. World Energy Statistics Yearbook*

PER CAPITA ENERGY CONSUMPTION BY REGION
(1982, in kg coal equivalent)

North America	6,784
U.S.S.R.	5,768
Oceania	5,196
Europe	4,193
South America	995
Asia	600
Africa	400
Rest of World	1,825

Diagram A: Ten leading countries in energy consumption, 1982

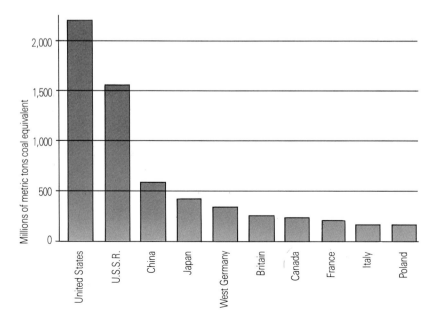

Diagram B: Electrical power production of ten selected countries, 1982

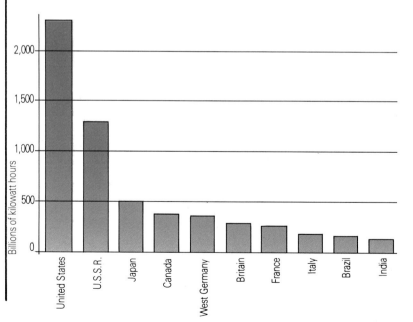

NOTE 1: Energy is measured here in terms of coal equivalent for convenience (it could as easily be converted to oil equivalent, for example). Fuels — coal, oil, and natural gas — have different calorific values but here have been converted to the one equivalent. (As an approximation, for example, one pound weight of oil is equivalent to one and a half pound weight of best coal.) Thus the U.S. national consumption figuré of 2,186 billion mtce (metric tons coal equivalent) is in fact made up of its combined consumption of all soures of energy.

NOTE 2: It is normal practise to calculate national energy consumption in metric tons but per capita energy consumption in terms of kilograms, otherwise per capita consumption would have to be expressed as fractions of tons. 1 metric ton = 1000 kg

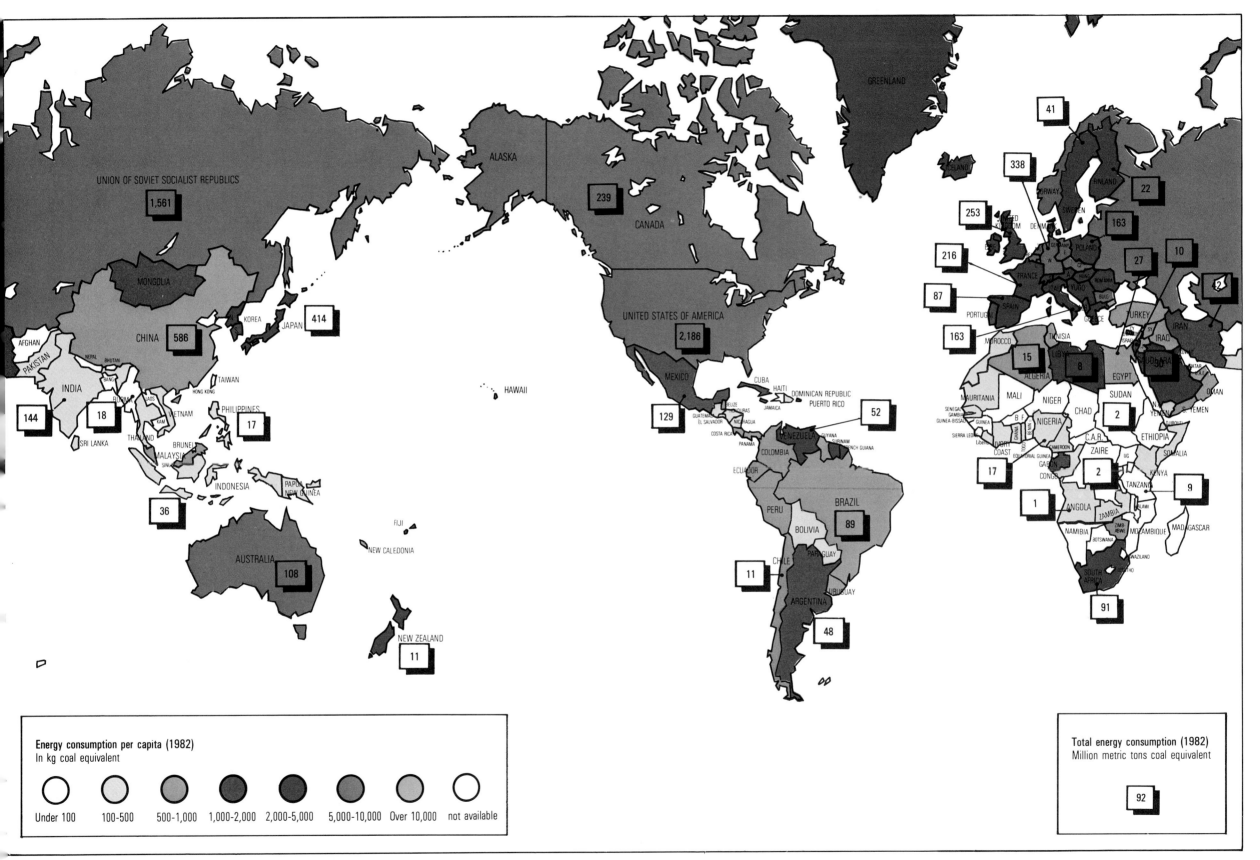

Energy consumption per capita (1982)
In kg coal equivalent

| Under 100 | 100-500 | 500-1,000 | 1,000-2,000 | 2,000-5,000 | 5,000-10,000 | Over 10,000 | not available |

Total energy consumption (1982)
Million metric tons coal equivalent

92

101

WORLD MANUFACTURING

The map shows the value of total manufacturing output in billions of dollars, and the output of two basic industrial indicators: motor vehicle production and steel production.

In terms of value of output the industrialized world consists of the major "powers:" the United States, the U.S.S.R., Japan, and the EEC. Within the EEC there are great variations; West Germany is at the top end of the production scale, and the small members, Greece, Ireland, and Portugal, are at the bottom.

In 1984 only the United States produced total manufactured goods valued at more than $500 billion. Manufactures of the U.S.S.R. and the EEC were between $400-500 billion, and those of Japan between $300-400 billion.

Steel production has always been regarded as a key to industrial strength although, with the coming of the electronic age, the pattern is changing. In 1984 the four top producers of crude steel were the U.S.S.R. (154 million tons), the EEC (133 million tons), Japan (106 million tons), and the United States (83 million tons). China produced 43 million tons of steel in 1984. Other important producers are Canada, Brazil, Poland, Mexico, Saudi Arabia, India, and Australia.

One reason for using motor vehicle production as an indicator of manufacturing is that vehicles are easily quantifiable units. One of the pie charts in Diagram A compares the number of cars produced in 1983 by the three major non-communist manufacturing areas. As can be seen, the EEC as a whole produced 12 million vehicles, Japan produced 11 million vehicles, and the United States produced 9 million.

Other manufacturing sectors such as chemicals or electrical goods are of great importance. On the map their contribution to industrial strength is included in the figure (in billions of dollars) for each country's total manufacturing output.

Diagram B shows how the industrial pattern is constantly changing. It charts the fortunes of six major industrial countries over the last quarter century. In 1950 the United States held 27.3 percent of the world market but its share had declined to 17.3 percent by 1984. Japan, which had only 3.4 percent in 1950, increased sixfold to 20.6 percent by 1984. France maintained its position almost unchanged (7.3 to 8.5 percent). West Germany nearly trebled her share from 7.3 percent in 1950 to 18.5 percent in 1984. Italy had a mere 1.2 percent share in 1950 but 7.4 percent by 1984. Britain has done worst of all. In 1950 it accounted for 25.5 percent, just below the United States, but by 1984 it had fallen by two-thirds to 7.9 percent.

Diagram A: Share in the total world production of steel, cars and sulphuric acid, between the United States, Japan, and the EEC, 1983

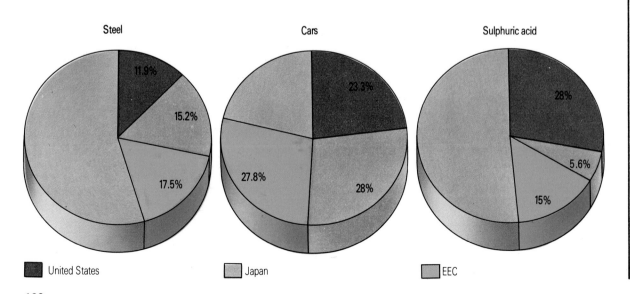

Steel

Cars

Sulphuric acid

■ United States   ▨ Japan   ▨ EEC

Diagram B: Percentage share in the world export of manufactured goods by six major industrial countries, 1950-1984

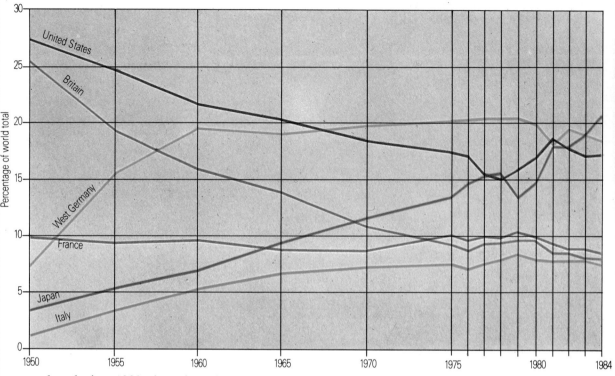

United States
Britain
West Germany
France
Japan
Italy

Percentage of world total

1950 1955 1960 1965 1970 1975 1980 1984

PRINCIPAL STEEL PRODUCERS, 1984
(millions of tons)

U.S.S.R.	154
Japan	106
United States	83
China	43
West Germany	39
Italy	24
Brazil	19
France	19
Poland	17
Canada	15
Britain	15
Spain	13
India	10
Saudi Arabia	8
Mexico	7
Australia	6

Source: *U.N. Monthly Bulletin of Statistics*

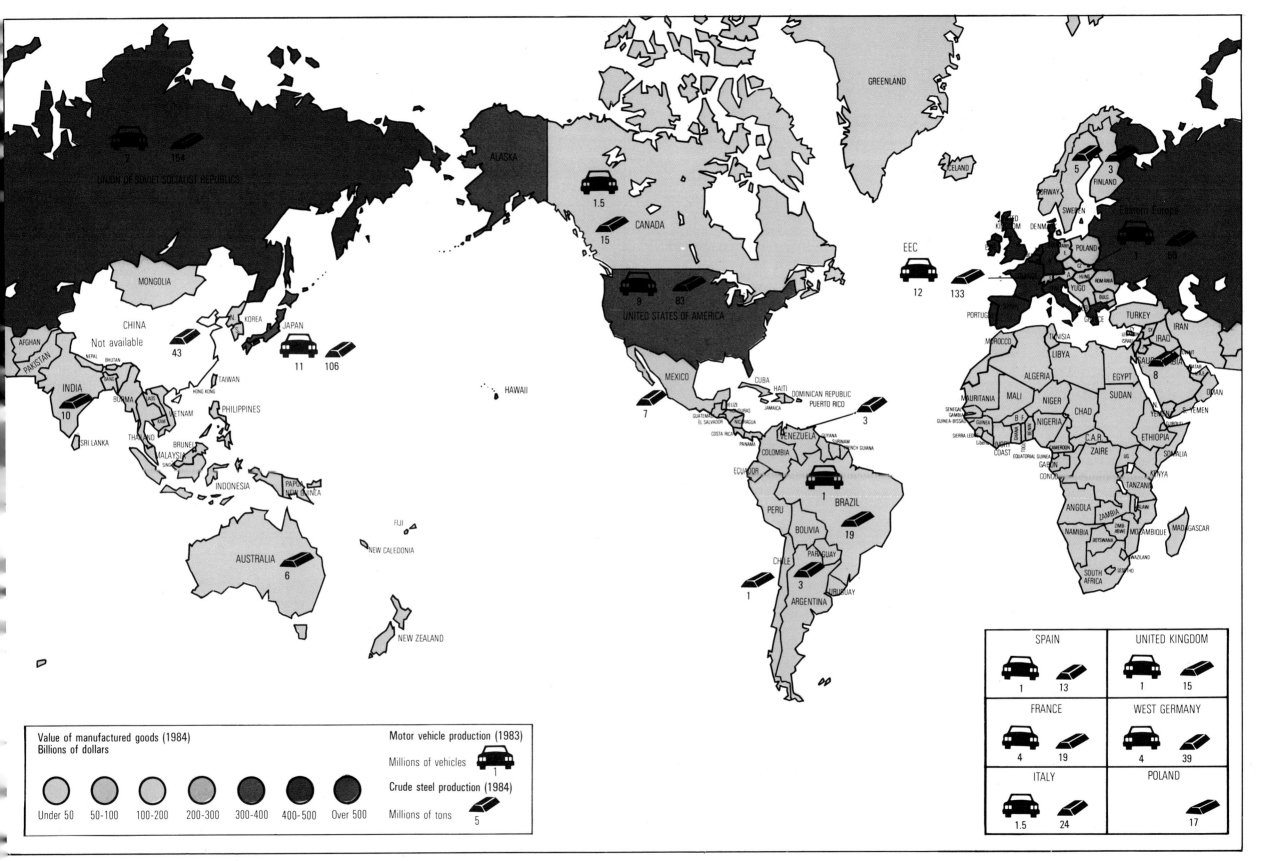

UNION OF SOVIET SOCIALIST REPUBLICS
2   154

GREENLAND

ALASKA

CANADA
1.5
15

ICELAND

NORWAY   SWEDEN   FINLAND
5   3

Eastern Europe
3   60

MONGOLIA

CHINA
Not available

AFGHAN
PAKISTAN
NEPAL   BHUTAN
INDIA
10
BURMA
SRI LANKA
THAILAND
MALAYSIA
INDONESIA
PAPUA
NEW GUINEA

N.
S.   KOREA

JAPAN
11   106

TAIWAN
HONG KONG
VIETNAM
PHILIPPINES

43

HAWAII

EEC
12   133

UNITED STATES OF AMERICA
9   83

MEXICO
7

CUBA
HAITI
DOMINICAN REPUBLIC
PUERTO RICO
3
BELIZE
GUATEMALA   JAMAICA
EL SALVADOR
NICARAGUA
COSTA RICA
PANAMA

VENEZUELA   GUYANA
COLOMBIA   SURINAM
FRENCH GUIANA
ECUADOR

PERU   BRAZIL
1
BOLIVIA
19
PARAGUAY

CHILE
3
1
ARGENTINA   URUGUAY

UNITED KINGDOM
DENMARK
POLAND
GERMANY
YUGO
TURKEY
PORTUGAL   SPAIN   GREECE   IRAN
ROMANIA
BULG

MOROCCO   TUNISIA   IRAQ
ISRAEL
LIBYA   EGYPT   SAUDI ARABIA
8
ALGERIA

MAURITANIA   MALI   NIGER   CHAD   SUDAN   S. YEMEN
SENEGAL
GAMBIA   GUINEA
GUINEA-BISSAU   NIGERIA   C.A.R.   ETHIOPIA
SIERRA LEONE   GHANA   CAMEROON   ZAIRE   SOMALIA
IVORY COAST   GABON   UG   KENYA
EQUATORIAL GUINEA   CONGO   TANZANIA

ANGOLA   ZAMBIA   MALAWI   MADAGASCAR
NAMIBIA   ZIMBABWE   MOZAMBIQUE
BOTSWANA   SWAZILAND
SOUTH   LESOTHO
AFRICA

AUSTRALIA
6

FIJI
NEW CALEDONIA

NEW ZEALAND

Value of manufactured goods (1984)
Billions of dollars

Under 50 | 50-100 | 100-200 | 200-300 | 300-400 | 400-500 | Over 500

Motor vehicle production (1983)

Millions of vehicles   1

Crude steel production (1984)

Millions of tons   5

SPAIN		UNITED KINGDOM	
1	13	1	15
FRANCE		WEST GERMANY	
4	19	4	39
ITALY		POLAND	
1.5	24		17

INTERNATIONAL TRADE

This map shows the imports and exports of the major trading countries in 1983, in billions of dollars. The difference between the heights of the two blocks in each country gives the trade balance for that year — a deficit if the left-hand block is the higher, and a surplus if the right-hand block is the higher.

Trade with the United States accounted for nearly 12 percent of total world trade, and resulted in a U.S. net trade deficit of $57.5 billion. In the following year, this deficit increased still further, to over $120 billion. In 1983, on the other hand, Japan showed an overall trade surplus of $20.6 billion, and West Germany achieved a $16.8 billion surplus.

The rise in total world exports since 1950 has been tremendous. But the increase has varied between countries or groups of countries and the proportion of the total accounted for by each has changed considerably. The proportion due to the trade of the United States fell from 1950 from 17 to 12 percent, that due to Western Europe rose from 25 percent to 41 percent. Japan; which in 1950 accounted for under 2 percent of world trade, was approaching 9 percent in 1983. The oil-producing countries accounted for about 7 percent in 1950, and this was still the case in 1973. But in 1975 the rise in oil prices brought about a rapid increase in the proportion to over 13 percent, a figure that remained unchanged in 1983.

Diagram A shows the imports and exports of the United States by region. Diagram B elaborates on this, giving the international picture showing the trade in 1983 between the United States,

Diagram A: United States imports and exports, 1984, by region

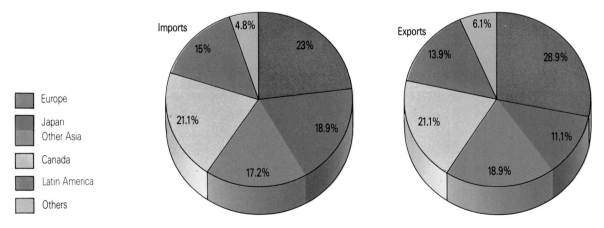

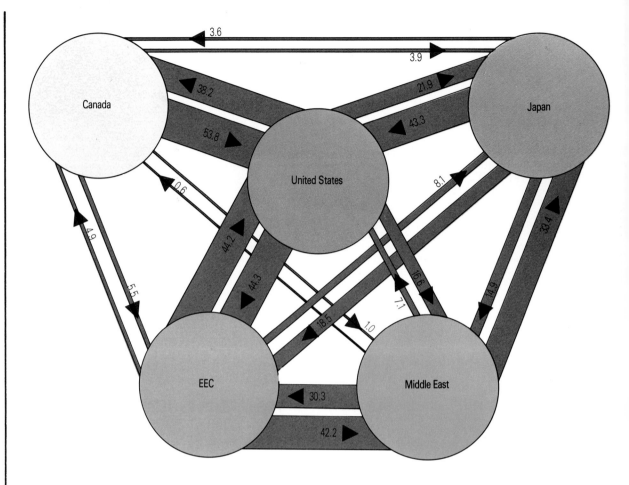

Canada, the countries of the European Economic Community (EEC), Japan, and the Middle East. U.S. imports from Canada form the largest single component of this picture, at $53.8 billion, followed by exports from the United States to the EEC countries ($44.3 billion).

The troublesome imbalance between Japan and the United States is clear to see — a deficit for the United States of $20.4 billion. And in 1984 this gap widened still further, to $36.8 billion. Japan showed trade surpluses of nearly this size in 1983 both with the EEC countries and with the Middle East.

Diagram B: International trade by selected countries in 1983, in billions of dollars

Sources: Organization for Economic Co-operation and Development; U.S. Bureau of the Census

104

UNION OF SOVIET SOCIALIST REPUBLICS

GREENLAND

ALASKA

CANADA

NORWAY

FINLAND

SWEDEN

UNITED KINGDOM

DENMARK

MONGOLIA

N. KOREA

JAPAN

POLAND

GERMANY

FRANCE

ROMANIA

ITALY

YUGO

BULG

GREECE

TURKEY

IRAN

AFGHAN

CHINA

PAKISTAN

NEPAL

BHUTAN

BANG

INDIA

BURMA

LAOS

TAIWAN

HONG KONG

VIETNAM

PHILIPPINES

SRI LANKA

THAILAND

CAM

BRUNEI

MALAYSIA

SING

INDONESIA

PAPUA NEW GUINEA

UNITED STATES OF AMERICA

MEXICO

HAWAII

CUBA

HAITI

DOMINICAN REPUBLIC

PUERTO RICO

BELIZE

GUATEMALA

HONDURAS

JAMAICA

EL SALVADOR

NICARAGUA

COSTA RICA

PANAMA

VENEZUELA

GUYANA

SURINAM

FRENCH GUIANA

COLOMBIA

ECUADOR

PERU

BRAZIL

BOLIVIA

CHILE

PARAGUAY

ARGENTINA

URUGUAY

PORTUGAL

SPAIN

MOROCCO

TUNISIA

LIBYA

ALGERIA

EGYPT

MAURITANIA

MALI

NIGER

CHAD

SUDAN

SENEGAL

GAMBIA

GUINEA-BISSAU

GUINEA

SIERRA LEONE

Liberia

IVORY COAST

GHANA

TOGO

BENIN

B F

NIGERIA

CAMEROON

EQUATORIAL GUINEA

GABON

CONGO

C.A.R.

ZAIRE

UG

KENYA

ETHIOPIA

SOMALIA

TANZANIA

ANGOLA

ZAMBIA

MALAWI

ZIMBABWE

MOZAMBIQUE

MADAGASCAR

NAMIBIA

BOTSWANA

SWAZILAND

SOUTH AFRICA

LESOTHO

LEBANON

SY

ISRAEL

IRAQ

JORDAN

SAUDI ARABIA

KUWAIT

QATAR

YEMEN

S. YEMEN

OMAN

AUSTRALIA

FIJI

NEW CALEDONIA

NEW ZEALAND

Foreign trade (1983)
In billions of US dollars

50
0
Imports

50
0
Exports

105

FOREIGN INVESTMENT

This map is concerned with foreign investment, both investments of U.S. companies in other countries, and direct investments of foreign companies in the United States. The amounts represented refer to the situation in 1983.

Direct investment abroad is defined as the "ownership or control, direct or indirect, by one U.S. person or business enterprise of 10 percent or more of the voting securities of an incorporated foreign business enterprise".

Foreign direct investment in the United States means "the ownership or control, directly or indirectly, by one foreign individual, branch, partnership, association, trust, corporation, or government of 10 percent or more of the voting securities of a U.S. business enterprise, or an equivalent interest in an unincorporated one." Only enterprises with assets of over $1 million, or owning 200 acres of land in the United States, are included. Book values of direct investments are given for the end of each year.

In 1983, the value of investments of U.S. companies overseas amounted to a total of $226 billion. Over one-fifth of this was in Canada, and almost exactly one-half in Western Europe. Of the European countries, the United Kingdom accounted for the largest single part, with nearly $31 billion U.S. investment. U.S. direct investment in Latin America totaled $30 million, $9 billion of this in Brazil.

On the other side of the coin, foreign investment in the United States in 1983 reached a total of $136 billion. The United Kingdom, with $32.5 billion, was the country with the largest single investment. It was closely followed by the Netherlands, whose nationals had $29 billion invested in the United States. A large proportion of this was in the petroleum industry. However, the 1983 situation represented a fall for the United Kingdom since 1970, as for Canada, while the Netherlands showed a sharp rise over the same period.

Diagram A is a pie chart, showing the distribution of foreign direct investment in the United States, among Canada, Europe, Japan, and the rest of the world. The predominance of European investors is clear, accounting for 68 percent of the total. In 1970, Japanese investment in the United States made up less than 2 percent of the total foreign direct investment, but by 1983, it equaled Canadian investment in importance.

The position of the United States as a world investor has changed dramatically over the past century as it became a world power. Before 1900, U.S. overseas investment was negligible. By 1908, it had risen to $2.5 billion. In 1929, the total of U.S. foreign investments was $7.5 billion, and of this total, $3.5 billion — 45

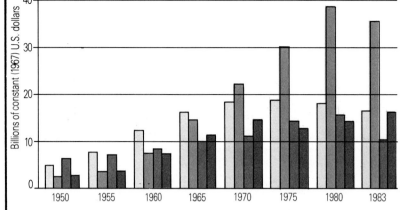

Diagram B: U.S. direct investment overseas, 1950-1983

percent — was in Latin America. In 1950, the Latin American proportion still stood at 40 percent. But investment in Europe, which in 1929 had represented only 15 percent of the total, rose rapidly in the 1950s and 1960s, overtaking the Latin American figure in 1962, and soon far outstripping it. In 1970, the income from U.S. investment abroad amounted to over $8 billion; in 1983 it was $21 billion.

Diagram B graphs part of this history. It shows the value of U.S. direct foreign investment, expressed in constant (1967) dollars, over the period 1950-1983, for Canada, Western Europe, Latin America, and other countries. The tremendous increase in the amount of U.S. investment in Europe, and the decline in U.S. investment in South American countries, stands out clearly.

Diagram C shows the distribution of investments abroad directly owned by U.S. companies. Again, the importance of Europe taken as a whole is obvious. A significant proportion of the "other" category refers to U.S. investment in the Middle East.

Diagram D gives the proportions of the total U.S. investment abroad in manufacturing, oil, finance, and other enterprises. Manufacturing makes up 40 percent of the total, followed by oil with 26 percent.

Source: U.S. Bureau of Economic Analysis

Diagram C: Distribution of U.S. direct investment overseas in 1983, by region

Diagram D: Distribution of U.S. direct investment overseas in 1983, by industry

Diagram A: Distribution of foreign direct investment in the United States, 1983

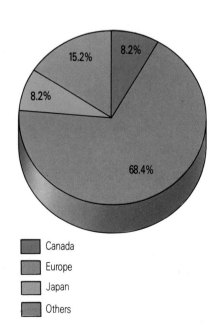

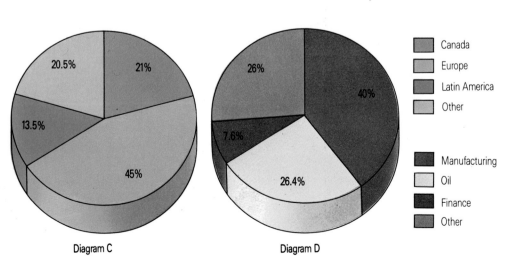

Diagram C   Diagram D

Canada
Europe
Latin America
Other

Manufacturing
Oil
Finance
Other

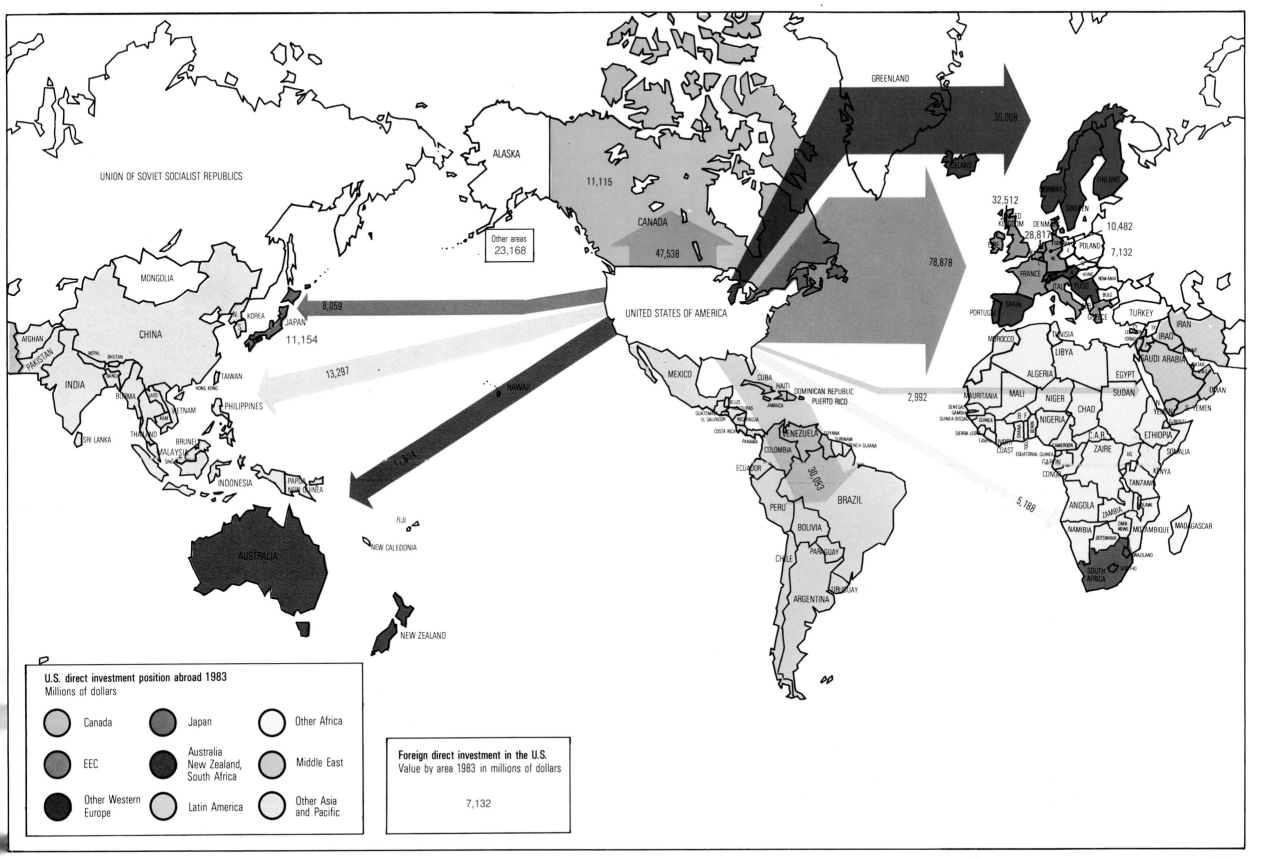

UNION OF SOVIET SOCIALIST REPUBLICS

GREENLAND

ALASKA

35,008

11,115

CANADA

32,512

Other areas
23,168

47,538

28,817

10,482

7,132

78,878

UNITED STATES OF AMERICA

MONGOLIA

8,059

JAPAN

11,154

CHINA

TURKEY

IRAN

AFGHAN

13,297

TAIWAN

PAKISTAN

NEPAL

BHUTAN

HONG KONG

INDIA

BURMA

VIETNAM

PHILIPPINES

SAUDI ARABIA

MEXICO

CUBA

HAITI

DOMINICAN REPUBLIC

PUERTO RICO

2,992

MOROCCO

LIBYA

EGYPT

OMAN

HAWAII

ALGERIA

MALI

NIGER

CHAD

SUDAN

MAURITANIA

THAILAND

GUATEMALA

BELIZE

HONDURAS

EL SALVADOR

NICARAGUA

COSTA RICA

PANAMA

VENEZUELA

GUYANA

SURINAM

FRENCH GUIANA

SENEGAL

GAMBIA

GUINEA-BISSAU

GUINEA

SIERRA LEONE

NIGERIA

LIBERIA

IVORY COAST

GHANA

C.A.R.

ETHIOPIA

SRI LANKA

BRUNEI

MALAYSIA

SINGAPORE

11,594

COLOMBIA

CAMEROON

EQUATORIAL GUINEA

GABON

ZAIRE

SOMALIA

INDONESIA

PAPUA NEW GUINEA

ECUADOR

30,063

CONGO

KENYA

FIJI

PERU

BRAZIL

5,188

TANZANIA

NEW CALEDONIA

BOLIVIA

ANGOLA

ZAMBIA

MALAWI

MOZAMBIQUE

MADAGASCAR

AUSTRALIA

CHILE

PARAGUAY

NAMIBIA

BOTSWANA

ZIMB

SWAZILAND

LESOTHO

SOUTH AFRICA

NEW ZEALAND

ARGENTINA

URUGUAY

NORWAY

SWEDEN

FINLAND

UNITED KINGDOM

DENMARK

POLAND

FRANCE

SPAIN

PORTUGAL

ITALY

YUGO

TUNISIA

U.S. direct investment position abroad 1983
Millions of dollars

- Canada
- Japan
- Other Africa
- EEC
- Australia New Zealand, South Africa
- Middle East
- Other Western Europe
- Latin America
- Other Asia and Pacific

Foreign direct investment in the U.S.
Value by area 1983 in millions of dollars

7,132

EXCHANGE RATES

This map shows how exchange rates — the relative values of the various international currencies — have changed over a five-year period in relation to the U.S. dollar. For example, in the years 1979-1984 the U.S. dollar increased in value between 50 and 100 percent against both the British pound sterling and the West German deutsche mark.

In a number of other cases, however, there has been no change at all. The countries where no change has taken place fall into three categories: those like El Salvador and Liberia whose currencies are tied to the U.S. dollar; those like Libya whose principal export is oil which is traded in dollars; and those like Albania which for all practical purposes has no dealings with the United States anyway.

In only three cases has the value of the dollar decreased in relation to other currencies: these are Qatar, the United Arab Emirates (UAE), and Romania. Qatar and the UAE in the Arabian Gulf are both virtually 100 percent dependent upon oil as the source of their currency strength and have become increasingly important over this period because the Gulf War between Iraq and Iran has threatened world oil supplies. Romania is another matter; the recent, more open trading policies of this communist country in COMECON have affected the value of its currency in relation to the dollar.

The most important countries to examine are those whose own currencies are "hard." Most world trade is conducted in these currencies because the economies that back them are sufficiently strong so that, like gold, the currencies are always negotiable.

The principal hard currencies, apart from the U.S. dollar, are the British pound sterling, the French franc, the West German deutsche mark, the Japanese yen, the Canadian dollar and the Italian lira. But all the currencies of the OECD (Organization for Economic Cooporation and Development) countries may be considered hard, that is, a reasonable exchange rate can be obtained for them around the world. (The position of communist countries is explained in the note on COMECON.) Most developing countries have weak currencies which are not internationally traded.

Certain countries have shown exceptional variations: for example, because of political upheaval in Argentina and high inflation in Israel enormous devaluations in their currencies have taken place over this period (Argentina 100,000 percent, Israel 18,000 percent).

Source: *U.N. Monthly Bulletin of Statistics*

Diagram A: Percentage increase in the value of the U.S. dollar against selected currencies, 1980-1985

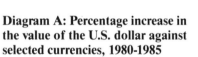

- France
- West Germany
- Italy
- Japan
- Britain

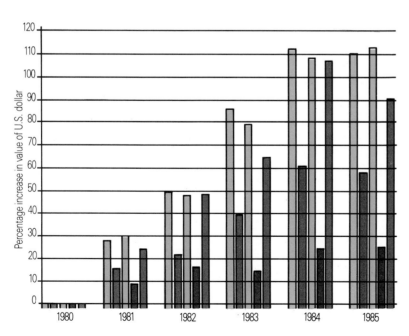

NATIONAL CURRENCY PER U.S. DOLLAR, APRIL 1985

Argentina (pesos)	448.45	Netherlands (guilders)	3.57
Australia (dollars)	1.53	New Zealand (dollars)	1.80
Brazil (cruzeiros)	4,980.00	Norway (kroner)	8.92
Canada (dollars)	1.37	Philippines (pesos)	18.49
Cuba (pesos)*	0.94	Poland (zlotych)*	138.25
Denmark (kroner)	11.20	Portugal (escudos)	173.17
Egypt (pounds)	0.70	Saudi Arabia (riyals)	3.60
France (francs)	9.50	Singapore (dollars)	2.22
Germany, East		South Africa (rand)	1.94
(marks)*	3.05	Spain (pesetas)	173.05
Germany, West		Sweden (kroner)	8.96
(deutsche marks)	3.10	Switzerland (francs)	2.59
Greece (drachmae)	136.71	U.S.S.R. (roubles)*	0.92
Iceland (kránur)	41.45	United Kingdom (pounds)	0.80
India (rupees)	12.49	Venezuela (bolivares)	7.50
Ireland (pounds)	0.99	Yugoslavia (new dinars)	263.14
Italy (lire)	1,975.00		
Japan (yen)	252.25		
Korea, South (won)	865.90	*Non-commercial rates applied	
Libya (dinars)	0.30	to tourism and to remittances	
Mexico (pesos)	215.20	from outside the rouble area.	

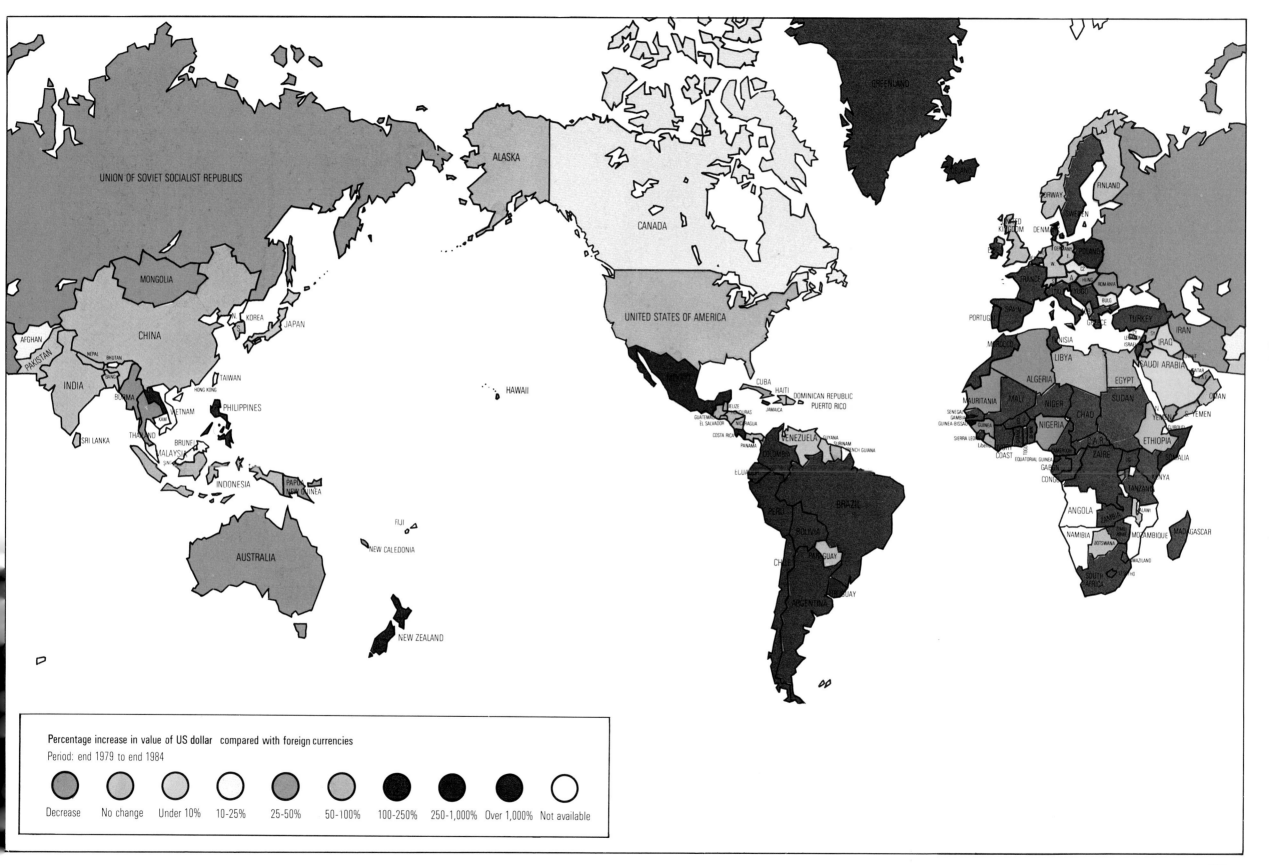

UNION OF SOVIET SOCIALIST REPUBLICS

MONGOLIA

ALASKA

CANADA

GREENLAND

FINLAND

NORWAY

SWEDEN

UNITED KINGDOM

DENMARK

POLAND

KOREA

JAPAN

CHINA

AFGHAN

PAKISTAN

NEPAL

BHUTAN

INDIA

BURMA

TAIWAN

HONG KONG

PHILIPPINES

VIETNAM

SRI LANKA

THAILAND

BRUNEI

MALAYSIA

INDONESIA

PAPUA NEW GUINEA

FIJI

NEW CALEDONIA

AUSTRALIA

NEW ZEALAND

UNITED STATES OF AMERICA

HAWAII

CUBA

HAITI

DOMINICAN REPUBLIC

PUERTO RICO

JAMAICA

BELIZE

HONDURAS

GUATEMALA

EL SALVADOR

NICARAGUA

COSTA RICA

PANAMA

VENEZUELA

GUYANA

SURINAM

FRENCH GUIANA

COLOMBIA

ECUADOR

PERU

BRAZIL

BOLIVIA

PARAGUAY

CHILE

ARGENTINA

URUGUAY

FRANCE

PORTUGAL

SPAIN

ITALY

YUGO

GREECE

TURKEY

IRAN

IRAQ

TUNISIA

LEBANON

ISRAEL

MOROCCO

LIBYA

SAUDI ARABIA

QATAR

EGYPT

ALGERIA

MAURITANIA

MALI

NIGER

CHAD

SUDAN

YEMEN

S. YEMEN

SENEGAL

GAMBIA

GUINEA-BISSAU

GUINEA

SIERRA LEONE

LIBERIA

IVORY COAST

TOGO

NIGERIA

C.A.R.

ETHIOPIA

CAMEROON

EQUATORIAL GUINEA

GABON

CONGO

ZAIRE

KENYA

SOMALIA

TANZANIA

ANGOLA

ZAMBIA

MALAWI

MOZAMBIQUE

MADAGASCAR

NAMIBIA

BOTSWANA

ZIMBABWE

SWAZILAND

SOUTH AFRICA

LESOTHO

Percentage increase in value of US dollar compared with foreign currencies

Period: end 1979 to end 1984

Decrease   No change   Under 10%   10-25%   25-50%   50-100%   100-250%   250-1,000%   Over 1,000%   Not available

109

WORLD ROAD AND RAIL TRANSPORT

This map is designed to show two things: the number of passenger vehicles a country has in relation to its total population, and the extent to which a country depends upon railroads for both passenger and freight movement.

In general terms the ratio of passenger vehicles to population is a good indicator of a country's prosperity. Only two countries have 500 vehicles or more to every 1,000 of the population: the United States and Australia.

No figures are available for the U.S.S.R., and given that country's historical concentration upon heavy industries at the expense of consumer goods perhaps that is not surprising.

The next group of countries (12 in all) have between 300 and 500 vehicles per 1,000 of the population. They are Belgium, Canada, France, West Germany, Iceland, Italy, Luxembourg, Netherlands, New Zealand, Norway, Sweden, and Switzerland. Apart from Canada and New Zealand, all are rich countries in Western Europe.

At the lower end of the scale come the countries with fewer than 10 passenger vehicles per 1,000 of the population. The great majority of these are in Africa and Asia.

The symbols on the map show the importance of the railroads in selected countries. The top segment carries a figure showing the net ton kilometers (in millions) on a monthly basis, while the figure in the lower segment of the circle represents passenger kilometers on a monthly basis (in millions).

As far as net ton kilometers are concerned, no country remotely approaches the U.S.S.R., with a monthly average of 300,000 million. The U.S. figure, for example, is a mere 97,405 million, less than a third of the Soviet figure. However, care should be taken in interpreting such differences. The U.S.S.R., with 8.6 million square miles of territory, is two and a half times the size of the United States and so has immense distances over which to transport goods. Further, a large proportion of U.S. freight is moved by road or by air, a far greater amount than in the U.S.S.R.

It should also be noted that data for a number of countries, especially in the developing world, is simply not available.

Diagram A shows the top 10 countries in terms of length of railroad. The amount of railroad has to be related to the size of the country and the remoteness of its various regions from urban and industrial centers. Diagram B shows the size of the same 10 countries. The United States, which has the most railroad, ranks fourth in size, whereas the U.S.S.R., which is by far the largest country in size, has the second greatest amount of railroad. West Germany is approximately 86 times smaller than the U.S.S.R., yet possesses nearly a seventh the amount of railroad.

Source: *U.N. Monthly Bulletin of Statistics*

Diagram A: The leading 10 countries in terms of kilometers of railroad

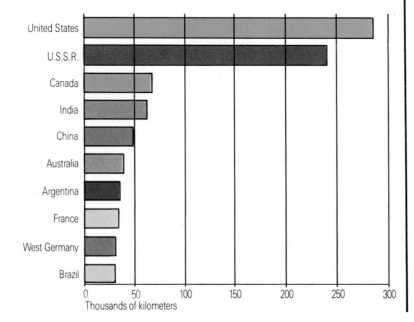

Diagram B: The size of the same 10 countries as shown in Diagram A

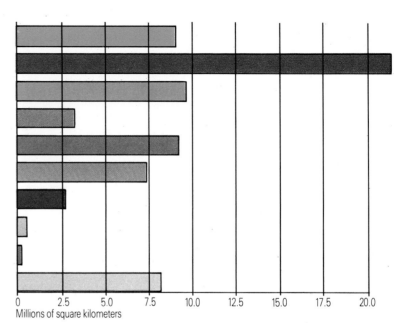

Note: for purposes of International comparison, metric measurements are used.

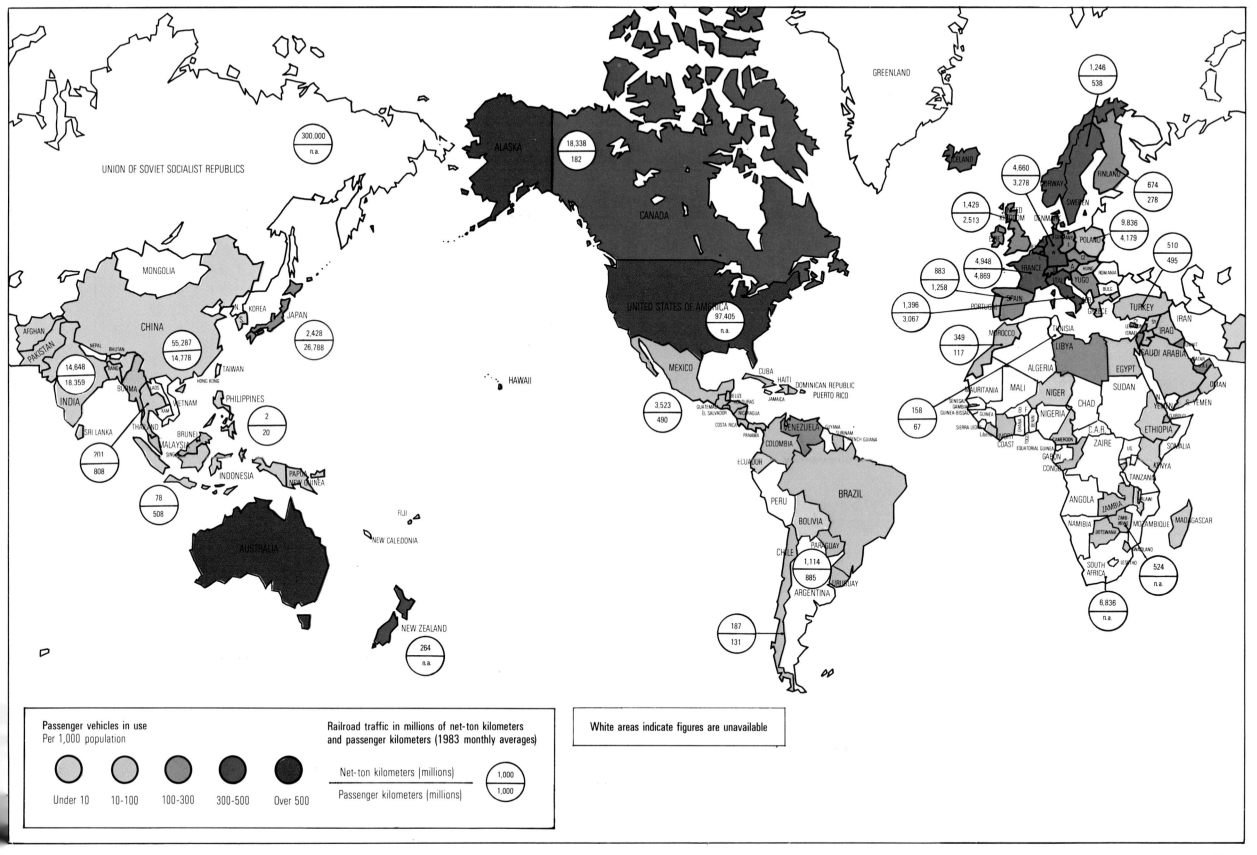

Passenger vehicles in use
Per 1,000 population

Under 10   10-100   100-300   300-500   Over 500

Railroad traffic in millions of net-ton kilometers and passenger kilometers (1983 monthly averages)

Net-ton kilometers (millions)
———————————————
Passenger kilometers (millions)

1,000
———
1,000

White areas indicate figures are unavailable

GREENLAND

UNION OF SOVIET SOCIALIST REPUBLICS

300,000
n.a.

MONGOLIA

N. KOREA

JAPAN
2,428
26,788

AFGHAN
CHINA
55,287
14,778

TAIWAN

HONG KONG

PAKISTAN
NEPAL BHUTAN
BANG

INDIA
14,648
18,359

BURMA
LAOS
VIETNAM
THAILAND
KAM

SRI LANKA

PHILIPPINES
2
20

MALAYSIA
SING

BRUNEI

201
808

INDONESIA

PAPUA
NEW GUINEA

78
508

AUSTRALIA

FIJI

NEW CALEDONIA

NEW ZEALAND
264
n.a.

ALASKA
18,338
182

CANADA

UNITED STATES OF AMERICA
97,405
n.a.

HAWAII

MEXICO
3,523
490

CUBA
HAITI
DOMINICAN REPUBLIC
PUERTO RICO
JAMAICA

BELIZE
GUATEMALA
HONDURAS
EL SALVADOR
NICARAGUA
COSTA RICA
PANAMA

VENEZUELA
GUYANA
SURINAM
FRENCH GUIANA

COLOMBIA

ECUADOR

PERU

BRAZIL

BOLIVIA

PARAGUAY

CHILE

ARGENTINA
1,114
885
URUGUAY

187
131

ICELAND

1,246
538

4,660
3,278
NORWAY
FINLAND
674
278
SWEDEN

1,429
2,513
UNITED KINGDOM
DENMARK
9,836
4,179
POLAND

883
1,258
4,948
4,869
FRANCE
ITALY
YUGO
HUNG
ROMANIA
510
495
BULG

1,396
3,067
PORTUGAL
SPAIN
GREECE
TURKEY
IRAN

349
117
MOROCCO
TUNISIA
LEB
SY
IRAQ
ISRAEL
LIBYA
EGYPT
SAUDI ARABIA
QATAR

ALGERIA
SUDAN
OMAN

158
67
MAURITANIA
MALI
NIGER
CHAD
YEMEN
S. YEMEN
DJIBOUTI

SENEGAL
GAMBIA
GUINEA-BISSAU
GUINEA
SIERRA LEONE
LIBERIA
IVORY COAST
B.F.
GHANA
TOGO
BENIN
NIGERIA
CAMEROON
C.A.R.
EQUATORIAL GUINEA
GABON
CONGO
ZAIRE
UG
ETHIOPIA
SOMALIA
KENYA
TANZANIA

ANGOLA
ZAMBIA
MALAWI
MOZAMBIQUE
MADAGASCAR

NAMIBIA
ZIMB
BOTSWANA
SWAZILAND
SOUTH AFRICA
LESOTHO
524
n.a.

6,836
n.a.

111

WORLD AIR AND SEA TRANSPORT

The ability to transport people and goods efficiently is a prime indicator of economic development. This map shows the extent of civil air traffic and the tonnage of goods shipped and landed by sea.

Air traffic is normally calculated by the number of kilometers in millions that are made both internally and overseas by a nation's citizens. The countries that register between 1,000 and 5,000 million kilometers monthly average (the second largest category) are mainly either major industrialized nations such as France, West Germany, Japan, and Britain, or second-ranked industrialized countries that are very large in size, such as Australia, India and Canada.

The United States is the only country registering over 5,000 million kilometers average a month. With a monthly average of 33,891 million passenger kilometers it accounts for nearly seven times as much passenger transport as its closest rival, Japan. It is natural that large countries such as the United States or Canada should register a high number of passenger kilometers since travel by air is generally the only practicable way to travel. Yet the U.S.S.R. registers only 860 million passenger kilometers a month despite its vast size.

The yellow rafts on the map indicate the average monthly metric tonnage of sea-borne goods loaded and unloaded. This is often a measure of a nation's external trade. Diagrams A and B show how the leading 8 nations for unloaded and loaded tonnage compare. A number of factors, however, must be taken into account when considering the figures. Panama, for instance, only appears in Diagram B because of the huge number of ships registered in that country for financial benefits. The Netherland's figures are boosted partly because it handles the imports and exports of other countries, and partly because it is a major center for refining and re-exporting oil products. On the other hand, the figures for West Germany are lower than might be expected because much of its trade is conducted by road rather than by sea.

The United States comes first and almost achieves an exact balance with a monthly average of 27,314,000 metric tons loaded, and 27,702,000 metric tons unloaded. No figures are available for the U.S.S.R. so comparisons are not possible. However, of the five principal industrial nations after the United States — Japan, West Germany, France, Britain, and Italy — only Britain achieves an approximate balance, with 10,809,000 metric tons loaded and 9,767,000 metric tons unloaded.

Japan shows a relatively small figure for goods loaded — 7,589,000 metric tons a month — but a huge 46,017,000 metric tons a month unloaded, despite the enormous trade imbalance in her favour. This is explained by the nature of Japan's economy: it is geared to importing heavy raw materials, such as iron ore, and exporting relatively light manufactured goods, such as televisions and cameras.

Source: *U.N. Monthly Bulletin of Statistics*

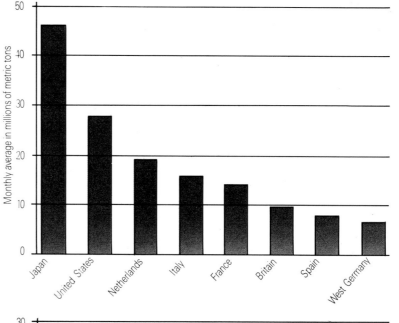

Diagram A: The leading 8 nations in terms of sea-borne imports, 1983, showing monthly averages of unloaded goods

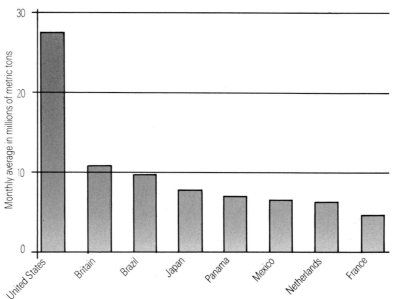

Diagram B: The leading 8 nations in terms of sea-borne exports, 1983, showing monthly averages of loaded goods

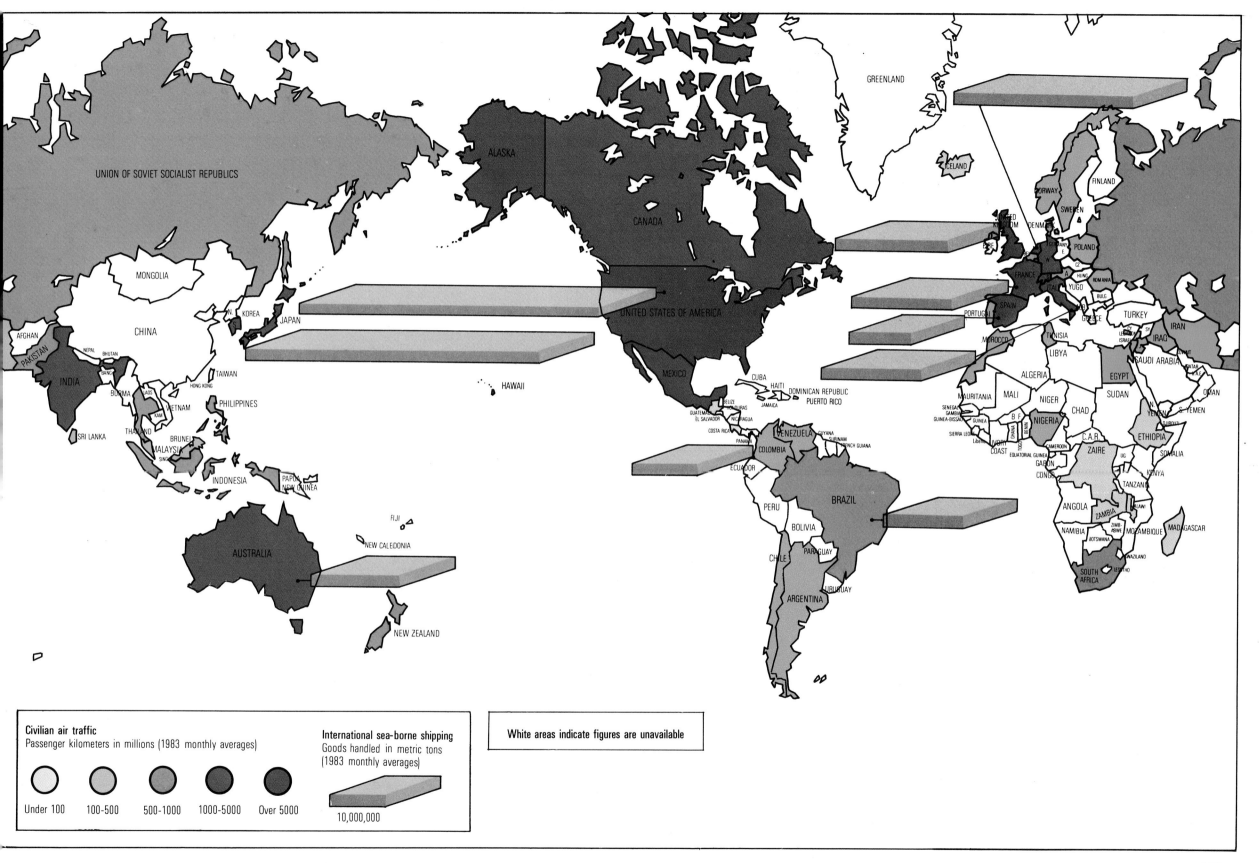

Civilian air traffic
Passenger kilometers in millions (1983 monthly averages)

Under 100   100-500   500-1000   1000-5000   Over 5000

International sea-borne shipping
Goods handled in metric tons
(1983 monthly averages)

10,000,000

White areas indicate figures are unavailable

GREENLAND

UNION OF SOVIET SOCIALIST REPUBLICS

ALASKA

CANADA

MONGOLIA

CHINA

KOREA

JAPAN

TAIWAN

HONG KONG

UNITED STATES OF AMERICA

MEXICO

CUBA
HAITI
DOMINICAN REPUBLIC
PUERTO RICO
JAMAICA

GUATEMALA
BELIZE
HONDURAS
EL SALVADOR
NICARAGUA
COSTA RICA
PANAMA

HAWAII

AFGHAN
PAKISTAN
NEPAL
BHUTAN
INDIA
BANG
BURMA
LAOS
VIETNAM
KAM
PHILIPPINES
THAILAND
SRI LANKA
MALAYSIA
SING
BRUNEI
INDONESIA

PAPUA
NEW GUINEA

FIJI

NEW CALEDONIA

AUSTRALIA

NEW ZEALAND

VENEZUELA
GUYANA
COLOMBIA
SURINAM
FRENCH GUIANA
ECUADOR
PERU
BRAZIL
BOLIVIA
PARAGUAY
CHILE
URUGUAY
ARGENTINA

ICELAND

NORWAY
SWEDEN
FINLAND
UNITED KINGDOM
DENMARK
IRE
GERMANY
POLAND
E
W
CZ
FRANCE
A
H
ROMANIA
YUGO
ITALY
BULG
SPAIN
PORTUGAL
GREECE
TURKEY
IRAN

MOROCCO
TUNISIA
LEB
SY
ISRAEL
IRAQ
KUWAIT
QATAR
U.A.E.
LIBYA
EGYPT
SAUDI ARABIA
OMAN

MAURITANIA
MALI
NIGER
CHAD
SUDAN
YEMEN
S-YEMEN
SENEGAL
GAMBIA
GUINEA-BISSAU
GUINEA
B.F
SIERRA LEONE
IVORY COAST
GHANA
TOGO
BENIN
NIGERIA
C.A.R.
ETHIOPIA
LIBERIA
CAMEROON
EQUATORIAL GUINEA
GABON
CONGO
ZAIRE
UG
SOMALIA
KENYA
TANZANIA
ANGOLA
ZAMBIA
MALAWI
ZIMB
ZIMBABWE
MOZAMBIQUE
MADAGASCAR
NAMIBIA
BOTSWANA
SWAZILAND
LESOTHO
SOUTH AFRICA

113

WORLD COMMUNICATIONS

This map shows the level of communications achieved in three areas: the number of telephones available per 100 of the population in 1981 (see color bands), the circulation of daily newspapers per 1,000 of the population, and the number of television receivers per 1,000 of the population in 1981. Countries left white are not included in the survey.

These are three of the most important indicators of the level of communications enjoyed in a country; a fourth indicator, not shown here, would be the number of radio sets available.

The number of telephones per 100 is an excellent pointer to the degree of technological efficiency (as well as wealth) which a country has attained. Only five countries are shown as having more than 50 telephones per 100 of the population: that is, more than one telephone for every two people. These are the United States, Canada, Sweden, Finland, and New Zealand. Most countries of Western Europe have between 20 and 50 telephones per 100, as do Japan, Israel, and Australia.

Africa is very poorly equipped with telephones. Where information is available, with the single exception of South Africa, all African countries have fewer than 10 and in many cases fewer than 5 telephones per 100 of the population.

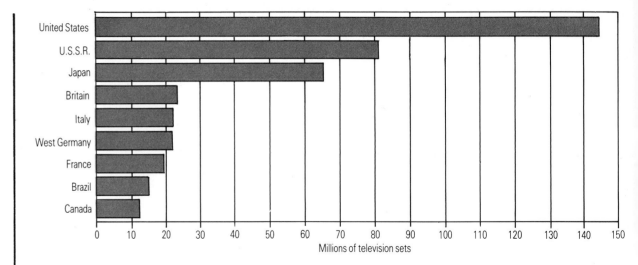

Millions of television sets

Diagram A: Comparison between daily newspaper circulation and television receivers among countries with over 50 telephones per 100 people

Newspapers

Televisions

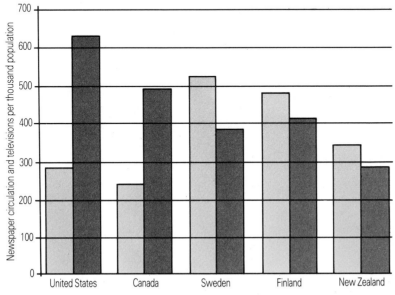

Newspaper circulation and televisions per thousand population

The number inside the symbol for newspapers alongside a country indicates daily circulation of newspapers per 1,000 of the population.

Only two countries shown have a circulation above 500 per 1,000 — Japan (569) and Sweden (526). (No figures are available for Britain but it also has one of the highest circulations in the world.) Two European countries, Finland and West Germany, have a circulation of more than 400 newspapers per 1,000, while the United States has only 282 per 1,000. Even the U.S.S.R. has a higher circulation at 396 per 1,000.

The second symbol alongside countries (a television set) indicates the number of receivers per 1,000. Television availability more than newspapers depends upon economic wealth. Only one country — the United States — has more than 600 sets per 1,000, at 631. At the other end of the scale, no country on the African continent achieves a figure of even 100 television sets per 1,000 of the population.

Diagram A shows how ownership of television receivers compares with the circulation of newspapers in countries with over 50 telephones per 100 people. Both United States and Canada have relatively low circulation figures. Diagram B shows how some 302 million television receivers are shared amongst the 9 countries with the highest total ownership.

Sources: Statistical Office of the United Nations, New York; United Nations Educational, Scientific and Cultural Organization, Paris

Diagram B: Number of television receivers available in 9 leading countries

---

SELECTED COUNTRIES WITH A CIRCULATION OF 300 OR MORE DAILY NEWSPAPERS PER 1,000 POPULATION

Japan	569
Sweden	526
Finland	480
West Germany	423
U.S.S.R.	396
New Zealand	345
Australia	336

SELECTED COUNTRIES WITH 300 OR MORE TELEVISION SETS PER 1,000 POPULATION

United States	631
Japan	551
Canada	489
Finland	414
Britain	411
Italy	390
Sweden	387
Australia	380
France	361
West Germany	348
U.S.S.R.	306

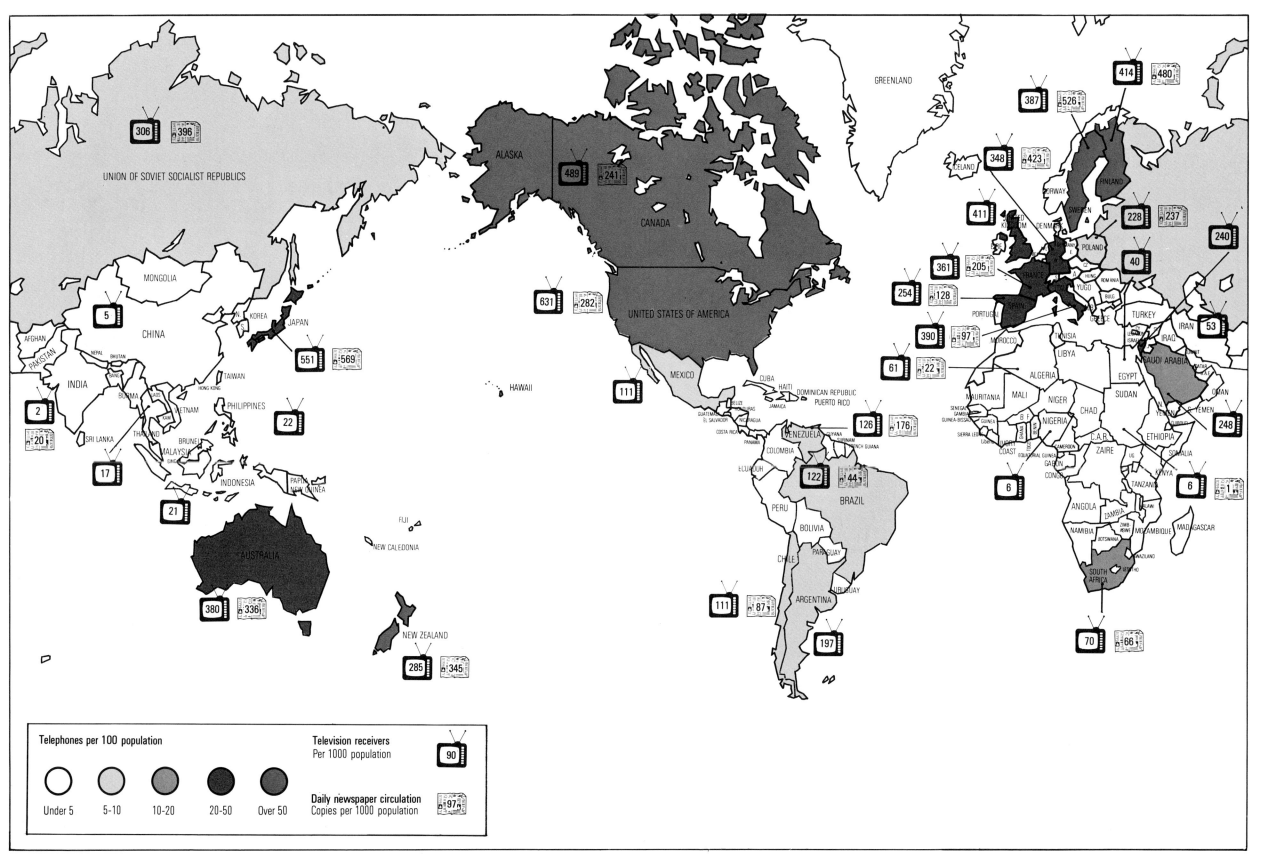

Telephones per 100 population

Television receivers
Per 1000 population

Daily newspaper circulation
Copies per 1000 population

Under 5	5-10	10-20	20-50	Over 50

115

LITERACY AND LEARNING

Diagram A: Distribution of world population, by primary school enrollment ratio, 1982

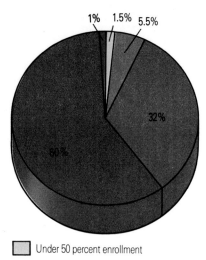

1% 1.5% 5.5%

32%

60%

- ☐ Under 50 percent enrollment
- ☐ 50-75 percent enrollment
- ☐ 75-100 percent enrollment
- ■ 100 percent and over enrollment
- ■ No data

This map shows the levels of education in different countries. The countries are colored according to the percentage enrollment in primary schools of the number of children of primary school age. "Primary school age" usually means from six to eleven years, but countries differ on this criterion. Most of the estimates relate to 1982, but where these are not available, the latest available data are given. The occurrence of percentages greater than 100 might appear surprising, but is easily explained. The enrollment in primary schools often includes children outside the usual primary school age, especially where those who repeat a year, or who started late, are still in primary school although they are over the upper age limit.

For the United States, Japan, the countries of Western Europe, and many others primary education is compulsory for all children. But in many parts of the world this is by no means the case. Diagram A is a pie chart showing the proportions of the world's population living in countries with primary enrollment ratios in the various bands. Although more than half the world falls into the "100 percent and more" band, a large proportion have ratios in the "75 and less than 100" group.

The map also shows two other indices of educational development for different countries: percentage literacy for males and females, and education expenditure as a percentage of GNP. Literacy here means the ability of adults — generally this means 15 years or older — to read and write.

The countries with primary school enrollment ratios of about 100 percent generally show literacy percentages of the same level. In some countries with lower standards of schooling, the difference between male and female literacy percentages is often an indicator of development.

The percentage of GNP spent on education is an interesting statistic. Of the countries shown on the map, Iran and Algeria, at 8.5 and 8.3 percent respectively, rank the highest. They are followed by Canada, with 7.7, and the U.S.S.R. with 7.0. Then comes the United States at 6.9. (The U.S.S.R. figure may not be comparable since "net material produced" is used instead of GNP.)

Diagram B plots some of the largest countries on a graph of primary school enrollment ratios against per capita GNP. Diagram C plots primary and secondary school enrollment. Despite the difficulties of comparison between countries with very different systems of education, the relationship between educational standards and GNP is fairly clear. The countries with low enrollment rates are the poorest ones. China, Indonesia, and Brazil stand out as interesting exceptions.

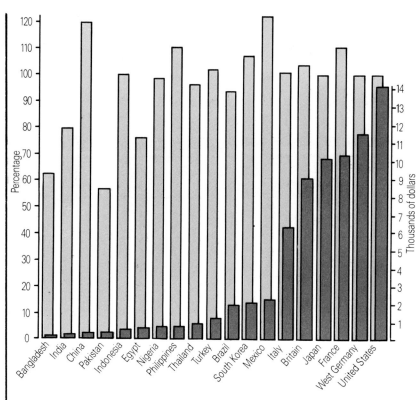

Diagram B: Primary school enrollment (yellow) compared with GNP per capita (brown), 1982

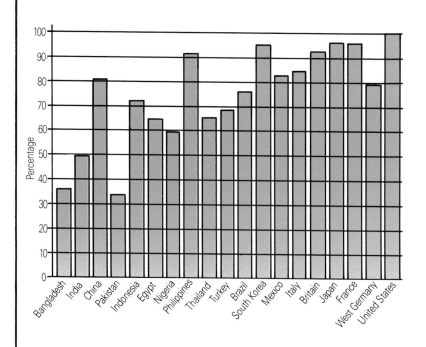

Diagram C: Primary and secondary school enrollment ratio, 1982

Sources: *The World Bank Atlas, 1985;*
UNESCO, *Statistical Yearbook, 1983;*
United Nations, *World Statistics in Brief, 1985;*
UNICEF, *State of the World's Children, 1984*

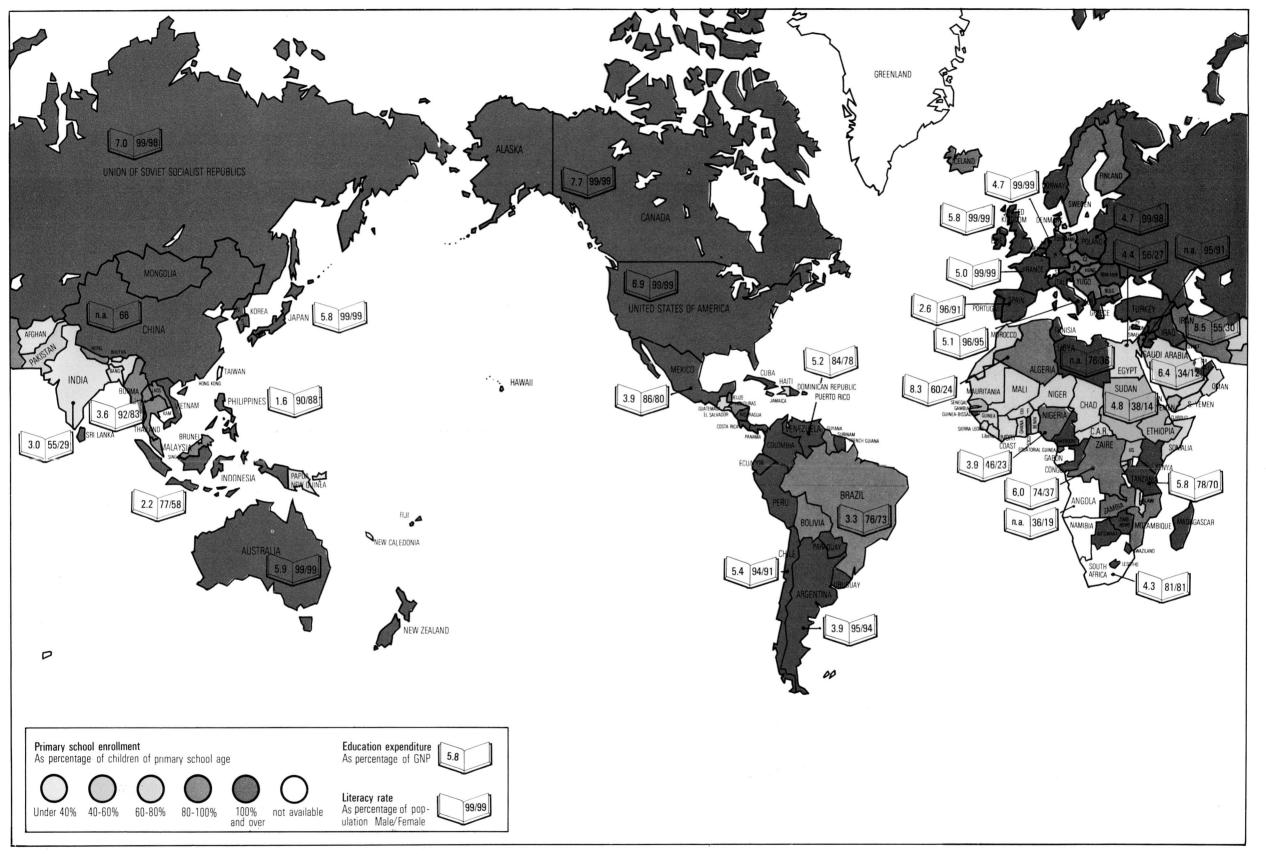

GREENLAND

UNION OF SOVIET SOCIALIST REPUBLICS
7.0 | 99/98

ALASKA

CANADA
7.7 | 99/99

UNITED STATES OF AMERICA
6.9 | 99/99

MONGOLIA

KOREA

JAPAN
5.8 | 99/99

CHINA
n.a. | 66

AFGHAN
PAKISTAN
INDIA
NEPAL BHUTAN
BANG
BURMA
3.6 | 92/83
LAOS
VIETNAM
TAIWAN
HONG KONG
PHILIPPINES
1.6 | 90/88
SRI LANKA
3.0 | 55/29
THAILAND
KAM
MALAYSIA
BRUNEI
SINGA
INDONESIA
PAPUA NEW GUINEA
2.2 | 77/58

HAWAII

MEXICO
3.9 | 86/80

CUBA
HAITI
JAMAICA
DOMINICAN REPUBLIC
PUERTO RICO
5.2 | 84/78

BELIZE
GUATEMALA HONDURAS
EL SALVADOR NICARAGUA
COSTA RICA
PANAMA

VENEZUELA
GUYANA
SURINAM
FRENCH GUIANA
COLOMBIA

ECUADOR
PERU
BRAZIL
3.3 | 76/73
BOLIVIA
PARAGUAY

CHILE
5.4 | 94/91
URUGUAY
ARGENTINA
3.9 | 95/94

FIJI
NEW CALEDONIA

AUSTRALIA
5.9 | 99/99

NEW ZEALAND

ICELAND
NORWAY
FINLAND
4.7 | 99/99
SWEDEN
UNITED KINGDOM
DENMARK
5.8 | 99/99
5.0 | 99/99
FRANCE
POLAND
4.7 | 99/98
4.4 | 56/27
n.a. | 95/91
GERMANY
CZ
HUNG
ROMANIA
YUGO
BULG
ITALY
SPAIN
2.6 | 96/91
PORTUGAL
GREECE
TURKEY
IRAN
8.5 | 55/30
5.1 | 96/95
MOROCCO
TUNISIA
ISRAEL
IRAQ
LEB
SYRIA
JORDAN
8.3 | 60/24
ALGERIA
LIBYA
n.a. | 76/36
EGYPT
SAUDI ARABIA
6.4 | 34/12
KUWAIT
OMAN
MAURITANIA
MALI
NIGER
CHAD
SUDAN
4.8 | 38/14
N. YEMEN
S. YEMEN
SENEGAL
GAMBIA
GUINEA-BISSAU
GUINEA
B F
NIGERIA
SIERRA LEONE
GHANA
IVORY COAST
LIBERIA
TOGO
BENIN
CAMEROON
C.A.R.
ETHIOPIA
SOMALIA
3.9 | 46/23
EQUATORIAL GUINEA
GABON
CONGO
ZAIRE
UG
KENYA
5.8 | 78/70
6.0 | 74/37
TANZANIA
ANGOLA
ZAMBIA
MALAWI
MADAGASCAR
n.a. | 36/19
NAMIBIA
ZIMB
BOTSWANA
MOZAMBIQUE
SWAZILAND
SOUTH AFRICA
LESOTHO
4.3 | 81/81

Primary school enrollment
As percentage of children of primary school age

○ ○ ○ ○ ● ○
Under 40% 40-60% 60-80% 80-100% 100% and over not available

Education expenditure
As percentage of GNP | 5.8 |

Literacy rate
As percentage of population Male/Female | 99/99 |

117

WORLD HEALTH

This map shows the state of world health in 1982. This is most easily measured by two factors: life expectancy at birth, and the availability of physicians in relation to a country's total population.

Countries with a life expectancy of 70 years or more coincide almost exactly with the richest nations of North America — Canada and the United States — and Europe (both Western Europe and the Eastern European countries). In addition, there are other countries such as Australia, New Zealand, Argentina, Chile, the United Arab Emirates, and Japan whose citizens also now enjoy maximum life expectancy.

These are the countries that have the resources to provide the best, most comprehensive medical services for their populations: they have the greatest number of physicians per 100,000 of the population.

There are, of course, other factors that make for good health that are not indicated on the map. These include the availability of pure drinking water, proper sanitation and enough food. But the two indicators used here are sufficient to convey the overall health picture.

Diagram A: Life expectancy at birth of the 10 most populous countries, with blocks for each country proportionate to the size of population

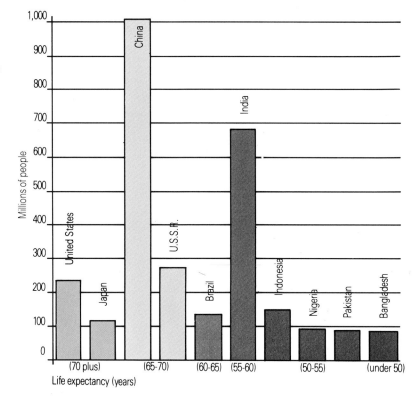

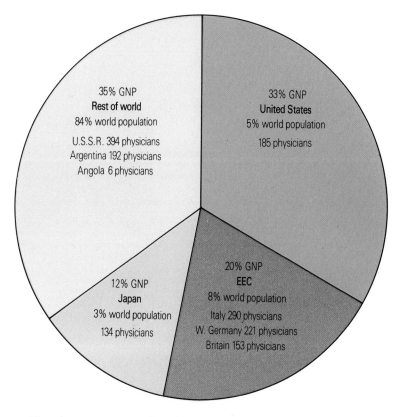

Diagram B: World share of GNP compared with population and physicians per 100,000 people. Selected countries for the EEC and the rest of the world show the range in the number of physicians among the various countries

To give two examples: in Britain there is on average one physician for every 653 people, while in Burkina Faso in West Africa the figure is one to 56,000 people. In India one child in eight dies before reaching its first birthday while the comparable figure for Britain is one child in 82.

It is easy to pick out from the map those countries with the longest life expectancies — they are almost all in North America and Europe — and these also have the most physicians available per 100,000 population.

On the other hand, the world's poorest, least developed regions — most of Africa and parts of Asia and Latin America — have the lowest life expectancy rates at birth and the fewest physicians available per 100,000 of their populations.

Diagram A compares the life expectancy of the 10 most populous nations with the size of each country's population. These countries, whose combined populations account for nearly three-fifths of the total world population, provide a good indication of the strides medicine has achieved in recent years. In economic terms it is not surprising to find the United States and Japan at the top end of the list. More interesting is the fact that China, with nearly four times the population of the U.S.S.R. and far less developed, nevertheless has the same life expectancy figure as the U.S.S.R.

Source: *The World Bank Atlas, 1985*

Note: Physicians are persons who are graduates of a medical school or faculty actually working in the country in any medical field (practice, teaching, administration, research, laboratory etc.)

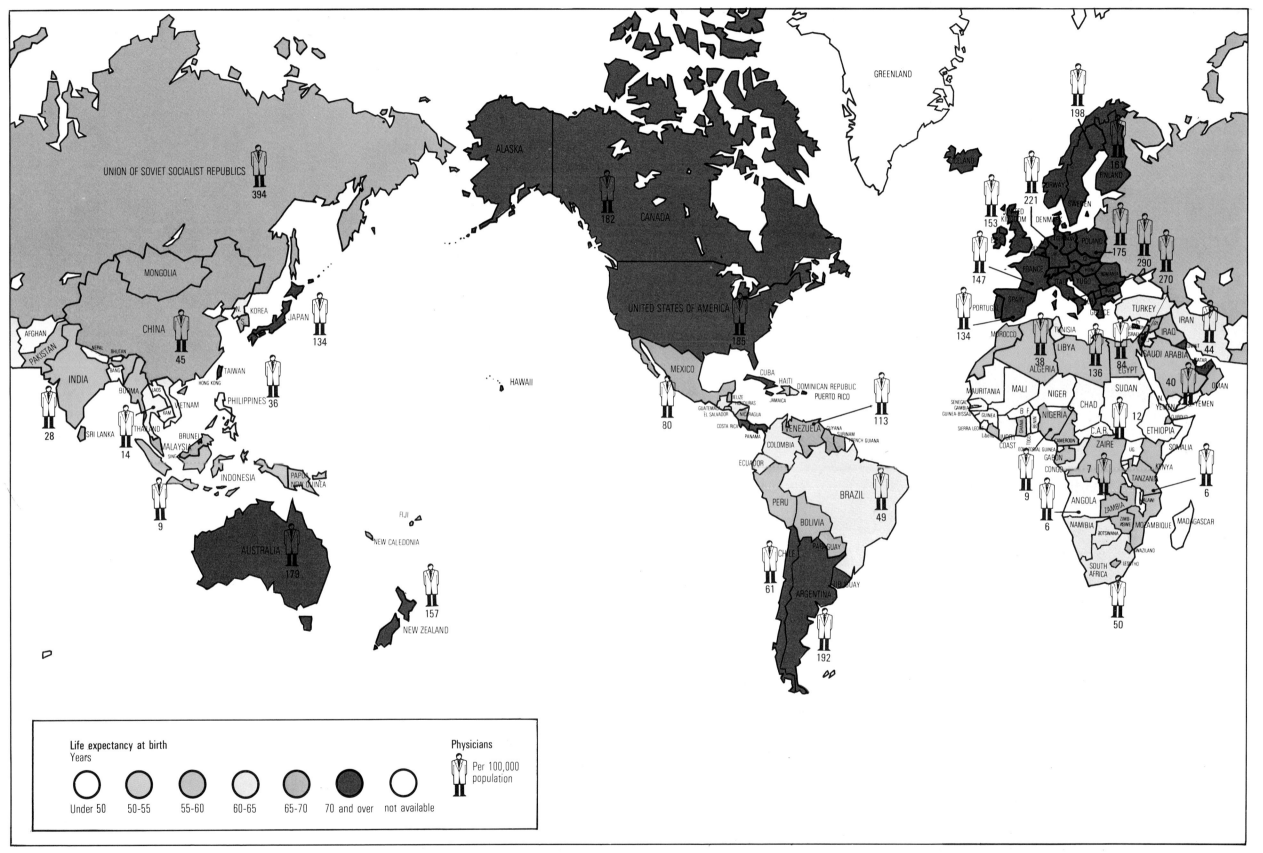

Life expectancy at birth
Years

Under 50 | 50–55 | 55–60 | 60–65 | 65–70 | 70 and over | not available

Physicians
Per 100,000 population

WORLD DEVELOPMENT

This map illustrates the relative positions of different countries on the path of social and economic development. Countries are colored according to the percentage of the population living in urban areas in 1980.

In the United States, this percentage is 77, and in some Western European countries it is even higher, for example, 91 percent in the United Kingdom. In many countries of Africa and Asia, on the other hand, the percentage is low.

The map also shows the percentages of males and females who are classified as "economically active" in some countries. Although the percentage for males does not vary very much, that for females is related to the general level of development. The figure for the U.S.S.R. is a combined figure for males and females. The figure for China is not available.

The diagram below brings together several indicators of development. Nineteen countries are ranked from left to right in order of their per capita GNP, and this quantity is represented by the height of the colored bar.

Also shown are the percentage of the labor force engaged in agriculture, the average life expectancy at birth, the number of passenger vehicles per 1,000 population, the per capita dietary energy supplies as a percentage of requirements, the percentage illiteracy, and the population per physician. Most of these refer to 1982, but some countries can only provide estimates for earlier years for some indicators.

Sources: UNICEF, *The State of the World's Children;*
United Nations, *World Statistics in Brief, 1983;*
The World Bank Atlas, 1985

Diagram A: GNP per capita for selected countries, plus six other indicators of development, including life expectancy and illiteracy

Country	Percentage of labor force engaged in agriculture	Passenger vehicles per thousand population	Per capita dietary energy supplies as a percentage of requirements	Population per physician	Life expectancy at birth (years)	Illiteracy as a percentage of adult population
Bangladesh	74%	0.5	85%	7,101	48	69%
India	70%	1.6	86%	3,586	55	58%
China	74%	0.2	107%	2,225	67	34%
Pakistan	60%	4	100%	4,658	50	72%
Indonesia	66%	5	108%	11,740	53	33%
Egypt	50%	10	117%	1,186	57	58%
Nigeria	56%	1.6	100%	11,330	50	66%
Philippines	47%	9	103%	2,793	64	11%
Thailand	76%	7	104%	7,215	63	13%
Turkey	61%	16	120%	1,648	63	36%
Brazil	36%	70	106%	2,028	64	25%
South Korea	30%	6	127%	1,693	67	8%
Mexico	41%	61	120%	1,251	65	17%
Italy	15%	311	148%	345	74	5%
Britain	1.5%	285	132%	654	74	0%
Japan	11%	209	n.a.	761	77	0%
France	9%	356	134%	580	75	0%
West Germany	6%	377	133%	452	73	0%
United States	4%	520	139%	542	75	0%

GNP per capita in U.S. dollars

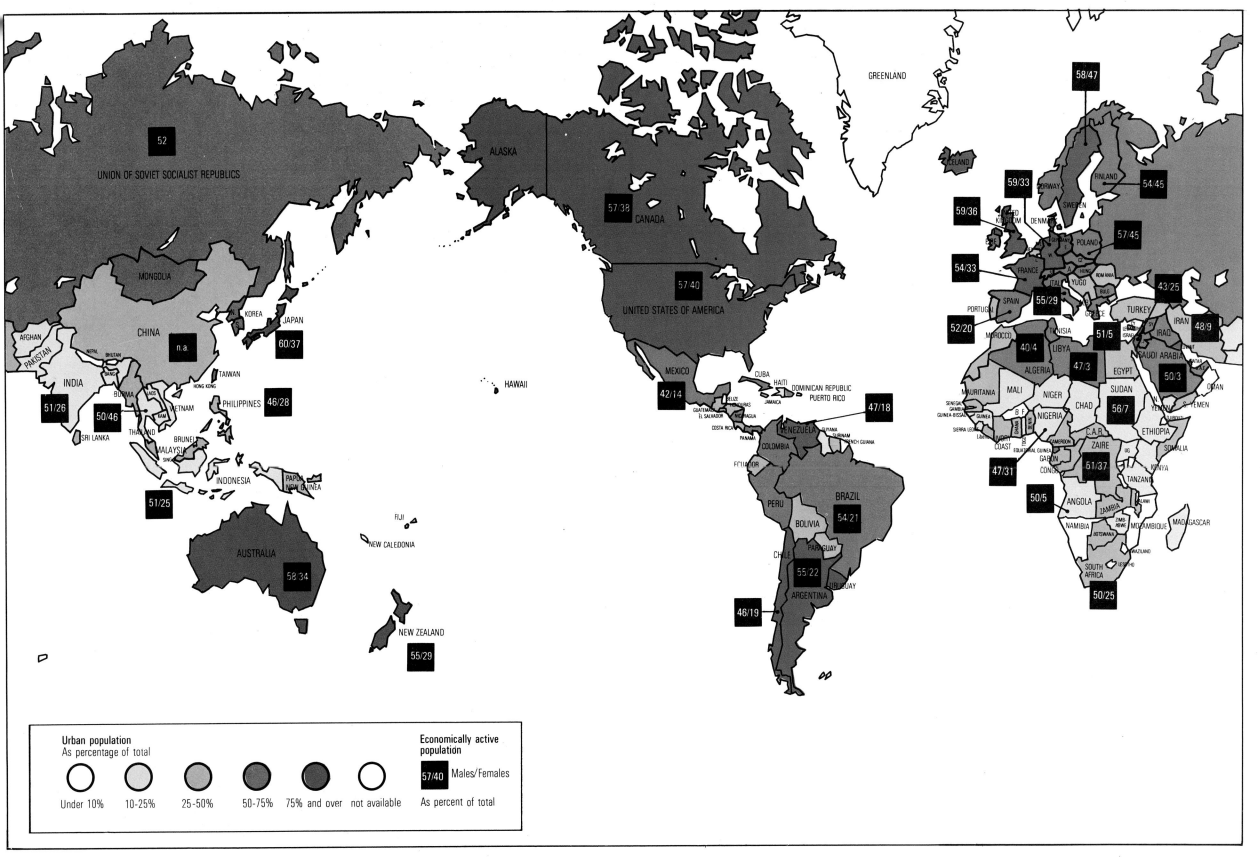

GREENLAND

58/47

52
UNION OF SOVIET SOCIALIST REPUBLICS

59/33
NORWAY
FINLAND
54/45

59/36
UNITED KINGDOM
DENMARK
SWEDEN
57/45
POLAND

ALASKA

57/38
CANADA

54/33
FRANCE
GERMANY
55/29
ITALY
YUGO
ROMANIA
BULG
GREECE
43/25
TURKEY

MONGOLIA

KOREA

JAPAN
60/37

AFGHAN
PAKISTAN
NEPAL
BHUTAN
CHINA
n.a.
TAIWAN
HONG KONG

52/20
PORTUGAL
SPAIN
MOROCCO
40/4
ALGERIA
47/3
LIBYA
51/5
SAUDI ARABIA
IRAN
48/9
IRAQ
KUWAIT
QATAR
50/3
OMAN

UNITED STATES OF AMERICA

57/40

INDIA
51/26
BURMA
50/46
VIETNAM
THAILAND
PHILIPPINES
46/28

SRI LANKA
MALAYSIA
SINGAPORE
BRUNEI

MEXICO
42/14
CUBA
HAITI
DOMINICAN REPUBLIC
PUERTO RICO
BELIZE
GUATEMALA
HONDURAS
JAMAICA
EL SALVADOR
NICARAGUA
COSTA RICA
PANAMA

MAURITANIA
MALI
NIGER
CHAD
SUDAN
56/7
EGYPT
YEMEN
S. YEMEN
DJIBOUTI

SENEGAL
GAMBIA
GUINEA-BISSAU
GUINEA
SIERRA LEONE
LIBERIA
IVORY COAST
GHANA
TOGO
B F
NIGERIA
BENIN
CAMEROON
EQUATORIAL GUINEA
GABON
CONGO
C.A.R.
ZAIRE
61/37
UG
ETHIOPIA
SOMALIA
KENYA
TANZANIA

47/31

50/5
ANGOLA
ZAMBIA
ZIMBABWE
MALAWI
MOZAMBIQUE
MADAGASCAR

INDONESIA
PAPUA NEW GUINEA

51/25

FIJI
NEW CALEDONIA

AUSTRALIA
58/34

VENEZUELA
47/18
GUYANA
SURINAM
FRENCH GUIANA
COLOMBIA
ECUADOR

PERU
BRAZIL
54/21
BOLIVIA

NAMIBIA
BOTSWANA
SOUTH AFRICA
SWAZILAND
LESOTHO
50/25

CHILE
PARAGUAY
55/22
URUGUAY
ARGENTINA
46/19

HAWAII

NEW ZEALAND
55/29

Urban population
As percentage of total

○ Under 10% ○ 10-25% ○ 25-50% ● 50-75% ● 75% and over ○ not available

Economically active population

57/40 Males/Females

As percent of total

121

ALLIANCES AND ASSOCIATIONS

This map shows the world's most important alliances and associations. These fall into several categories, the main ones being military alliances such as the North Atlantic Treaty Organization (NATO) and economic groupings such as the European Economic Community (EEC). There are also associations of like-minded states such as the Organization of American States (OAS) and the Arab League.

The United States belongs to 3 of the groupings illustrated on the map: NATO, ANZUS and the OAS. The most important of these for the United States is NATO, the principal military alliance of the West, which was formed in 1949 to combat the growing military threat posed by the Soviet dominated communist bloc. The Warsaw Pact, which was formed in 1955, is the communist military alliance opposed to NATO.

The United States also has a military alliance with Australia and New Zealand (ANZUS) for mutual security in the Pacific region.

The United States does not belong to any of the world's economic groupings; with a GNP equivalent to 33 percent of the total world GNP, U.S. wealth is half as much again as that of the EEC (see Diagram A). The EEC is the world's most powerful economic grouping, yet the combined GNP of its member countries comes to only 20 percent of total world GNP. Diagram A shows the size of the U.S. economy in relation to other world groupings. This should be taken into account when considering Diagram B. This shows the percentage of GDP spent on defense by the United States and its principal allies compared with the percentage spent by the U.S.S.R.

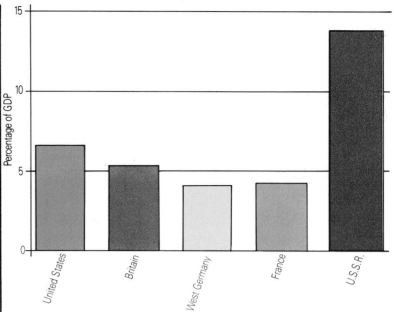

Diagram B: The percentage of GDP spent on defense by the United States and its principal allies compared with the percentage spent by the U.S.S.R. in 1984

Other systems shown on the map include the Council for Mutual Economic Assistance (COMECON) and the European Free Trade Association (EFTA) which are both economic groupings, the former covering the communist economies, the latter covering smaller countries in Europe that remain outside the EEC. The Organization of Petroleum Exporting Countries (OPEC) is really an international cartel to control the selling price of its members' oil.

There are other associations and alliance systems not shown on the map. The most important of these are: the Commonwealth of Nations, the Organization of African Unity (OAU), and the Association of Southeast Asian Nations (ASEAN).

Diagram A: The U.S. share of world GNP in comparison with the EEC, Japan and the rest of the world

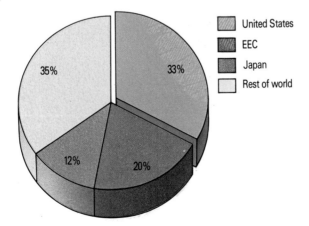

- United States
- EEC
- Japan
- Rest of world

ECONOMIC GROUPINGS

EEC	COMECON	OPEC
Belgium	Bulgaria	Algeria
Britain	Cuba	Ecuador
Denmark	Czechoslovakia	Gabon
France	East Germany	Indonesia
Greece	Hungary	Iran
Ireland	Mongolia	Iraq
Italy	Poland	Kuwait
Luxembourg	Romania	Libya
Netherlands	U.S.S.R.	Nigeria
Portugal	Vietnam	Qatar
Spain	Yugoslavia	Saudi Arabia
West Germany		United Arab Emirates
		Venezuela

MILITARY ALLIANCES

NATO	Warsaw Pact
Belgium	Bulgaria
Britain	Czechoslovakia
Canada	East Germany
Denmark	Hungary
France	Poland
West Germany	Romania
Greece	U.S.S.R.
Iceland	
Italy	**ANZUS**
Luxembourg	Australia
Netherlands	New Zealand
Norway	United States
Portugal	
Spain	
Turkey	
United States	

GREENLAND

ALASKA

CANADA

UNITED STATES OF AMERICA

HAWAII

MEXICO

CUBA
HAITI
DOMINICAN REPUBLIC
PUERTO RICO
BELIZE
GUATEMALA HONDURAS JAMAICA
EL SALVADOR NICARAGUA
COSTA RICA
PANAMA
VENEZUELA GUYANA
COLOMBIA SURINAM
FRENCH GUIANA
ECUADOR

PERU BRAZIL

BOLIVIA

CHILE PARAGUAY

ARGENTINA URUGUAY

UNION OF SOVIET SOCIALIST REPUBLICS

MONGOLIA

CHINA

KOREA JAPAN

AFGHAN
PAKISTAN
NEPAL BHUTAN
INDIA
BANG TAIWAN
BURMA HONG KONG
LAOS
VIETNAM PHILIPPINES
THAILAND KAM
SRI LANKA BRUNEI
MALAYSIA
INDONESIA PAPUA NEW GUINEA

FIJI
NEW CALEDONIA

AUSTRALIA

NEW ZEALAND

ICELAND

NORWAY FINLAND
SWEDEN
UNITED KINGDOM DENMARK
EIRE POLAND
FRANCE
ITALY YUGO
PORTUGAL SPAIN GREECE TURKEY IRAN
MOROCCO TUNISIA IRAQ
ALGERIA LIBYA SAUDI ARABIA OMAN
EGYPT
MAURITANIA MALI NIGER SUDAN YEMEN S YEMEN
SENEGAL CHAD
GAMBIA NIGERIA C.A.R. ETHIOPIA
GUINEA-BISSAU GUINEA
SIERRA LEONE IVORY CAMEROON ZAIRE SOMALIA
LIBERIA COAST EQUATORIAL GUINEA KENYA
GABON CONGO TANZANIA
ANGOLA ZAMBIA MOZAMBIQUE MADAGASCAR
ZIMBABWE
NAMIBIA BOTSWANA SWAZILAND
SOUTH LESOTHO
AFRICA

Alliances and associations membership

European Economic Community

European Free Trade Association

Council for Mutual Economic Assistance (COMECON)

Arab League

Organization of American States

North Atlantic Treaty Organization

Warsaw Treaty Organization

ANZUS

123

TOP TEN: LEADING MILITARY SPENDERS, 1982
(millions of dollars)

	Amount $m	% GNP
U.S.S.R	257,000	15.0
United States	196,345	6.4
China	49,500	7.1
Britain	27,368	5.1
France	25,618	4.2
Saudi Arabia	24,754	15.4
West Germany	24,351	3.4
Poland	13,494	7.2
Japan	12,159	1.0
Iraq	11,689	46.4

MILITARY EXPENDITURE BY THE NATO POWERS, 1982
(millions of dollars)

United States	196,345
Britain	27,368
France	25,612
West Germany	24,351
Italy	9,778
Canada	6,139
Netherlands	4,755
Spain	4,123
Belgium	3,507
Turkey	3,375
Greece	2,782
Norway	1,823
Denmark	1,575
Portugal	900
Total	**312,433**

Diagram A: Share of military expenditure by the NATO powers, in millions of U.S. dollars (figures for all members are listed above)

MILITARY EXPENDITURE

This map shows national levels of military expenditure in 1982. The total amount spent on the military establishment is related to two principal factors: the total number of the armed forces that have to be serviced, and the sophistication and range of weapons with which they are supplied.

When comparing the United States with the U.S.S.R., therefore, account must be taken of the fact that the U.S.S.R. currently maintains 4.4 million military personnel while the United States maintains some 2.1 million personnel. Consequently, although Soviet expenditure (1982) comes to $257,000 million, while U.S. expenditure only reaches $196,000 million, the U.S.S.R. has to pay for twice as many military personnel before finances can be used for weapons. The result is that for less money spent the United States may still devote a greater amount to providing and developing more sophisticated weapons.

The United States plus all its NATO allies, including Britain, France, West Germany, Canada, and Italy, together spend about $12,000 million more than the U.S.S.R. and its Warsaw Pact allies. As can be seen from Diagram A, the United States contributes just under two-thirds of the total NATO expenditure. Britain, France and West Germany account for just under one-quarter, and the remaining NATO powers make up the balance. Diagram B shows that the U.S.S.R. carries proportionately a far larger share of the total Warsaw Pact expenditure than does the United States within NATO.

Several other countries (not in NATO or the Warsaw Pact) have very high military expenditures. These include China, Iran and Iraq (since the Gulf War which began in 1980), Japan (although its expenditure is only a small amount when related to its total GNP), and Saudi Arabia. The ten highest spenders in 1982 were (in millions of dollars):

China	49,500
Japan	12,159
Iraq	11,689
Iran*	7,140
India	6,223
Israel	5,838
South Korea	4,783
Australia	4,415
Sweden	3,878
South Africa	3,161

*Figure given is for 1981

A number of countries are extremely high spenders when their military budget is calculated as a percentage of their GNP. These include Bulgaria (10 percent), Israel (25.5 percent), North Korea (21.6 percent), Oman (28.5 percent), and Syria (14.4 percent).

Source: U.S. Arms Control and Disarmament Agency, *World Military Expenditures and Arms Transfers*

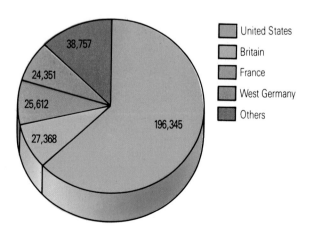

☐	United States
☐	Britain
☐	France
☐	West Germany
☐	Others

38,757 / 24,351 / 25,612 / 27,368 / 196,345

Diagram B: Share of military expenditure by the Warsaw Pact powers, in millions of U.S. dollars (figures for all members are listed below)

MILITARY EXPENDITURE BY THE WARSAW PACT POWERS, 1982
(millions of dollars)

U.S.S.R.	257,000
Poland	13,494
East Germany	10,236
Czechoslovakia	7,634
Romania	4,790
Bulgaria	3,761
Hungary	3,108
Total	**300,023**

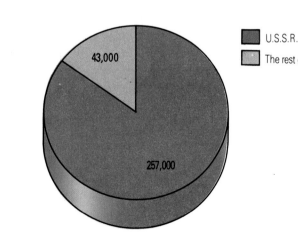

43,000 / 257,000

☐	U.S.S.R.
☐	The rest of the Warsaw Pact

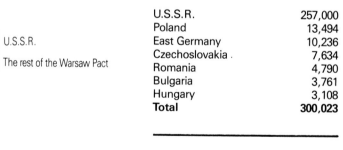

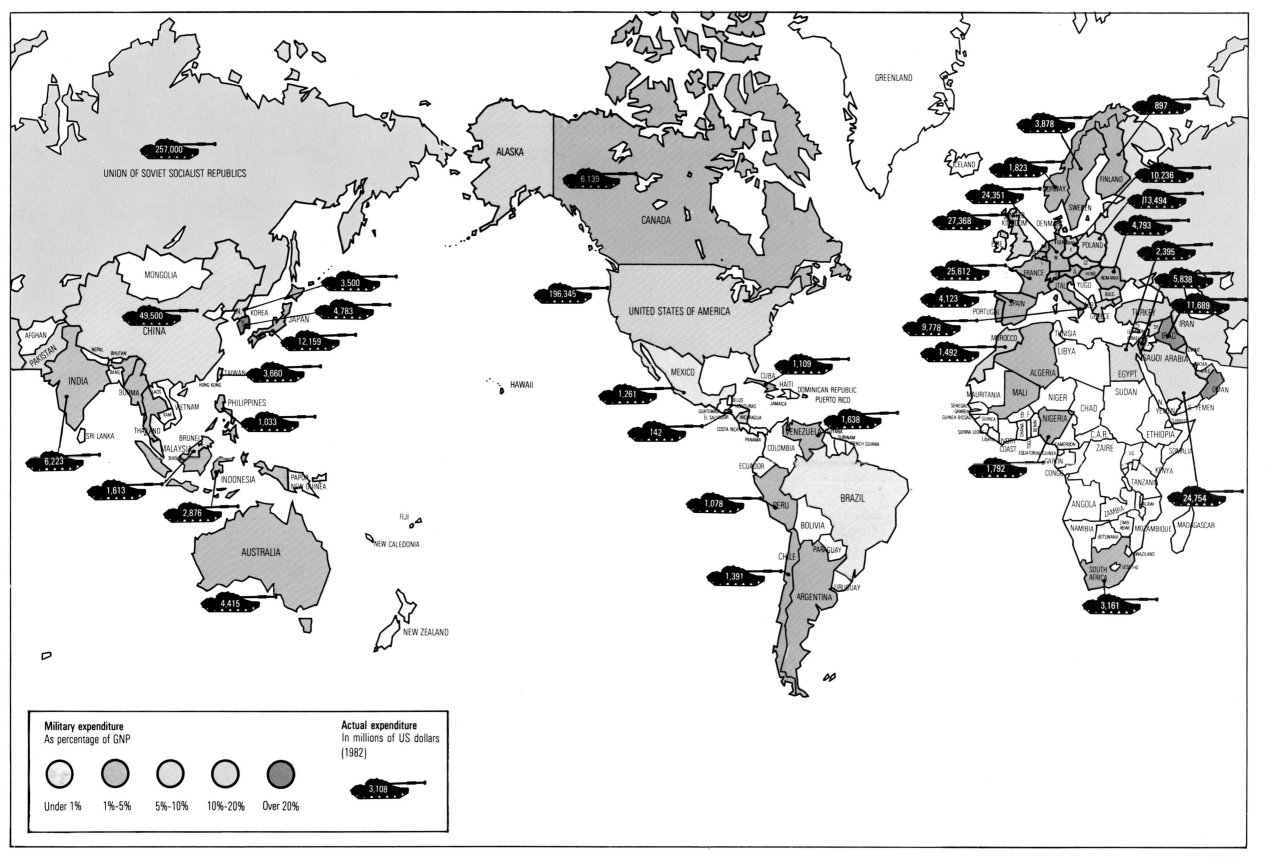

GREENLAND

UNION OF SOVIET SOCIALIST REPUBLICS

ALASKA

CANADA

UNITED STATES OF AMERICA

MONGOLIA

257,000

3,500

49,500
CHINA

4,783

12,159

AFGHAN

PAKISTAN

NEPAL BHUTAN

KOREA

JAPAN

TAIWAN

3,660

INDIA

BANG

BURMA

LAOS

HONG KONG

VIETNAM

KAM

THAILAND

SRI LANKA

PHILIPPINES

BRUNEI

MALAYSIA

SING

6,223

INDONESIA

PAPUA
NEW GUINEA

1,613

2,876

FIJI

NEW CALEDONIA

AUSTRALIA

4,415

NEW ZEALAND

196,345

MEXICO

1,109

CUBA

HAITI

DOMINICAN REPUBLIC

PUERTO RICO

JAMAICA

1,261

BELIZE

GUATEMALA
EL SALVADOR

HONDURAS

NICARAGUA

COSTA RICA

PANAMA

142

VENEZUELA

1,638

GUYANA

SURINAM

FRENCH GUIANA

COLOMBIA

ECUADOR

PERU

1,078

BRAZIL

BOLIVIA

PARAGUAY

CHILE

1,391

URUGUAY

ARGENTINA

HAWAII

ICELAND

1,823

NORWAY

SWEDEN

FINLAND

3,878

897

10,236

24,351

113,494

U.K.

KINGDOM

DENMARK

27,368

E GERMANY

W GERMANY

POLAND

4,793

CZ

2,395

25,612

FRANCE

AUS

HUNG

ROMANIA

BULG

5,838

4,123

PORTUGAL

SPAIN

ITALY

YUGO

GREECE

TURKEY

11,689

IRAN

9,778

MOROCCO

TUNISIA

ALGERIA

LIBYA

EGYPT

IRAQ

SAUDI ARABIA

KUWAIT

QATAR

1,492

MAURITANIA

MALI

NIGER

CHAD

SUDAN

YEMEN

OMAN

YEMEN

DJIBOUTI

SENEGAL

GAMBIA

GUINEA-BISSAU

GUINEA

SIERRA LEONE

Liberia

IVORY
COAST

B F

BENIN

TOGO

GHANA

NIGERIA

C.A.R.

ETHIOPIA

SOMALIA

1,792

EQUATORIAL GUINEA

GABON

CAMEROON

CONGO

ZAIRE

UG

KENYA

TANZANIA

24,754

ANGOLA

ZAMBIA

MALAWI

MOZAMBIQUE

MADAGASCAR

NAMIBIA

ZIMB
ABWE

BOTSWANA

SWAZILAND

SOUTH
AFRICA

LESOTHO

3,161

6,139

Military expenditure
As percentage of GNP

Actual expenditure
In millions of US dollars
(1982)

Under 1%   1%-5%   5%-10%   10%-20%   Over 20%

3,108

125

MILITARY MIGHT

This map shows the ratio of military personnel to total population for each country. Countries are banded (see key) according to the number of military personnel per 1,000 of the population in 1982.

Canada, for example, has less than 5 people per 1,000 in its armed forces and these only amount to 82,000 personnel altogether. Yet the sophistication of weaponry makes Canada an important member of NATO and militarily far more effective than some countries with far higher numbers in their services.

China also has less than 5 people per 1,000 in her armed forces yet these still amount to 4,490,000 because of the enormous size of the Chinese population.

The United States falls into the second category on the map, with 9.1 people per 1,000 in the armed forces and has a total of 2,108,000 men in its services. The U.S.S.R. falls into the fourth category on the map, with 16.3 per 1,000 of the population in the armed forces, which in its case comes to 4,400,000 personnel, double the figure for the United States.

Comparisons, however, are not easy to make. The U.S.S.R., with armed forces totaling approximately the same as China, has only a quarter of China's population from which to recruit them. Britain has 322,000 in its military services, while Ethiopia has 250,000. However, any comparison between the two makes little sense since Britain is one of the world's leading nations in its ability to produce the sophisticated weaponry with which its forces are equipped.

A number of factors have to be considered when assessing military might. The first is the actual size of the armed forces; the second is the size of the total population from which reinforcements may be drawn; the third factor consists of the level of sophistication of available military equipment and the training

in its use. A small army which is properly trained and which is equipped with the most up-to-date weapons can defeat a much larger army that is badly trained and ill-equipped.

Finally, there is the question of nuclear weapons. Only four countries possess strategic missiles (intercontinental and submarine-launched ballistic missiles): the United States and the U.S.S.R., which are in a class of their own, and Britain and France. But even Britain and France, with relatively tiny nuclear arsenals, have devastating "kill" power. China does have a nuclear strike force but delivery depends upon medium range bombers and medium range ballistic missiles.

Diagrams A and B are pie charts showing the share of military personnel by NATO and the Warsaw Pact respectively. As can be seen, whereas the United States provides approximately two-fifths of the total NATO manpower, the U.S.S.R. contributes four-fifths of personnel to the Warsaw Pact.

Source: U.S. Arms Control and Disarmament Agency, *World Military Expenditures and Arms Transfers*

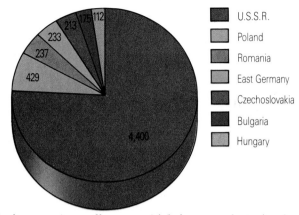

Diagram B: Warsaw Pact shares of military personnel, in thousands of men

U.S.S.R.
Poland
Romania
East Germany
Czechoslovakia
Bulgaria
Hungary

TOP MILITARY POWERS ACCORDING TO NUMBERS IN ARMED FORCES

China	4,490,000
U.S.S.R.	4,400,000
United States	2,108,000
Vietnam	1,200,000
India	1,120,000
North Korea	710,000
Turkey	638,000
South Korea	600,000
Iraq	517,000
France	485,000
West Germany	480,000
Pakistan	478,000
Iran	470,000
Taiwan	464,000
Brazil	460,000
Poland	429,000
Italy	391,000
Spain	353,000
Britain	322,000

Diagram A: NATO shares of military personnel, in thousands of men

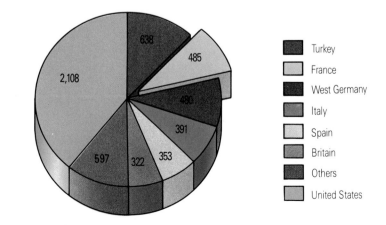

Turkey
France
West Germany
Italy
Spain
Britain
Others
United States

Note: Although France has adopted an independent policy and does not allow NATO forces to be stationed on its territory for the purpose of Western defence it may be considered a full member of NATO.

COMPARATIVE NUCLEAR STRENGTHS
(launchers/warheads are given under each heading)

	Strategic missiles		Intermediate missiles
	Land-based (ICBM)	Sea-launched (SLBM)	land-based
United States	1045/2145	568/5152	41/?
U.S.S.R.	1398/5654	980/2688	599/1320
Britain	—	64/192	—
France	—	80/80	18/18

(Figures are for August 1983; they exclude tactical and aircraft-borne nuclear weapons)

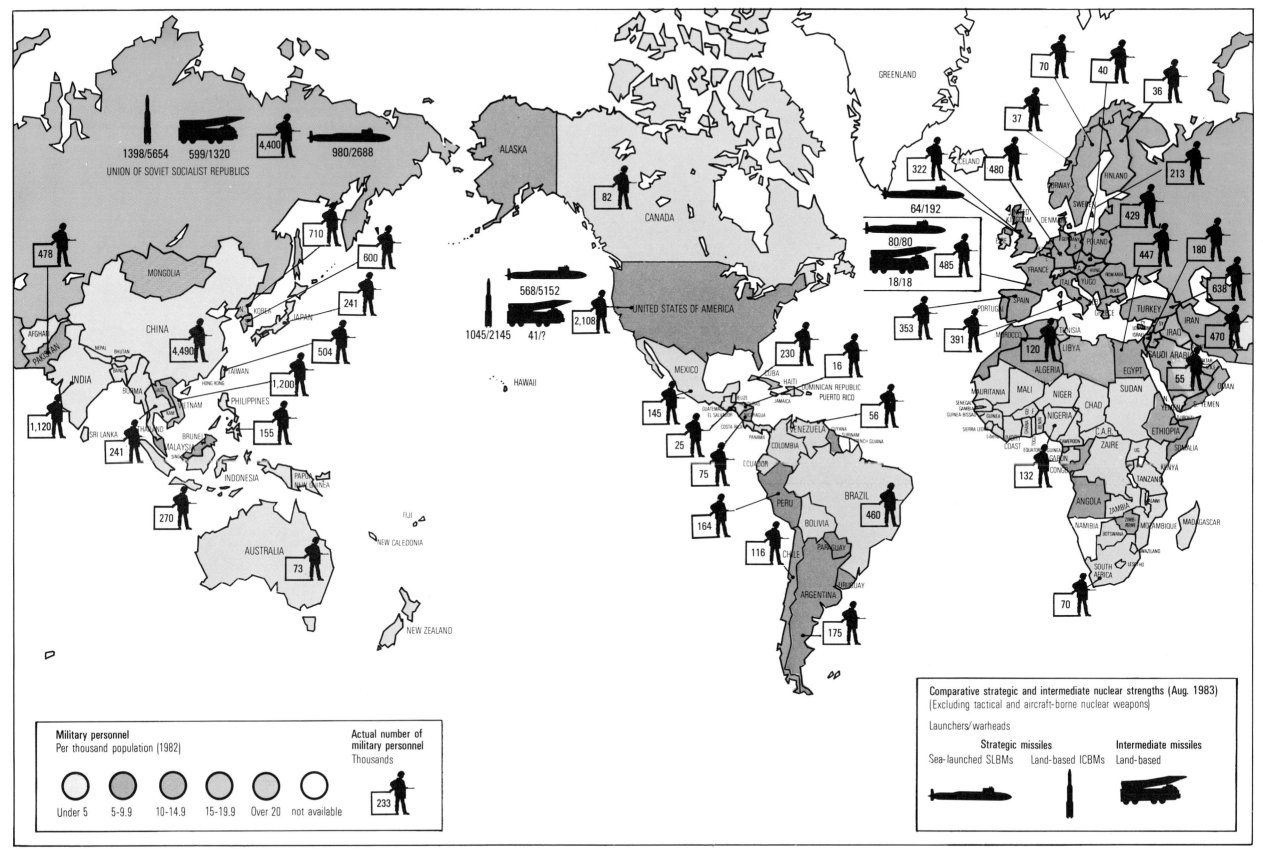

UNION OF SOVIET SOCIALIST REPUBLICS
1398/5654   599/1320   4,400   980/2688

ALASKA
82   CANADA

GREENLAND

70   40   36
37
322   ICELAND   480   213
NORWAY   FINLAND
64/192   SWEDEN   429
80/80   485   UNITED   DENMARK
18/18   KINGDOM   POLAND   447   180
FRANCE   ITALY   YUGO   638
353   SPAIN   GREECE   TURKEY
391   PORTUGAL   MOROCCO   TUNISIA   IRAN   470
120   ALGERIA   LIBYA   EGYPT   SAUDI ARABIA   55
MAURITANIA   MALI   NIGER   CHAD   SUDAN   OMAN
SENEGAL   GAMBIA   YEMEN   S. YEMEN
GUINEA-BISSAU   GUINEA   B F   NIGERIA   DJIBOUTI
SIERRA LEONE   Liberia   IVORY COAST   GHANA   BENIN   CAMEROON   C.A.R.   ETHIOPIA   SOMALIA
132   EQUATORIAL GUINEA   GABON   CONGO   ZAIRE   KENYA
TANZANIA
ANGOLA   ZAMBIA   MALAWI   MOZAMBIQUE   MADAGASCAR
NAMIBIA   ZIMBABWE   BOTSWANA   SWAZILAND
SOUTH AFRICA   LESOTHO
70

710
600
478   MONGOLIA   241
CHINA   504
AFGHAN   4,490   KOREA   JAPAN
PAKISTAN   NEPAL   BHUTAN   TAIWAN   1,200
INDIA   BANG   HONG KONG
1,120   BURMA   VIETNAM   PHILIPPINES
SRI LANKA   THAILAND   CAM   155
241   MALAYSIA   BRUNEI
SINGA
INDONESIA   PAPUA NEW GUINEA
270
FIJI
NEW CALEDONIA
AUSTRALIA   73
NEW ZEALAND

UNITED STATES OF AMERICA
568/5152
1045/2145   41/?   2,108
230
16
MEXICO   CUBA   HAITI
145   BELIZE   DOMINICAN REPUBLIC
GUATEMALA   JAMAICA   PUERTO RICO   56
HAWAII   EL SALVADOR   HONDURAS
NICARAGUA
25   COSTA RICA   VENEZUELA   GUYANA
PANAMA   SURINAM
COLOMBIA   FRENCH GUIANA
75   ECUADOR
PERU   BRAZIL
164   BOLIVIA   460
116   CHILE   PARAGUAY
ARGENTINA   URUGUAY
175

Comparative strategic and intermediate nuclear strengths (Aug. 1983)
(Excluding tactical and aircraft-borne nuclear weapons)

Launchers/warheads

Strategic missiles		Intermediate missiles
Sea-launched SLBMs	Land-based ICBMs	Land-based

Military personnel
Per thousand population (1982)

Under 5	5-9.9	10-14.9	15-19.9	Over 20	not available

Actual number of military personnel
Thousands

233

127